A French Review Grammar

BOYD G. CARTER
PROFESSOR OF ROMANCE LANGUAGES
UNIVERSITY OF NEBRASKA

CHARLES G. ROWE
PROFESSOR OF ROMANCE LANGUAGES
SCHREINER INSTITUTE

SECOND EDITION

THE RONALD PRESS COMPANY • NEW YORK

Library of Congress Catalog Card Number: 57-6798
PRINTED IN THE UNITED STATES OF AMERICA

PREFACE

This book, intended for second-year students, or those entering college with two units of high school French, offers (a) a review of verbs and idioms, (b) a general review of grammar, and (c) practical conversation. These were the objectives of the First Edition and they remain those of this revision.

Each of the eighteen regular chapters consists of a grammar section followed by a variety of exercises illustrating the constructions, verb forms, and idioms involved. The optional translations included in each lesson test the student's understanding of formal grammar and his ability to compose correct French sentences. Beginning with the fifth chapter a short reading passage (usually incorporating many of the idioms presented under the heading of Idiomatic Expressions) follows each lesson. The questions based thereon are simple but allow the student to express himself in his own words, a dangerous but necessary adventure.

In separate sections following the regular chapters are eighteen units devoted to irregular verbs and their idiomatic uses. These sections may be covered concurrently with the regular lessons or as review, supplementary, or special assignments. An exercise on the irregular verbs is included in the Oral and Written Exercises of each lesson. It is suggested that mastery of the irregular verbs be considered the responsibility of the student, tested by an occasional examination.

The aim of the Conversations is to supply simple mechanical responses to a variety of questions and commands. The questions are simple and require simple answers; they should always be answered in complete sentences. We ask the student to accept as an arbitrary principle that the only possible answers to the question "Did you go?," for example, are "Yes, I went" or "No, I did not go." Likewise, the only possible answers to "Etes-vous. . . ?" would be "Oui, je suis. . . ." or

"Non, je ne suis pas. . . ." The commands are to be carried out, not merely understood.

Many students blank out linguistically for a few seconds when asked the simplest question. Our conversation exercises are designed to overcome this tendency by speeding up linguistic response to the point that the French-English-French translation circuit is eliminated.

Obviously two of the most basic functions of communication involve the asking and answering of questions and the carrying out of directions. For this reason, the ability to ask questions, understand the answers, and to follow directions should continue to be stressed assiduously in conversation exercises on the second-year level. We suggest that the conversation exercises constitute a spontaneous feature of classroom procedure. By this we mean that the questions, answers, and commands should not be assigned for class study. In this way the teacher can move in on the exercises vigorously and dramatically without the hindrance of preformed translation to English language patterns. It is urged that each Conversation be covered, at least briefly, before the optional translation of the corresponding lesson is assigned. Most of the translations call for the use of expressions found in the Conversations, and it is preferable that oral-aural acquaintance precede writing.

Of late, most language teachers have been seeking to impart a more active command of the spoken language than was thought possible of attainment a few years ago. The authors are confident that this edition will meet present-day requirements and will enjoy the same favorable reception as did the original from those institutions which maintain a high standard of accomplishment.

The authors take this opportunity to thank Professor Alphonse V. Roche of Northwestern University for his contributions to this edition.

C. G. R.

January, 1957 B. G. C.

CONTENTS

PART ONE

EXERCISES IN GRAMMAR AND CONVERSATION

PART TWO

IRREGULAR VERBS, IDIOMS, AND EXERCISES

Part One

EXERCISES IN GRAMMAR AND CONVERSATION

CHAPTER 1

VERBS : SIMPLE TENSES OF THE **-er** CONJUGATION

GRAMMAR

French verbs may be classified into three conjugations, according to the ending of their infinitives: **-er, -ir, -re.** A few verbs end in **-oir.** When a verb is conjugated, it is limited as to person, number, and time (tense) by endings which are added to its stem. Tenses thus formed are known as *simple tenses.*

There are seven simple tenses in French: *present, imperfect, future, conditional, past definite, present subjunctive,* and *imperfect subjunctive.* In the case of regular verbs, the stem is constant throughout, and the sets of endings do not vary from one verb to another of the same conjugation. Thus all regular verbs whose infinitives end in **-er** are conjugated in all tenses like the models in this lesson. The same observation holds true for all regular verbs in the **-ir** and **-re** conjugations. Cf. Chapter 2 and Chapter 3.

OBSERVATION

Other names for some of these tenses are: *imperfect* = *past descriptive*; *past definite* = *simple past* or *past absolute.*

Irregularities in those verbs that are classified as irregular * are to be found mainly in the stems. Irregularities occur less

* The irregular verbs, their idiomatic construction, and exercises based upon them, are grouped in a special section of this book, *Irregular Verbs, Idioms and Exercises,* §§127–162. Some irregular verbs, which may appropriately be studied as a supplementary exercise along with the *Oral and Written Exercises,* are given in each chapter.

frequently in the endings, which, with few exceptions, are the same as those of the regular verbs.

1. The Present Indicative. This tense is formed by dropping the infinitive ending **-er** and adding **-e, -es, -e, -ons, -ez, -ent** in its place.

Infinitive	**donner**	to give
Past Participle	**donné**	given
Present Participle	**donnant**	giving

I give, am giving, do give		*We give, are giving, do give*	
Je donn*e*	I give, etc.	**Nous donn*ons***	We give, etc.
Tu donn*es*	You give, etc.	**Vous donn*ez***	You give, etc.
Il donn*e*	He gives, etc.	**Ils donn*ent***	They give, etc.
Elle donn*e*	She gives, etc.	**Elles donn*ent***	They give, etc.

OBSERVATIONS

(1) The present tense in French, with the exception of its various translations, is almost identical in usage with the English present. For idiomatic meanings cf. §40 and §41.

(2) The first person singular and the third person singular of this conjugation are always identical in form.

(3) The pronouns **elle** and **elles** always take the same form of the verb, in all conjugations and tenses, that **il** and **ils** take. For this reason the feminine forms will be omitted from the conjugations from now on.

2. The Imperfect Indicative. With the exception of **être,** all regular and irregular verbs that have a complete conjugation form the imperfect by dropping the **-ons** ending of the *first person plural* of the present indicative and adding the endings **-ais, -ais, -ait, -ions, -iez, -aient.**

I was giving, used to give, gave		*We were giving, used to give, gave*	
Je donn*ais*	I was giving, etc.	**Nous donn*ions***	We were giving, etc.
Tu donn*ais*	You were giving, etc.	**Vous donn*iez***	You were giving, etc.
Il donn*ait*	He was giving, etc.	**Ils donn*aient***	They were giving, etc.

OBSERVATIONS

(1) For the use of the imperfect, and for a comparison of it with other tenses, cf. §42 and §43.

(2) The first person singular and the second person singular of this tense are always identical in form.

3. The Future Indicative. This tense is formed by adding the endings **-ai, -as, -a, -ons, -ez, -ont** to the infinitive. These endings are the same as the present tense forms of **avoir,** the **av-** which occurs in the first person and the second person plural being dropped. The future endings are the same for all verbs, regular or irregular.

I shall (will) give		*We shall (will) give*	
Je donner*ai*	I shall (will) give	**Nous donner*ons***	We shall (will) give
Tu donner*as*	You will give	**Vous donner*ez***	You will give
Il donner*a*	He will give	**Ils donner*ont***	They will give

OBSERVATIONS

(1) On the whole, the future tense is used in French as it is in English. The future tense is presented in detail in Chapter 13.

(2) The future stem always ends in **r** or **rr,** whether the verb is regular or irregular. Note carefully the irregular future stems and learn them by heart.

4. The Conditional. This tense is formed by adding the imperfect endings **-ais, -ais, -ait, -ions, -iez, -aient** to the future stem. These endings are the same for all verbs, regular or irregular.

I should (would) give		*We should (would) give*	
Je donner*ais*	I should (would) give	**Nous donner*ions***	We should (would) give
Tu donner*ais*	You would give	**Vous donner*iez***	You would give
Il donner*ait*	He would give	**Ils donner*aient***	They would give

OBSERVATION

The verbs *should* and *would* are past forms of *shall* and *will*. The conditional is presented in detail in Chapter 13.

5. The Past Definite. This tense (cf. §43) is the equivalent of the English simple past, but in French its use is restricted to literature and formal discourse. The perfect replaces the past definite in conversation and informal composition. (Cf. the *Observation* at the beginning of Chapter 4.)

Verbs of the **-er** conjugation form this tense by dropping the **-er** and adding the endings **-ai, -as, -a, -âmes, -âtes, -èrent.**

I gave, did give		*We gave, did give*	
Je donn*ai*	I gave, etc.	**Nous donn*âmes***	We gave, etc.
Tu donn*as*	You gave, etc.	**Vous donn*âtes***	You gave, etc.
Il donn*a*	He gave, etc.	**Ils donn*èrent***	They gave, etc.

OBSERVATION

The singular past definite endings of this conjugation are identical in form with the singular future endings. Do not confuse the two tenses.

6. The Present Subjunctive. This tense is formed by dropping the **-ent** of the third person plural, present indicative, of all three conjugations, and adding the endings **-e, -es, -e, -ions, -iez, -ent.** The endings are the same for all conjugations.

(that) I give, shall (will) give, may give, etc.		*(that) we give, shall (will) give, may give, etc.*	
(que) je donn*e*	(that) I give, etc.	**(que) nous donn*ions***	(that) we give, etc.
(que) tu donn*es*	(that) you give, etc.	**(que) vous donn*iez***	(that) you give, etc.
(qu') il donn*e*	(that) he gives, etc.	**(qu') ils donn*ent***	(that) they give, etc.

OBSERVATIONS

(1) There is no particular way to translate the present subjunctive. It is usually translated by the English present indica-

tive or by the future, or by the infinitive, depending upon the idea that is expressed in the principal clause. For an analysis of the present subjunctive and its grammatical usage cf. Chapter 14.

(2) Note that the subjunctive endings **-e, -es, -e, -ent,** are identical with the present indicative endings of the **-er** conjugation, and that the endings **-ions, -iez** are identical with the similar imperfect endings.

7. The Imperfect Subjunctive. Like the past definite, the imperfect subjunctive is exclusively a literary tense and is not used either in conversation or informal composition.

Verbs of the **-er** conjugation form this tense by dropping **i,** the last letter of the first person singular of the *past definite,* and adding the endings **-sse, -sses, -^t, -ssions, -ssiez, -ssent.**

(that) I might, would give, etc.		*(that) we might, would give, etc.*	
(que) je donna*sse*	(that) I might give, etc.	**(que) nous donna*ssions***	(that) we might give, etc.
(que) tu donna*sses*	(that) you might give, etc.	**(que) vous donna*ssiez***	(that) you might give, etc.
(qu') il donnâ*t*	(that) he might give, etc.	**(qu') ils donna*ssent***	(that) they might give, etc.

OBSERVATION

As is true of the present subjunctive, there is also no particular way of translating the imperfect subjunctive. It may be translated by *might* or *would,* or by the imperfect indicative, or by the infinitive. For an analysis of this tense and its grammatical usage cf. Chapter 15.

8. Simple Negation. The sentence is made negative in French by placing **ne** before the verb form and **pas** or some other negative word after it. (Cf. §120.) Note that the word order in simple tenses is *subject* > **ne** > *pronoun* > *verb* > **pas** or some other negative adverb. (Cf. §87 and §88.)

Je ne parle pas.	I do not speak, am not speaking.
Ils ne nous le montreront pas.	They will not show it to us.

9. Interrogation. The method to be used when forming an interrogative sentence is determined by the sort of subject the sentence has.

(1) When the subject is a personal pronoun, the interrogative is formed by inverting the sentence, or by placing **est-ce que . . . ?** literally, *Is it that?* before the affirmative. **Est-ce que . . . ?** is usually found in the first person singular, and in this person it is preferable to the inverted form.

Do I speak, am I speaking?		*Do we speak, are we speaking?*	
Est-ce que je parle?	Do I speak? etc.	**Parlons-nous?**	Do we speak? etc.
Parles-tu?	Do you speak? etc.	**Parlez-vous?**	Do you speak? etc.
Parle-t-il?	Does he speak? etc.	**Parlent-ils?**	Do they speak? etc.
Parle-t-elle?	Does she speak? etc.	**Parlent-elles?**	Do they speak? etc.

(2) When the subject is a noun, the word order is *noun* > *verb* > *pronoun:* **Marie est-elle ici?** If **est-ce que . . . ?** is used, the word order after **que** is the same as that of a declarative sentence. **Est-ce que Marie est ici?** For a more extended treatment of the interrogative sentence cf. Chapter 11.

OBSERVATIONS

(1) The use of **est-ce que . . . ?** is obligatory with verbs of one syllable in the first person singular, except **ai-je? suis-je? dis-je? dois-je? fais-je? puis-je? sais-je? vais-je? vois-je?**

(2) In the third person singular **(parle-t-il? parle-t-elle?)** the **t** is inserted between the vowels for sound only; it does not alter the meaning. Note also the forms **parlera-t-il?** and **donna-t-il?**

10. The Imperative. The imperative is formed by omitting the subject pronouns *tu, vous, nous* of the present indicative. The **-s** of the familiar **tu** form, the second person singular, of the **-er** conjugation is dropped.

Donne	Give	**Ne le lui donne pas.**	Do not give it to him.
Donnez	Give	**Ne me le donnez pas.**	Do not give it to me.
Donnons	Let us give	**Ne le lui donnons pas.**	Let us not give it to him.

11. Orthographic Changes. Certain changes take place in the spelling of various verbs. Some of these are explained in the paragraphs that follow.

(1) Verbs that end in **-oyer** and **-uyer** undergo a vowel change before mute **-e, -es,** and **-ent** in the present tense, the **y** becoming **i.** This change is optional in verbs that end in **-ayer.**

employer *to employ*		**essuyer** *to wipe*	
J'emplo*i*e	**Nous employons**	**J'essu*i*e**	**Nous essuyons**
Tu emplo*i*es	**Vous employez**	**Tu essu*i*es**	**Vous essuyez**
Il emplo*i*e	**Ils emplo*i*ent**	**Il essu*i*e**	**Ils essu*i*ent**

Like the above verbs are these: **envoyer** to send, **nettoyer** to clean, **appuyer** to support, to lean, **ennuyer** to bore, **balayer** to sweep, **essayer** to try, to try on, **payer** to pay, to pay for.

(2) For reasons of pronunciation, a verb whose stem contains a mute **e** adds a grave accent in all persons of the singular, and in the third person plural. Instead of adding the accent, many verbs in **-ter** and **-ler** double the **t** and the **l.** Verbs whose stem contains an **é** change this to **è.**

mener *to take, to lead*		**jeter** *to throw*	
Je mène	**Nous menons**	**Je je*tt*e**	**Nous jetons**
Tu mènes	**Vous menez**	**Tu je*tt*es**	**Vous jetez**
Il mène	**Ils mènent**	**Il je*tt*e**	**Ils je*tt*ent**

Espérer to hope: **j'espère, tu espères, il espère, ils espèrent.** BUT **nous espérons, vous espérez.**

Like **mener: promener** to take for a walk, **emmener** to lead away, **acheter** to buy, **geler** to freeze, **modeler** to model.

Like **jeter: appeler** to call, **rappeler** to recall, **épeler** to spell.

Like **espérer: céder** to yield, **répéter** to repeat, **accélérer** to accelerate, **pécher** to sin.

(3) Orthographic changes also occur in the future and the conditional. The orthographic irregularities of the present tense occur in *all* persons of the future and the conditional. The single exception is the class of verbs like **espérer** whose **-é-** is unchanged in the future and the conditional.

The forms below illustrate, respectively, those principles of orthographic change that have just been explained in the paragraphs above.

Present	*Future*
Je mène	**Je mènerai**
Nous menons	**Nous mènerons**
Je m'ennuie	**Je m'ennuierai**
Nous nous ennuyons	**Nous nous ennuierons**
J'appelle	**J'appellerai**
Nous appelons	**Nous appellerons**

BUT

J'espère	**J'espérerai**
Nous espérons	**Nous espérerons**

(4) A verb whose stem ends in **-c** adds the cedilla to that **-c** before the **-o** and the **-a** of personal endings. A verb whose stem ends in **-g** adds an **e** before the **-o** or the **-a** of a personal ending. In the present tense the cedilla or the **e** occurs only in the first person plural.

Je commence	**Nous commençons**

BUT

Je mange	**Nous mangeons**

IDIOMATIC EXPRESSIONS

donner sur	to open on	**La porte donne sur la rue.**
donner raison (à)	to side with	**Il donne raison à son père.**
fermer à clef	to lock	**Elle ferme la porte à clef.**
aimer mieux	to prefer	**J'aime mieux cette maison-là.**

Cela me regarde. That concerns me.

à bientôt	So long!	**d'abord**	first, in the first place
à l'instant	at once	**de nouveau**	again
au revoir	good-by	**s'il vous plaît**	please

I

ORAL AND WRITTEN EXERCISES 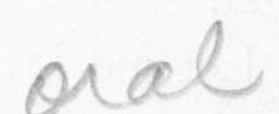

A. *Review of regular verbs in* **-er. aimer** to like, to love, **apporter** to bring, **baiser** to kiss, **baisser** to lower, **chercher** to look for, **coûter** to cost, **demander** to ask for, **demeurer** to dwell, to live, **désirer** to desire, **donner** to give, **écouter** to listen to, **emporter** to take away, **enseigner** to teach, **étudier** to study, **fermer** to close, **jouer** to play, **laisser** to leave, to let, **monter** to climb, **montrer** to show, **oser** to dare, **ôter** to take off, **oublier** to forget, **parler** to speak, to talk, **penser** to think, **porter** to wear, to carry, **prêter** to lend, **raconter** to tell, **ramasser** to pick up, **regarder** to look at, **regretter** to be sorry, **rencontrer** to meet, **souhaiter** to wish, **tirer** to pull, to draw, **tomber** to fall, **travailler** to work, **tromper** to deceive, **trouver** to find, **tuer** to kill.

B. *Consulting Ex. A, write the following verb forms. Then try to give the French from the English very rapidly without referring to Ex. A. Repeat the pronoun subject with each verb form.* 1. You love, bring, kiss, lower, look for, ask for. 2. We dwell, desire, give, listen, take away, teach. 3. I study, close, win, keep, play, let, climb. 4. He shows, dares, takes off, forgets, speaks. 5. They think, carry, lend, tell, pick up, look at. 6. You (tu) regret, meet, wish, pull, fall, work. 7. I was deceiving, finding, killing, loving, bringing. 8. They used to teach, study, close, win, keep, play. 9. I shall let, climb, show, dare, take off, forget. 10. He would desire, give, listen, take away, teach. 11. (*Past Definite*) He met, pulled, fell, worked, killed. 12. They brought, lowered, looked for, asked.

C. *Write and repeat the following verb forms which are based on* **Orthographic Changes,** *explained in* §11. 1. I employ, support, try, throw, buy, call, hope, begin, eat. 2. We employ, support, try, throw, buy, call, hope, begin, eat. 3. Put the forms in sentences 1 and 2 in the *future* and *conditional.*

D. ORAL. *Model:* **Aimez-moi.** Love me. *Say:* 1. Give me. 2. Let me **jouer.** 3. Show me. 4. Forget me. 5. Speak to me. 6. Lend me **votre livre.** 7. Tell me **une histoire.** 8. Look at me. 9. Find me. 10. Pay me. *Make the above sentences negative.* E.g., **Ne m'aimez pas.**

E. ORAL. *Model:* **Donnez-le-moi.** Give it to me. *Say:* 1. Show it to me. 2. Lend it to me. 3. Throw it to me. 4. Bring it to me. 5. Tell it to me.

F. ORAL. *Model:* **Ne me le donnez pas.** Do not give it to me. *Make the sentences in E negative.*

G. ORAL. *Model:* **Donnons-le-lui.** Let's give it to him. 1. Let's show it to him. 2. Let's lend it to him. 3. Let's throw it to him. 4. Let's bring it to him. 5. Let's tell it to him.

H. ORAL. *Model:* **Ne le lui donnons pas.** Let's not give it to him. *Make the sentences in G negative.*

I. *Make the following sentences and verb forms (a) negative and (b) interrogative.* 1. Je pensais. 2. Il les trouve. 3. Ils le ramassent. 4. Le maître grondait l'élève. 5. Il en achètera.

IRREGULAR VERBS

J. *Consult:* **aller** (§127), **envoyer** (§128), **falloir** (§141). (a) *Translate:* 1. Ils vont. 2. Ils iront. 3. Il irait. 4. J'allais. 5. Ils allèrent. 6. Ils enverront. 7. Il envoya. 8. Il enverra. 9. Il faut qu'il y aille. 10. Il faut que nous y allions.

(b) *Write:* 1. He goes. 2. He will go. 3. They were going. 4. You would go. 5. He went (Past Def.) 6. He sends. 7. He would send. 8. They sent (Past Def.) 9. I must go there. 10. You must go there.

II

OPTIONAL

K. *Translate. Consult:* **Idiomatic Expressions,** Chap. 1, **Unit** 1. 1. My window opened on the garden. 2. He always sides with me. 3. I am going to lock the door. 4. Does that concern you? 5. First, let's send for our friends. 6. Tell me a story, please. 7. Your dress does not become you. 8. Your life is at stake. 9. He will send for me at once.

L. *Pronounce and translate.* 1. J'osais. 2. J'ôtais. 3. Je montrai. 4. Je montrerai. 5. Je montrais. 6. Je montai. 7. Je monterai. 8. Il raconta. 9. Il rencontra. 10. Elle rencontrera. 11. Ils baissèrent la fenêtre. 12. Ils lui baisèrent la main. 13. Vous montriez. 14. Vous montreriez. 15. Vous montiez. 16. Commencera-t-il? 17. Commença-t-il? 18. Joueriez-vous? 19. Vous donnerait-il raison? 20. Cela ne vous regarde pas. 21. Elle aimait mieux partir à l'instant. 22. Elle ferma sa porte à clef. 23. Ma porte donnait sur le jardin. 24. Ils regrettèrent de vous dire au revoir. 25. Il oublia de vous le donner.

III

CONVERSATION 1

1. Parlez-vous anglais (français, espagnol, latin, chinois, italien, allemand, russe)? —Oui, monsieur, je parle anglais, etc. Non, monsieur, je ne parle pas chinois, etc.

2. Comprenez-vous l'anglais (le français, etc.)? —Je (ne) comprends (pas) l'anglais. Je le comprends très bien (un peu, assez bien). Je ne le comprends pas du tout.

3. Savez-vous écrire (lire) l'anglais, etc.? —Je (ne) sais (pas) écrire (lire) l'anglais. Je (ne) sais (pas) l'écrire (le lire).

4. Savez-vous comment on dit *bonjour* (*au revoir, adieu, merci, très bien, mon ami, oui, non, monsieur,* etc.) en espagnol, etc.? —On dit *buenos días.*

5. Demandez-moi si je parle français, si je comprends le russe, si je sais écrire le chinois, si je sais comment on dit *café* en japonais.

6. Allez-vous bien travailler cette année-ci? . . . travailler mieux que l'année passée? . . . étudier tous les jours? . . . essayer de parler correctement? . . . oublier tout ce que je vous dis? . . . commencer à travailler tout de suite? . . . écouter bien le professeur? . . . —Oui, monsieur, je vais. . . .

7. Espérez-vous trouver le français plus facile? . . . comprendre mieux la grammaire? . . . faire des progrès? . . . corriger votre accent? . . . apprendre beaucoup de mots? . . . recevoir de bonnes (meilleures) notes? —Oui, monsieur, j'espère. . . .

8. Aimez-vous le café, le sport, les bonbons, les fleurs, les oiseaux, la musique, le travail, la nature, les femmes, etc.? —Je (ne) l'aime (pas). Je (ne) les aime (pas). Je l' (les) adore. Je ne peux pas le (la, les) souffrir.

9. Aimez-vous mieux les blondes ou les brunes (l'été ou l'hiver, la ville ou la campagne, les chats ou les chiens, le cinéma ou la télévision, la pluie ou le beau temps, le rouge ou le bleu, les riches ou les pauvres, la musique moderne ou la musique classique, la cuisine française ou la cuisine chinoise, parler ou écouter, travailler ou vous amuser, manger ou dormir)? —J'aime mieux les blondes que les brunes. J'aime mieux parler que d'écouter.

CHAPTER 2

VERBS : SIMPLE TENSES OF THE -ir CONJUGATION

GRAMMAR

12. The Present Indicative. This tense is formed by dropping the final **-r** of the infinitive and adding the endings **-s, -s, -t, -ssons, -ssez, -ssent.**

Infinitive	**finir**	to finish
Past Participle	**fini**	finished
Present Participle	**finissant**	finishing

I finish, am finishing, do finish		*We finish, are finishing, do finish*	
Je finis	I finish, etc.	**Nous finissons**	We finish, etc.
Tu finis	You finish, etc.	**Vous finissez**	You finish, etc.
Il finit	He finishes, etc.	**Ils finissent**	They finish, etc.

13. The Imperfect Indicative. The imperfect of the **-ir** conjugation is formed in the same manner as the imperfect of the **-er** conjugation. (Cf. §2.)

I was finishing, used to finish, finished		*We were finishing, used to finish, finished*	
Je finissais	I was finishing, etc.	**Nous finissions**	We were finishing, etc.
Tu finissais	You were finishing, etc.	**Vous finissiez**	You were finishing, etc.
Il finissait	He was finishing, etc.	**Ils finissaient**	They were finishing, etc.

14. The Future Indicative. The future of the **-ir** conjugation is formed in the same manner as the future of the **-er** conjugation. (Cf. §3.)

I shall (will) finish		*We shall (will) finish*	
Je finir*ai*	I shall (will) finish	**Nous finir*ons***	We shall (will) finish
Tu finir*as*	You will finish	**Vous finir*ez***	You will finish
Il finir*a*	He will finish	**Ils finir*ont***	They will finish

15. The Conditional. The conditional of the **-ir** conjugation is formed in the same manner as the conditional of the **-er** conjugation. (Cf. §4.)

I should (would) finish		*We should (would) finish*	
Je finir*ais*	I should (would) finish	**Nous finir*ions***	We should (would) finish
Tu finir*ais*	You would finish	**Vous finir*iez***	You would finish
Il finir*ait*	He would finish	**Ils finir*aient***	They would finish

16. The Past Definite. Verbs of the **-ir** conjugation form this tense by dropping the **-ir** and adding the endings **-is, -is, -it, îmes, -îtes, -irent.**

I finished, did finish		*We finished, did finish*	
Je fin*is*	I finished, etc.	**Nous fin*îmes***	We finished, etc.
Tu fin*is*	You finished, etc.	**Vous fin*îtes***	You finished, etc.
Il fin*it*	He finished, etc.	**Ils fin*irent***	They finished, etc.

OBSERVATION

Note that the forms of the first, second, and third persons singular are identical with the present indicative forms.

17. The Present Subjunctive. The present subjunctive of the **-ir** conjugation is formed in the same manner as the present subjunctive of the **-er** conjugation. (Cf. §6.)

(that) I finish, shall (will) finish, may finish, etc.		*(that) we finish, shall (will) finish, may finish, etc.*	
(que) je fin*isse*	(that) I finish, etc.	**(que) nous fin*issions***	(that) we finish, etc.
(que) tu fin*isses*	(that) you finish, etc.	**(que) vous fin*issiez***	(that) you finish, etc.
(qu') il fin*isse*	(that) he finishes, etc.	**(qu') ils fin*issent***	(that) they finish, etc.

18. The Imperfect Subjunctive. Verbs of the **-ir** conjugation form this tense by dropping **-s,** the last letter of the first person singular of the *past definite,* and adding the endings **-sse, -sses, -^t, -ssions, -ssiez, -ssent.** (Cf. §7.)

(that) I might, would finish, etc.		*(that) we might, would finish, etc.*	
(que) je fini*sse*	(that) I might finish, etc.	**(que) nous fini*ssions***	(that) we might finish, etc.
(que) tu fini*sses*	(that) you might finish, etc.	**(que) vous fini*ssiez***	(that) you might finish, etc.
(qu') il finî*t*	(that) he might finish, etc.	**(qu') ils fini*ssent***	(that) they might finish, etc.

OBSERVATION

Note that the imperfect subjunctive forms of the **-ir** conjugation, with the exception of the third person singular, are identical with the present subjunctive forms.

19. Negative-Interrogative. A negative-interrogative sentence usually presupposes an affirmative answer. Such sentences are formed in the following ways:

(1) By using **est-ce que . . . ?**

Est-ce qu'il ne finit pas?	Isn't he finishing?
Est-ce que Jean n'étudie pas?	Doesn't John study?

(2) By inversion.

N'ira-t-il pas en ville?	Will he not go down town?
Ne vous loue-t-il pas sa maison?	Isn't he renting his house to you?
Jean n'étudiait-il pas?	Wasn't John studying?
Pourquoi ne les cherchera-t-il pas?	Why won't he look for them?

20. The Imperative. The imperative is formed by omitting the subject pronouns **tu, nous, vous** of the present indicative.

Finis	Finish	**Ne les finis pas.**	Do not finish them.
Finissez	Finish	**Ne la finissez pas.**	Do not finish it.
Finissons	Let us finish	**Ne les finissons pas.**	Let us not finish them.

IDIOMATIC EXPRESSIONS

finir par	literally, end up by (finally)	**Il finira par me le donner.** The translation of **finir par** depends upon the tense of **finir** and upon the infinitive which follows. The example above is translated thus: He will finally give it to me.
à n'en plus finir	interminably	**Elle parle à n'en plus finir.**
en finir avec	to be done (through) with	**En finit-il avec cette affaire?**
aimer beaucoup	to be fond of	**J'aime beaucoup les cerises.**
regarder par	to look out	**Elle regarde par la fenêtre.**
regarder de près	to examine thoroughly	**Il a regardé de près tout le terrain.**

à demain	good-by (until tomorrow)	**à voix basse**	in a whisper, in a low voice
à haute voix	aloud	**au moins**	at least (*quantity*)
à la fois	at the same time	**du moins**	at least (*concession*)
à propos	by the way	**là-bas**	over there, yonder

I

ORAL AND WRITTEN EXERCISES

A. *Review of regular verbs in* **-ir. agir** to act, **avertir** to warn, **bâtir** to build, **bénir** to bless, **choisir** to choose, **éblouir** to dazzle, **établir** to establish, **s'évanouir** to faint, **fournir** to furnish, **franchir** to cross, **grandir** to grow tall, **grossir** to grow fat, **guérir** to cure, to get well, **haïr** * to hate, **jouir de** to enjoy, **maigrir** to grow thin, **obéir** to obey, **s'obscurir** to grow dark, **rajeunir** to grow young, **réussir** to succeed, **rougir** to blush, **saisir** to seize, **subir** to undergo, **trahir** to betray, **vieillir** to grow old.

* The diaeresis (¨) occurs in all forms of **haïr** except the present indicative singular and the imperative singular.

B. *Write the following verb forms and then repeat them orally without referring to the written translations.* 1. He acts, warns, builds, blesses, chooses, dazzles. 2. They establish, faint, furnish, cross, grow tall. 3. We grow fat, get well, hate, enjoy, grow thin. 4. You obey, grow young, succeed, blush, seize. 5. I was acting, warning, building, blessing. 6. He will faint, furnish, cross, grow tall. 7. They grew young, succeeded, blushed, seized. 8. I must undergo (build, bless, choose, establish) it. (See **falloir,** §141.)

C. *Pronounce and translate.* 1. Quand je lui ai dit qu'elle vieillissait elle a rougi. 2. Elle a fini par s'évanouir. 3. En grandissant, souvent on maigrit. 4. Je vous avertis que si vous n'agissez pas tout de suite vous ne réussirez pas à établir votre innocence. 5. En regardant par la fenêtre j'ai vu que le jour s'obscurcissait. 6. Si vous allez me dire des choses pareilles, du moins parlez à voix basse. 7. Le jeune homme parlait à n'en plus finir. 8. Elle voulait en finir avec lui, car elle l'aimait et le haïssait à la fois. 9. Elle avait au moins vingt ans. 10. Il regardait de près sa nourriture avant de la manger.

D. *Make the following affirmative statements negative, interrogative (two ways), and negative-interrogative (two ways). E.g.,* **Il finit. Il ne finit pas. Finit-il? Est-ce qu'il finit? Ne finit-il pas? Est-ce qu'il ne finit pas?** 1. Elle marche. 2. Ils guérissent. 3. Il y va. 4. Il la racontera. 5. Marie vous regarde. 6. On * parle beaucoup. 7. Les étudiants travaillent. 8. Tu aimes.

E. *Using the order of tenses in the example that follows, give a synopsis of the following verbs in the person indicated. E.g.,* **Il saisit, il saisissait, il saisira, il saisirait, il saisit, qu'il saisisse.** 1. Je réussis. 2. Nous choisissons. 3. Ils agissent. 4. Vous obéissez. 5. Nous étudions. 6. Il achète.

* When used as the subject of a verb form that ends in a vowel, **on,** like **il** and **elle,** requires a **-t-** in the inverted position. **Parle-t-on? S'en ira-t-on?**

IRREGULAR VERBS

F. *Consult:* **dormir** (§129) **tenir** (§130), **Unit** 2.

(a) *Translate:* 1. Dormons. 2. Ne vous endormez pas. 3. Il faut que je mente. 4. Ils partirent. 5. Ils partiront. 6. Il sort. 7. Il sortit. 8. Il vient. 9. Il vint. 10. Ils vinrent. 11. Ils viendront. 12. Nous nous en souviendrons.

(b) *Write:* 1. He sleeps. 2. He is falling asleep. 3. He is lying. 4. I serve. 5. I feel. 6. I hold. 7. We come. 8. They become. 9. I shall return. 10. He will remember it. 11. I must sleep. 12. He must obtain it.

II

OPTIONAL

G. *Translate. Consult:* **Idiomatic Expressions** (Chap. 2), **Exercise** C, **Unit** 2 and **Conversation** 2: 1. I told him he was growing old. 2. He finally obeyed me. 3. On growing old one often gets fat. 4. Why do you insist on saying such things to me? 5. He loved her and hated her at the same time. 6. Choose one of your friends. 7. Ask him whether he knows how to write Chinese. 8. What are you doing? 9. Tell him not to look at you. 10. Will you please get up? 11. You write your name and I write my name. 12. Raise your hand. 13. Do not raise it. 14. Lower it. 15. He takes a piece of chalk and draws something. 16. Sit down. 17. Tell him to sit down. 18. I sit down. 19. Tell him to go to the blackboard.

III

CONVERSATION 2

1. Le Professeur: Monsieur Leblanc, choisissez quelqu'un (un des élèves, un de vos camarades). Leblanc: Je choisis M. Lenoir. Lenoir (à Leblanc): Vous me choisissez? Leblanc: Oui, monsieur, je vous choisis.

2. Le Professeur (à Leblanc) : Demandez-lui s'il parle français, comprend l'italien, sait écrire le chinois, va bien travailler, aime les enfants, etc.

3. Le Professeur, s'adressant à un étudiant : Regardez-moi. (Regardez la fenêtre. Levez la main. Baissez-la. Fermez les yeux. Ouvrez-les. Ouvrez votre livre. Fermez-le. Fermez l'oeil droit. Levez-vous. Allez au tableau noir. Prenez un morceau de craie. Ecrivez votre nom. Effacez-le. Dessinez quelque chose. Retournez à votre place. Asseyez-vous.

4. Le Professeur : Qu'est-ce que vous faites? —Je vous regarde; je regarde la fenêtre; je lève la main; je la baisse; je ferme les yeux; je les ouvre; j'ouvre mon livre; je le ferme; je ferme l'oeil droit; je me lève; je vais au tableau noir; je prends un morceau de craie; j'écris mon nom; je l'efface; je dessine un avion; je retourne à ma place; je m'assieds.

5. Le Professeur, s'adressant à Lenoir qui vient de choisir un de ses camarades : Dites-lui de vous regarder (regarder la fenêtre; lever la main, la baisser; fermer les yeux, les ouvrir; ouvrir son livre, le fermer; fermer l'oeil droit, fermer l'oeil gauche; se lever, aller au tableau noir, prendre un morceau de craie, écrire son nom, l'effacer, dessiner une auto, etc.; retourner à sa place, s'asseoir).

6. Le Professeur : Choisissez quelqu'un. . . . Dites-lui de ne pas vous regarder (se lever, lever la main gauche, baisser la main droite, la baisser, s'asseoir, etc.) —Ne me regardez pas. Ne vous levez pas. Ne levez pas la main gauche. Ne baissez pas la main droite. Ne la baissez pas. Ne vous asseyez pas.

7. Le Professeur : Voulez-vous bien me regarder, regarder la fenêtre . . . vous lever, etc.? L'élève à qui on parle, en faisant l'action indiquée : Mais certainement, avec plaisir.

CHAPTER 3

SIMPLE TENSES OF THE -re CONJUGATION

GRAMMAR

21. The Present Indicative. This tense is formed by dropping the **-re** and adding the endings **-s, -s, -t, -ons, -ez, -ent.** If the verb stem ends in **-d,** which it usually does, the **t** is not added.

Infinitive	**vendre**	to sell
Past Participle	**vendu**	sold
Present Participle	**vendant**	selling

I sell, am selling, do sell		*We sell, are selling, do sell*	
Je vend*s*	I sell, etc.	**Nous vend*ons***	We sell, etc.
Tu vend*s*	You sell, etc.	**Vous vend*ez***	You sell, etc.
Il vend	He sells, etc.	**Ils vend*ent***	They sell, etc.

OBSERVATIONS

(1) The forms in the singular have the same pronunciation.

(2) When linked, the final **-d** is pronounced as a **t:** *E.g.,* **vend-il?**

22. The Imperfect Indicative. The imperfect tense of the **-re** conjugation is formed in the same manner as the imperfect of the **-er** and **-ir** conjugations. (Cf. §2, §13.)

I was selling, used to sell, sold		*We were selling, used to sell, sold*	
Je vend*ais*	I was selling, etc.	**Nous vend*ions***	We were selling, etc.
Tu vend*ais*	You were selling, etc.	**Vous vend*iez***	You were selling, etc.
Il vend*ait*	He was selling, etc.	**Ils vend*aient***	They were selling, etc.

23. The Future Indicative. The future of the **-re** conjugation is formed by dropping the final **-e** of the infinitive and adding the future endings. (Cf. §3, §14.)

I shall (will) sell		*We shall (will) sell*	
Je vendr*ai*	I shall (will) sell	**Nous vendr*ons***	We shall (will) sell
Tu vendr*as*	You will sell	**Vous vendr*ez***	You will sell
Il vendr*a*	He will sell	**Ils vendr*ont***	They will sell

24. The Conditional. The conditional of the **-re** conjugation is formed in the same manner as the conditional of the **-er** and **-ir** conjugations; that is, by adding personal endings to the future stem. (Cf. §4, §15.)

I should (would) sell		*We should (would) sell*	
Je vendr*ais*	I should (would) sell	**Nous vendr*ions***	We should (would) sell
Tu vendr*ais*	You would sell	**Vous vendr*iez***	You would sell
Il vendr*ait*	He would sell	**Ils vendr*aient***	They would sell

25. The Past Definite. Verbs of the **-re** conjugation form the past definite tense by dropping the **-re** and adding the endings **-is, -is, -it, -îmes, -îtes,** and **-irent.**

I sold, did sell		*We sold, did sell*	
Je vend*is*	I sold, etc.	**Nous vend*îmes***	We sold, etc.
Tu vend*is*	You sold, etc.	**Vous vend*îtes***	You sold, etc.
Il vend*it*	He sold, etc.	**Ils vend*irent***	They sold, etc.

OBSERVATION

The endings of the **-ir** and **-re** conjugations are identical. Remember, however, that the endings of the **-er** conjugation are entirely different.

26. The Present Subjunctive. The present subjunctive tense of the **-re** conjugation is formed in the same manner as the present subjunctive of the **-er** and **-ir** conjugations. (Cf. §6, §17.)

(that) I sell, shall (will) sell, may sell, etc.		*(that) we sell, shall (will) sell, may sell, etc.*	
(que) je vend*e*	(that) I sell, etc.	**(que) nous vend*ions***	(that) we sell, etc.
(que) tu vend*es*	(that) you sell, etc.	**(que) vous vend*iez***	(that) you sell, etc.
(qu') il vend*e*	(that) he sell, etc.	**(qu') ils vend*ent***	(that) they sell, etc.

OBSERVATION

The singular forms and the third person plural have the same pronunciation.

27. The Imperfect Subjunctive. Verbs of the **-re** conjugation form the imperfect subjunctive tense by dropping **-s**, the last letter of the first person singular of the *past definite* tense, and adding the endings **-sse, -sses, -^t, -ssions, -ssiez, -ssent.** (Cf. §7, §18.)

(that) I might, would sell, etc.		*(that) we might, would sell, etc.*	
(que) je vendi*sse*	(that) I might sell, etc.	**(que) nous vendi*ssions***	(that) we might sell, etc.
(que) tu vendi*sses*	(that) you might sell, etc.	**(que) vous vendi*ssiez***	(that) you might sell, etc.
(qu') il vendî*t*	(that) he might sell, etc.	**(qu') ils vendi*ssent***	(that) they might sell, etc.

28. Reflexive Verbs. If a verb expresses an action that is performed directly or indirectly by the subject upon itself, then the verb is said to be reflexive. The reflexive pronouns that correspond to the subject pronouns are **me, te, se, nous, vous, se.** The following conjugated verb shows the relationship of the reflexive pronouns to the respective subject pronouns and verb forms.

I wash, do wash, am washing (myself)		*We wash, do wash, are washing (ourselves)*	
Je me lave	I wash, etc.	**Nous nous lavons**	We wash, etc.
Tu te laves	You wash, etc.	**Vous vous lavez**	You wash, etc.
Il se lave	He washes, etc.	**Ils se lavent**	They wash, etc.

OBSERVATIONS

(1) The reflexive verb is used much more extensively in French than in English, and its force as a reflexive is often not felt at all. For the use of the reflexive to replace the passive voice cf. §126, 2.

(2) The forms of the reflexive verb, as these appear in the other simple tenses, are set out below.

Imperfect	**Je me lavais**	I was washing, etc.
Future	**Je me laverai**	I shall (will) wash, etc.
Conditional	**Je me laverais**	I should (would) wash, etc.
Past Definite	**Je me lavai**	I washed, etc.
Present Subjunctive	**que je me lave**	that I wash, etc.
Imperfect Subjunctive	**que je me lavasse**	that I might wash, etc.

Full conjugation of the above simple tenses is analogous to that of the present tense given above. Conjugate each of these tenses in full.

(3) The negative, interrogative, and negative-interrogative uses of reflexive verbs are illustrated by the specimen sentences given below.

NEGATIVE

Je ne me lave pas.	I do not wash.

INTERROGATIVE

Est-ce que nous nous laverons?	Shall we wash?
Nous laverons-nous?	Shall we wash?

NEGATIVE-INTERROGATIVE

Est-ce que nous ne nous laverons pas?	Shall we not wash?
Ne nous laverons-nous pas?	Shall we not wash?

(4) Any transitive verb may be used reflexively if its sense permits of so doing. The verb may assume an idiomatic meaning, however, when it is used reflexively.

amuser	to amuse	**s'amuser**	to have a good time
appeler	to call	**s'appeler**	to be named (called)
battre *	to beat	**se battre (avec)**	to fight
demander	to ask for	**se demander**	to wonder
lever	to raise	**se lever**	to get up
marier	to marry off	**se marier (avec)**	to get married to
porter	to carry	**se porter**	to be (of health)
rendre	to give back	**se rendre (à)**	to surrender, to go (to)
sauver	to rescue, to save	**se sauver**	to escape, to run away
tromper	to deceive	**se tromper**	to be mistaken
trouver	to find	**se trouver**	to be (location), to happen to be

Jean bat son ennemi.	John beats his enemy.
Jean et son ennemi se battent.	John and his enemy fight.
Il appelle Jean.	He calls John.
Il s'appelle Jean.	His name is John.
M. Dupin marie sa fille.	Mr. Dupin is marrying off his daughter.
Elle se marie avec Jean Leblanc.	She is marrying Jean Leblanc.
Je trouve un canif.	I find a knife.
Je me trouve dans le jardin.	I am (happen to be) in the garden.

(5) The reflexive verb frequently translates the English phrase *each other* or *one another*. This reciprocal meaning is often re-enforced by the presence of **l'un(e) l'autre, l'un(e) à l'autre, mutuellement,** *etc.*

Ils se flattent (l'un l'autre).	They flatter each other.
Elles se parlent (l'une à l'autre).	They speak to each other.
Ils se rencontrent.	They meet each other.

29. The Imperative. All imperatives are formed by omitting the subject pronouns **tu, nous, vous** of the present indicative.

* The verb **battre** is irregular in the present indicative singular. *E.g.,* **je bats, tu bats, il bat.**

Vends	Sell	**Ne les vends pas.**	Do not sell them.
Vendez	Sell	**Ne le vendez pas.**	Do not sell it.
Vendons	Let us sell.	**Ne les vendons pas.**	Let us not sell them.

The reflexive imperatives are formed in the same way as those above. Note that in the *affirmative imperative* the reflexive pronoun is placed after the verb, and that **te,** in order to carry the pronunciation stress, becomes **toi.** Also observe, however, that the **te** form is used in the *negative imperative.*

Lave-toi	Wash	**Ne te lave pas.**	Don't wash
Lavez-vous	Wash	**Ne vous lavez pas.**	Don't wash
Lavons-nous	Let us wash	**Ne nous lavons pas.**	Let us not wash

OBSERVATION

Do not confuse the interrogative of nonreflexive verbs with the affirmative imperative of reflexive verbs. Note the examples below:

Partez-vous?	Are you leaving?
Levez-vous.	Get up.

IDIOMATIC EXPRESSIONS

assister à	to attend, to be present at	**Assiste-t-il au cours?**
entendre dire	to hear (someone say)	**J'ai entendu dire qu'il est parti.**
entendre parler de	to hear of	**J'entends souvent parler de lui.**
perdre de vue	to lose sight of	**L'enfant perd de vue sa mère.**
pousser un cri	to utter a cry	**Elle pousse un cri.**
rendre visite à	to visit, to call on	**Il rend visite à son père.**
rendre compte de	to account for	**Il nous rend compte de son argent.**
se rendre compte de	to realize	**Je me rends compte de cela.**

à droite	to the right	**de temps en temps**	from time to time
à gauche	to the left	**en même temps**	at the same time
à perte de vue	as far as the eye can see	**peu à peu**	little by little
bien entendu	of course	**tant mieux**	so much the better
C'est entendu!	agreed!	**tant pis**	so much the worse
de temps à autre	from time to time	**tout droit**	straight ahead

I

ORAL AND WRITTEN EXERCISES

A. *Review of regular verbs in* **-re.** **Attendre** to wait for, **battre** to beat, **confondre** to confound, to confuse, **défendre** to defend, to forbid, **entendre** to hear, **étendre** to spread, to expand, **fondre** to melt, **pendre** to hang, **perdre** to lose, **prétendre** to lay claim to, to pretend, **rendre** to give back, **répandre** to spread, **répondre** to answer, **rompre** to break, **tondre** to shear, **vendre** to sell.

B. *Write the following verb forms and then repeat them orally without referring to the written translations.* 1. I wait for you, beat you, confuse you, defend you, hear you. 2. They spread it, break it, shear it, sell it, wait for it. 3. We melt them, hang them, lose them, give them back. 4. He was not spreading it, breaking it, shearing it. 5. We would sell some, melt some, hear some, lose some. 6. They will not answer us, break us, sell to us, beat us. 7. (Past Def.) He waited for her, defended her, lost her. 8. They hanged him, sheared him, sold him, beat him. 9. He must wait, defend himself, hang himself, hear himself.

C. *Pronounce and translate.* 1. Ne les perdez pas de vue. 2. A qui rendez-vous visite demain? 3. De temps en temps les chats poussaient des cris. 4. A qui donne-t-il raison? A ses amis, bien entendu! 5. Ecoutez, mon fils! Vous allez me rendre compte de l'argent que vous dépensez. 6. Ont-ils assisté à la conférence de M. Michaud? 7. J'ai entendu dire qu'il a prononcé un fort beau discours. 8. Peu à peu il se rendait compte des petits problèmes de la vie. 9. C'est entendu! Moi, j'irai à gauche, vous et vos amis, vous irez à droite, et toi, mon petit, va tout droit. 10. Le lieutenant rendait compte de sa mission au capitaine. 11. Il amuse tout le monde mais il ne s'amuse pas. 12. Le vieux maria sa fille. 13. Vous vous trompez, mon vieux. Votre fille ne va pas se marier. 14. Un homme qui se bat avec sa femme court des risques bien graves.

Put the following present indicative verb forms into the other simple tenses. Prefix **que (qu')** *to the subjunctive forms. E.g.,* **J'attends, j'attendais, j'attendrai, j'attendrais, j'attendis, que j'attende, que j'attendisse.** 1. Il espère. 2. Ils la racontent. 3. Ils s'amusent. 4. Je le perds. 5. Il le lui montre. 6. Nous les choisissons. 7. Vous nous défendez. 8. Vous les cherchez. 9. Elle m'écoute. 10. Tu finis.

IRREGULAR VERBS

D. *Consult:* **mettre** (§131), **prendre** (§132), **Unit** 3.

(a) *Translate:* 1. Il promet. 2. Il permit. 3. Comprenez-vous? 4. J'apprendrais. 5. Permettez-moi. 6. Il mettra. 7. Il faut qu'il comprenne. 8. Je ne promettais rien. 9. On le surprit. 10. Ils apprirent.

(b) *Write:* 1. I permit. 2. We understand. 3. I was learning. 4. We would take. 5. They will promise. 6. I must learn. 7. I must put. 8. He took (Past Def.) 9. He was learning. 10. He promised (Past Def.)

II

OPTIONAL

E. *Translate the following sentences, using expressions found in the* **Idiomatic Expressions** *of the first three lessons and in the first three* **Conversations.** 1. Will you attend his lecture? 2. Little by little she was realizing his insincerity. 3. So much the better! I am glad you realize your stupidity. 4. I have heard that she always locks her door. 5. Of course. It opens on the street. 6. Do you know how to say hello in Italian? 7. I do not know how to speak Spanish, but I know how to read it. 8. Where is the door? There it is. 9. What is it? 10. What is that? 11. One smells with the nose. 12. Ask him what he does with his eyes. 13. That hat does not become her. 14. Does that concern you? 15. They used to live in this house.

16. The young man talked interminably. 17. Look out of the window and speak to me in a whisper. 18. They wonder what her name is. 19. Ask him if he can write these sentences.

III

CONVERSATION 3

1. Voici ma bouche, mon nez, ma tête, mon oeil droit (gauche), ma langue, mon front, mon menton, ma main droite, mon bras, ma jambe, mon pied, mon oreille, mes yeux, mes dents, mes doigts, mes cheveux, mes genoux. Montrez-moi votre bouche, vos yeux, etc. —Voici ma bouche, etc.

2. Où est votre bouche; votre nez, etc.? —La voici; le voici. Où sont vos yeux, etc.? —Les voici.

3. Où est la porte, la table, le plafond, le plancher, le tableau noir? —La voilà *ou* le voilà. Où sont les fenêtres, les chaises, les murs, etc.? —Les voilà.

4. Qu'est-ce que c'est (que ça, cela)? —C'est la porte, un livre, etc. Ce sont les fenêtres, des arbres, etc.

5. Est-ce que c'est mon nez? Voici ma bouche, n'est-ce pas? C'est la porte, n'est-ce pas? Ce sont mes oreilles, n'est-ce pas? —Oui, c'est votre nez. Mais non, ce n'est pas votre bouche; c'est votre front. Ce ne sont pas vos oreilles; ce sont vos dents.

6. Qu'est-ce qu'on fait avec les yeux (les oreilles, le nez, la bouche, la langue, les mains, les pieds, les dents)? —On voit (entend, sent, mange, parle, touche, marche) avec les yeux, etc.

7. Avec quoi voit-on (entend-on, sent-on, parle-t-on, touche-t-on, marche-t-on)? —On voit avec les yeux, etc.

8. Est-ce que vous voyez (entendez, sentez, mangez, parlez, touchez, marchez) avec les yeux, etc.? —Oui, je vois avec les yeux. Mais non, je ne touche pas avec les yeux; je touche avec les mains.

9. Choisissez un des élèves. Dites-lui (Priez-le) de vous montrer sa bouche, son nez, ses yeux, etc. Demandez-lui où est son menton, où sont ses genoux, etc.

10. Montrez-lui quelque chose et demandez-lui ce que c'est.

11. Demandez-lui ce qu'on fait avec les yeux, etc.; avec quoi on entend, etc.; s'il sent avec les pieds, etc.

12. Voyez-vous mon nez (ma bouche, mes yeux, etc.)? (En posant les questions le professeur laisse voir et se cache tour à tour le nez, la bouche, les yeux, etc.) —Oui, je le (la, les) vois. Non, je ne le (la, les) vois pas.

13. Demandez à quelqu'un s'il voit votre nez, etc.

14. Combien de bouches (nez, mains, doigts, etc.) avez-vous? —J'ai une bouche, etc. J'en ai une.

15. Combien de sœurs, (frères, cousins, cousines, tantes, oncles, neveux, nièces, amis, professeurs, etc.) avez-vous? —J'ai . . . sœurs. J'en ai. . . . Je n'ai pas de frères. Je n'en ai pas.

CHAPTER 4 *

THE COMPOUND TENSES

GRAMMAR

I

The compound tenses are formed by conjugating the auxiliary verbs **avoir** and **être** in the simple tenses and by placing a past participle after them. If the simple tenses of **avoir** and **être** are thoroughly learned, if the manner of forming past participles from regular verbs is mastered, and if the irregular past participles are committed to memory as they occur, the student can without difficulty form the seven compound tenses of French verbs whether the latter are regular or irregular. The seven compound tenses are named in the right-hand column below.

Simple Tenses	*Compound Tenses*
1. Present	1. Perfect
2. Imperfect	2. Pluperfect
3. Future	3. Future Perfect
4. Conditional	4. Conditional Perfect
5. Past Definite	5. Past Anterior
6. Present Subjunctive	6. Perfect Subjunctive
7. Imperfect Subjunctive	7. Pluperfect Subjunctive

OBSERVATION

The perfect tense is sometimes called the past indefinite, **passé indéfini,** or **passé composé.** The pluperfect tense is at times called the past perfect. The conditional perfect tense is often referred to as the past conditional.

* This chapter may be regarded as consisting of two parts, and handled accordingly. The second part opens with §38.

30. Formation of Past Participles. The past participle of **-er** verbs is formed by dropping the **-r** of the infinitive and placing an acute accent on the **-e;** thus, **é.** The **-ir** verbs drop the **-r.** The **-re** verbs drop the **-re** and add **-u.** Irregular verbs usually have irregular past participles.

Regular Verbs			*Irregular Verbs*		
fermer	**fermé**	closed	**tenir**	**tenu**	held
choisir	**choisi**	chosen	**mettre**	**mis**	put
vendre	**vendu**	sold	**prendre**	**pris**	taken
			avoir	**eu**	had
			être	**été**	been

OBSERVATION

There are no irregular past participles in the **-er** conjugation.

31. The Perfect Indicative. An action which is *perfect* is an action which is completed. This tense, which translates the English *perfect* and *simple past,* occurs most frequently in conversation and informal composition.

FORMULA: The perfect = the *present* of **avoir** or **être** + a *past participle.*

avoir to have		**être** to be	
J' ai	I have	**Je suis**	I am
Tu as	You have	**Tu es**	You are
Il a	He has	**Il est**	He is
Nous avons	We have	**Nous sommes**	We are
Vous avez	You have	**Vous êtes**	You are
Ils ont	They have	**Ils sont**	They are

j'ai fermé { I closed / I have closed / I did close

je suis parti { I left / I have left / I did leave

OBSERVATIONS

(1) When used as an auxiliary in the active voice, forms of **être** have the meanings of forms of **avoir.** But when used with an adjective or alone, they have their regular verbal meanings. **Il est parti** means *He has left* but **Il est riche** means *He is rich.*

(2) In English the present perfect tense is used to indicate that an action has taken place within the unit of time in which the speaker considers himself to be. If some past unit of time is mentioned or implied, the simple past is used. This distinction is not made in French, the *perfect* tense being used indiscriminately in both cases.

Avez-vous été à Paris?	Have you been to Paris? (*i.e.*, in your lifetime)
Oui, j'y suis allé en 1923.	Yes, I went there in 1923.
Je l'ai vu récemment. Je l'ai vu la semaine passée.	I have seen him recently. I saw him last week.

32. The Pluperfect. Since a *perfect* action is one which is completed, a pluperfect action is one which is *more than perfect,* that is, more than completed. A pluperfect action, then, is one which was already completed before some other past action took place. If we say *A storm came up,* we have expressed a completed action. But if we say *John had closed the door when the storm came up,* we have expressed the sequence of two past events which took place. The action of closing the door preceded the arrival of the storm.

FORMULA: The pluperfect = the *imperfect* of **avoir** or **être** + a *past participle.*

avoir		**être**	
I had, used to have, was having, etc.		*I was, used to be, etc.*	
J'avais	I had, etc.	**J'étais**	I was, etc.
Tu avais	You had, etc.	**Tu étais**	You were, etc.
Il avait	He had, etc.	**Il était**	He was, etc.
Nous avions	We had, etc.	**Nous étions**	We were, etc.
Vous aviez	You had, etc.	**Vous étiez**	You were, etc.
Ils avaient	They had, etc.	**Ils étaient**	They were, etc.

Il avait fini son travail quand son père est rentré.	He had finished his work when his father came home.
J'étais déjà parti quand vos amis sont arrivés.	I had already left when your friends arrived.
Ils s'étaient déjà couchés quand le feu a éclaté.	They had already gone to bed when the fire broke out.

OBSERVATION

The imperfect forms of **être**, when used with intransitive verbs which require it as an auxiliary, or with reflexive verbs, are translated *had*.

33. The Future Perfect. This tense expresses an action which is viewed as having been completed at some given time in the future. *E.g.,* He will have arrived (finished, left, etc.) by noon. (Cf. §93, §97.)

FORMULA: The future perfect = the *future* of **avoir** or **être** + a *past participle.*

	avoir		être
J'aurai	I shall (will) have	**Je serai**	I shall (will) be
Tu auras	You will have	**Tu seras**	You will be
Il aura	He will have	**Il sera**	He will be
Nous aurons	We shall (will) have	**Nous serons**	We shall (will) be
Vous aurez	You will have	**Vous serez**	You will be
Ils auront	They will have	**Ils seront**	They will be

J'aurai bientôt fini.	I shall have soon finished.
Elle sera venue à midi demain.	She will have come by noon to-morrow.
Ils se seront levés à huit heures.	They will have got up by eight.

34. The Conditional Perfect. For a discussion of this tense and its grammatical usage cf. Chapter 13, §95 and §97.

FORMULA: The conditional perfect = the *conditional* of **avoir** or **être** + a *past participle.*

	avoir		être
J'aurais	I should (would) have	**Je serais**	I should (would) be
Tu aurais	You would have	**Tu serais**	You would be
Il aurait	He would have	**Il serait**	He would be
Nous aurions	We should (would) have	**Nous serions**	We should (would) be
Vous auriez	You would have	**Vous seriez**	You would be
Ils auraient	They would have	**Ils seraient**	They would be

Il aurait complété sa thèse il y a deux ans, s'il s'était appliqué.	He would have finished his thesis two years ago if he had worked.
Ils seraient arrivés cette nuit, s'ils n'avaient pas eu de panne.	They would have arrived last night if they had not had car trouble.
Nous nous serions amusés au Mexique, si nous n'avions pas perdu notre argent.	We would have had a good time in Mexico if we had not lost our money.

OBSERVATION

Remember that when the verb requires **être**, the conditional forms of this auxiliary are to be translated *would have* or *should have.*

35. The Past Anterior. The past anterior tense is sometimes called the *second pluperfect.* Like the pluperfect, this tense denotes an action which happened before another took place; that is, the one action was anterior to the other. The past anterior is seldom used, however, except after conjunctions that indicate time, among which are **lorsque, quand, après que, dès que,** and some others. This tense is not used in conversation or informal composition. It occurs only in formal literary style after the conjunctions just named whenever the verb of the main clause is in the past definite tense.

FORMULA: The past anterior = the *past definite* of **avoir or être** + a *past participle.*

avoir		**être**	
J'eus	I had	**Je fus**	I was
Tu eus	You had	**Tu fus**	You were
Il eut	He had	**Il fut**	He was
Nous eûmes	We had	**Nous fûmes**	We were
Vous eûtes	You had	**Vous fûtes**	You were
Ils eurent	They had	**Ils furent**	They were

Dès qu'il eut parlé, la foule s'en alla.	As soon as he had spoken, the crowd left.
Après qu'elle fut sortie, ils y entrèrent.	After she had gone out, they went in.

Lorsque les soldats se furent couchés, la mère outragée mit le feu à sa maison.	When the soldiers had gone to bed, the outraged mother set fire to her house.

OBSERVATION

Remember that the past definite forms of **être,** when used with verbs that require this auxiliary, are translated *had.*

36. The Perfect Subjunctive. It is as difficult to state a definite rule for translating the perfect subjunctive as it is for translating the present subjunctive. (Cf. §6, Obs. 1.) Usually, however, it translates the English *perfect indicative* or *simple past,* which it replaces in the subordinate clause, contingent upon the thought that is expressed in the principal clause. For the use of the perfect subjunctive cf. Chapter 14, §103.

FORMULA: The perfect subjunctive = the *present subjunctive* of **avoir** or **être** + a *past participle.*

avoir		**être**	
(*that*) *I have, shall* (*will*) *have, may have, etc.*		(*that*) *I am, shall* (*will*) *be, may be, etc.*	
(que) j'aie	(that) I have, etc.	**(que) je sois**	(that) I am, etc.
(que) tu aies	(that) you have, etc.	**(que) tu sois**	(that) you are, etc.
(qu') il ait	(that) he has, etc.	**(qu') il soit**	(that) he is, etc.
(que) nous ayons	(that) we have, etc.	**(que) nous soyons**	(that) we are, etc.
(que) vous ayez	(that) you have, etc.	**(que) vous soyez**	(that) you are, etc.
(qu') ils aient	(that) they have, etc.	**(qu') ils soient**	(that) they are, etc.

Il est content qu'elle ait manqué le train.	He is glad that she missed (has missed) the train.
Elle regrette que vous soyez venu.	She is sorry that you came (have come).
Il est possible que Jean se soit déjà couché.	It is possible that John has already gone to bed.

OBSERVATIONS

(1) Note that in the last two examples the subjunctive forms of **être** are translated *have come, has . . . gone.* Why?

(2) The subjunctive forms of **avoir** and **être** are used to express the imperative.

aie *	have	**sois**	be
ayons	let us have	**soyons**	let us be
ayez	have	**soyez**	be

37. The Pluperfect Subjunctive. Like the past definite, past anterior, and imperfect subjunctive, the *pluperfect subjunctive* is exclusively a literary tense and does not occur in conversation or informal composition. Although its meaning varies, as in the case of the other subjunctive tenses, it is usually translated by the English conditional perfect, pluperfect indicative, or simple past. For the use of this tense cf. Chapter 15, §107 and §108.

FORMULA: The pluperfect subjunctive = the *imperfect subjunctive* of **avoir** or **être** + a *past participle.*

avoir		**être**	
(that) I might (would) have, etc.		*(that) I might (would) be, etc.*	
(que) j'eusse	(that) I might have, etc.	**(que) je fusse**	(that) I might be, etc.
(que) tu eusses	(that) you migh' have, etc.	**(que) tu fusses**	(that) you might be, etc.
(qu') il eût	(that) he might have, etc.	**(qu') il fût**	(that) he might be, etc.
(que) nous eussions	(that) we might have, etc.	**(que) nous fussions**	(that) we might be, etc.
(que) vous eussiez	(that) you might have, etc.	**(que) vous fussiez**	(that) you might be, etc.
(qu') ils eussent	(that) they might have, etc.	**(qu') ils fussent**	(that) they might be, etc.

Elle regrettait qu'il l'eût perdu.	She was sorry that he had lost it.
Ils avaient peur que Jean ne fût parti.	They were afraid that John had (might have) left.
Sa mère était contente qu'ils se fussent mariés.	His mother was glad that they married (had got married).

* Note that the **-s** of the subjunctive form **aies** is omitted.

ORAL AND WRITTEN EXERCISES

A. *Pronounce and translate the past participles of the following verbs.* 1. perdre 2. entendre 3. écouter 4. raconter 5. rencontrer 6. vieillir 7. être 8. tenir 9. consentir 10. avoir 11. apprendre 12. promettre 13. guérir 14. mourir 15. naître.

B. *Put the following sentences (1) In the perfect. (2) In the pluperfect. (3) In the future perfect. (4) In the conditional perfect. (5) In the perfect subjunctive. Prefix* **je regrette que (qu')** *to the perfect subjunctive. E.g.,* **Il parle.** (*1*) **Il a parlé.** (*2*) **Il avait parlé.** (*3*) **Il aura parlé.** (*4*) **Il aurait parlé.** (*5*) **Je regrette qu'il ait parlé.** 1. Il ferme la porte. 2. Elle finit la leçon. 3. Ils vendent des fleurs. 4. Nous partons. 5. Tu rougis. 6. Vous vous trompez. 7. Il a froid. 8. Elle est malheureuse. 9. Il le raconte. 10. Il le rencontre.

C. *Translate:* 1. I have eaten and you have eaten. 2. I have lost my money and you have lost your money. 3. I have chosen my friends and you have chosen your friends. 4. I have been at home **(chez moi)** and you have been at home. 5. I have had my troubles (**chagrins,** m.) and you have had yours **(les vôtres).** 6. I have gone over there and you have gone over there. 7. I was born in New York and you were born there **(y).** 8. I got up and you got up.

(a) *Repeat the above, making the second clause negative. E.g.,* **J'ai mangé mais vous n'avez pas mangé.**

(b) *Repeat, substituting* **he** *and* **we** *for* **I** *and* **you.**

(c) *Repeat, substituting the pluperfect, future perfect, and conditional perfect for the perfect.*

(d) *Repeat, prefacing each sentence of Exercise C with* **Il regrette que . . .** *E.g.,* **Il regrette que j'aie mangé et que vous ayez mangé.**

II

38. Agreement of the Past Participles. A past participle adds **-e** to indicate the feminine gender and an **-s** to indicate the plural. The nature of this agreement is determined by the auxiliary — **être** or **avoir** — that is required in the verbal construction.

1. VERBS CONJUGATED WITH **avoir**

The past participle of a verb that is conjugated with **avoir** agrees in gender and number with the *preceding direct object*, noun or pronoun. There is no agreement with **en.**

Vous avez fermé la porte.	You closed the door.
Vous l'avez fermé*e*.	You closed it.
A-t-il vendu les vaches?	Did he sell the cows?
Les a-t-il vendu*es*?	Did he sell them?
Elle avait mis sa robe.	She had put on her dress.
Quelle robe avait-elle mis*e*?	Which dress had she put on?
Les devoirs qu'il a fini*s*.	The exercises which he finished.

2. INTRANSITIVE VERBS CONJUGATED WITH **être**

Certain (not all) intransitive verbs of motion and a few that express state or change of condition are conjugated with **être** instead of **avoir.** The past participle agrees in gender and number with the *subject,* noun or pronoun. The following is a list of such verbs:

aller	to go	**venir (venu)**	to come
arriver	to arrive	**revenir (revenu)**	to come back
entrer (dans)	to enter	**devenir (devenu)**	to become (of)
rentrer	to go back (home)	**partir**	to leave
retourner	to return	**sortir**	to go out
monter	to climb	**descendre**	to descend
tomber	to fall	**naître (né)**	to be born
rester	to remain	**mourir (mort)**	to die

Il est rentré de bonne heure.	He came home early.
Ils sont restés là-bas.	They remained over there.
Elle est arrivée à huit heures.	She arrived at eight.
Ses amies sont mortes.	His friends died (have died, are dead).

OBSERVATION

Certain of these verbs, **descendre, sortir, monter,** for example, may have a transitive meaning. In that case they are conjugated with **avoir.**

Ils sont sortis de la maison.
They went out of the house.
Je suis descendu de l'auto.
I got out of the car.
Il est monté me voir.
He came up to see me.

Ils ont sorti leurs pipes.
They got out their pipes.
J'ai descendu mon fusil.
I got down my gun.
Elle a monté (descendu) l'escalier en courant.
She ran up (*or* down) the stairs.

3. REFLEXIVE VERBS WITH être

All reflexive verbs are conjugated with **être.** The past participle agrees in gender and number with the *preceding direct object,* which is usually the reflexive pronoun.

Il s'est levé.	He got up, has got up.
Elle s'est levée.	She got up, has got up.
Ils s'étaient couchés.	They had gone to bed.
Les hommes s'étaient couchés.	The men had gone to bed.
Nous nous serons lavé(e)s.	We shall have washed.
BUT	
Ils se sont parlé.	They spoke to each other.
Elle s'est lavé la figure.	She washed her face.

Note that in the last two examples, the object that precedes the verb is *indirect* rather than *direct*; hence there is no agreement. If in addition to the indirect reflexive object, however, there is also a preceding direct object, then the past participle does make an agreement. *E.g.,* **Les dentelles qu'elle s'est achetées.** *The laces which she bought herself.*

4. CHOICE OF THE AUXILIARY: **avoir** OR **être**

a) If the verb is one of the intransitive verbs listed above (Learn them by heart!), it is conjugated with **être.**

b) If it is reflexive, it is conjugated with **être.**

c) All other verbs are conjugated with **avoir.**

OBSERVATION

Inasmuch as the simple tenses of **être** are used with a past participle to form the *passive voice,* care must be taken not to confuse verb phrases with **être** in the active voice with those in the passive. (Cf. §125 and §126.)

Active Voice	*Passive Voice*
Elle est allée en ville. She went downtown.	**Le conférencier est applaudi par les assistants.** The lecturer is applauded by the audience.
Quand elle fut allée au cinéma . . . When she had gone to the movies . . .	**Le piéton fut renversé par un chien.** The pedestrian was tripped by a dog.

39. **Word Order.** In compound tenses, the auxiliary assumes the verbal functions. It can be made negative, interrogative, or negative-interrogative. The pronouns precede it, and most short adverbs (**beaucoup, trop, assez, bien,** and such) follow it immediately. Of the various negative forms (**ne . . . jamais, ne . . . plus, ne . . . rien, ne . . . que, ne . . . personne,** and such) (cf. §87), only **que** and **personne** follow the past participle.

Subject	***ne***	*Pronoun*	*Auxiliary*	*Second Part of Negation*	*Adverb*	*Past Participle*
Ils	**ne**	**m'**	**ont**	**jamais**	**beaucoup**	**demandé.**

Nous ne les avons pas cherchés.	We didn't look for them.
Ils n'avaient trouvé que des ruines.	They had found only ruins.
Ils ne s'étaient jamais beaucoup aimés.	They had never loved each other very much.

OBSERVATION

The following adverbs always follow the past participle: **aujourd'hui, hier, demain, autrefois, tôt, tard, ici, là, ailleurs, partout.**

IDIOMATIC EXPRESSIONS

avoir l'air de to seem (to be)	**Il a l'air d'être malade.**
avoir beau* +inf. no matter how much . . ., to waste one's efforts (or time)	**Vous avez beau étudier, vous n'apprendrez rien.**
avoir envie de to feel like	**J'ai envie de partir.**
avoir lieu to take place	**L'examen aura lieu demain.**

Qu'est-ce qu'il y a?	What's the matter (trouble)?
Il y a que j'ai faim.	(The matter is) I'm hungry.
Qu'avez-vous?	What's the matter (with you)?

avoir chaud	to be warm	**avoir soif**	to be thirsty
avoir froid	to be cold	**avoir peur (de)**	to be afraid
avoir raison	to be right	**avoir sommeil**	to be sleepy
avoir tort	to be wrong	**avoir honte (de)**	to be ashamed
avoir faim	to be hungry	**avoir besoin (de)**	to need

I

ORAL AND WRITTEN EXERCISES

A. *Translate the following idiomatic sentences.* 1. J'ai beau manger, j'ai toujours faim. 2. «J'aurai l'air misérable comme tout,» dit Mme Loisel. 3. On dit que tout le monde avait envie de pleurer. 4. «Qu'est-ce qu'il y a?» s'écria mon père. «Il y a que le petit Jacques a mangé un ver de terre,» répondis-je, la mort dans l'âme. 5. «Qu'avez-vous, mon ami? Vous avez mauvaise mine ce matin.» «Je vous assure que je n'ai rien,»

* Note that when **avoir beau** is used it is always followed by a clause that expresses result. Perhaps the simplest way to render this expression into idiomatic English is to introduce the sentence with *No matter how much . . .*, and to translate the dependent infinitive in the person, number, and tense in which **avoir** is used. Thus the sentence above would read: *No matter how much you study, you will not learn anything.*

dit-il. 6. Le mariage a eu lieu il y a plusieurs jours. 7. De quoi avez-vous besoin? 8. Puisque vous avez sommeil vous avez raison de vous coucher. 9. Il avait tort de ne pas prendre un parti. 10. J'avais chaud et soif mais personne ne s'en rendit compte.

B. *Model:* **J'avais déjà fait ce qu'il a fait.** *Translate:* 1. I had already taken what he took. 2. I had already been where he has been. 3. I had already chosen what he chose. 4. I had already sold the car he sold. 5. I had already paid for what he paid for.

Repeat, changing **I** *and* **he** *to* **you** *and* **they.** *E.g.,* **Vous aviez déjà fait ce qu'ils ont fait.**

C. *Model:* **Si vous vous étiez amusé je me serais amusé.** *Translate:* 1. If you had been mistaken I would have been mistaken. 2. If you had married I would have married. 3. If you had got up I would have got up. 4. If you had run away I would have run away. 5. If you had entered it **(y)** I would have entered it.

Repeat, making both clauses negative. E.g., **Si vous ne vous étiez pas amusé je ne me serais pas amusé.**

D. *Translate the French to English and vice-versa:* 1. Elle a vendu la vache. Where is the cow which she sold? 2. J'ai écrit une phrase. Look at the sentence which I have written. 3. Vous avez perdu vos livres. Find the books which you have lost. 4. Il a choisi une cravate. Which necktie did he choose? 5. J'avais acheté une maison. I sold the house which I had bought.

IRREGULAR VERBS

E. *Consult:* **naître** (§133) **vivre** (§134) **mourir** (§135), **Unit** 4.

(a) *Translate:* 1. Etes-vous né hier? 2. Qui est mort? 3. Elle a vécu. 4. Je mourrais. 5. Je mourais. 6. Il mourut. 7. Il faut qu'il meure. 8. Vit-il? 9. Nous vivions. 10. Il naîtra.

(b) *Write:* 1. I was born here. 2. We were dying. 3. You will die. 4. You must die. 5. They were living. 6. They are dying. 7. They must die. 8. You were being born. 9. You must be born again (renaître). 10. You have lived.

II

OPTIONAL

F. *Translate, using expressions from the* **Idioms** *in this lesson and from* **Conversation** 4. 1. No matter how much he drinks, he is still thirsty. 2. They say that he looks miserable. 3. Do you feel like laughing? 4. What does he need? 5. What is the matter? 6. The marriage will take place next week. 7. He assured me that he had made up his mind. 8. She always looks well when she is not sleepy. 9. No one realizes it. 10. Since he is thirsty he needs to drink. 11. Did you sleep well? 12. Did you fall asleep before midnight? 13. Did you go out last night? 14. I did not understand the grammar. 15. She got the book out of the library. 16. The hats that she bought for herself are on the table. 17. Ask him what he bought yesterday. 18. I saw a flying saucer last night while I was looking at the stars. 19. What did you buy downtown? 20. How many letters have you written today?

III

CONVERSATION 4

1. Est-ce que vous avez (Avez-vous) bien dormi, bien mangé, étudié la leçon, travaillé beaucoup hier, fait une promenade, été en ville, appris les verbes de la leçon, compris la grammaire, pris un taxi pour venir à l'école, eu un accident en venant, perdu votre livre? —Oui, j'ai bien dormi, etc. Non, je n'ai pas bien mangé, etc.

2. Est-ce que vous êtes (Etes-vous) arrivé à l'heure (en retard), allé en ville hier, resté chez vous, sorti hier soir, rentré

de bonne heure, tombé dans la boue, né en France (en Amérique, hier) ? —Oui (Non), je (ne) suis (pas) arrivé à l'heure, etc.

3. Est-ce que vous vous êtes (Vous êtes-vous) couché tard hier soir, levé de bonne heure ce matin, lavé la figure, bien amusé à la fête (au bal, au match), endormi avant minuit, brossé les dents avant de vous coucher, vite déshabillé, habillé, rasé, fait couper les cheveux récemment, souvenu de vos camarades pendant l'été, rendu compte de la situation, fait mal en tombant, mis à travailler, fait gronder? —Oui (Non), je (ne) me suis (pas) couché tard, etc.

4. Demandez à quelqu'un s'il a bien dormi, etc., s'il est arrivé à l'heure, etc., s'il s'est couché tard hier soir, etc.

5. Qu'est-ce que vous avez (Qu'avez-vous) acheté (appris, mangé, bu, lu, vu, écrit) hier? —Hier j'ai acheté un stylo, des cigarettes, du papier, etc. (appris bien des choses, etc.; mangé des œufs, un filet mignon; bu du café, du lait; lu le journal, un roman; vu un beau film, une soucoupe volante; écrit une lettre, un thème, un sonnet).

6. Où êtes-vous allé hier? —Hier je suis allé à mes classes, à la bibliothèque, en ville, au cinéma, à l'église, chez le médecin, chez le dentiste, au parc, à la campagne, à la chasse, à la pêche, à la poste, au magasin, à la pharmacie, au cabaret, etc.

7. Combien de fois vous êtes-vous brossé les dents (lavé les mains, peigné, rasé, maquillé, habillé, déshabillé) hier (ce matin, la semaine passée) ? Je me suis . . . . . . fois.

8. Demandez à quelqu'un ce qu'il a acheté hier, etc.; où il est allé; combien de fois il s'est brossé les dents, etc.

CHAPTER 5

TENSES AND THEIR IDIOMATIC PECULIARITIES

GRAMMAR

40. The Present Tense. In general, the present tense has about the same functions in French as in English. Note, however, the peculiarities of French usage that are more fully explained below.

(1) In conversational style the present tense may be used to express the future if it is reinforced by an adverb or an expression of time.

Il vient tout à l'heure.	He will come presently. He is going (is coming) in a little while.

(2) With certain verbs, and especially with **arriver, rentrer, revenir, sortir, venir,** the present tense is used to indicate an immediate past.

Elle arrive de Paris.	She has just arrived from Paris.
Il rentre de l'école.	He has just returned from school.
D'où venez-vous?	Where did you come from?

(3) The present tense is used instead of a past tense whenever a climax in a narrative is being reached. This use of the present tense is often known as the *historical present.*

On frappa à la porte: mon père laisse tomber son journal, ma mère se sauve du côté de la cuisine et mon frère se cache dans l'armoire. J'ouvre. C'était le facteur!	Someone knocked. My father dropped his paper, my mother ran towards the kitchen, and my brother hid in the closet. I opened the door. It was the postman!

OBSERVATION

The English continuous present or progressive past may be expressed by **en train de** + an *infinitive*.

Il est (était) en train de prendre son café.	He is (was) drinking his coffee.

41. The Progressive Present-Perfect concept of time in English and French. The present indicative is used in French to express an action that was begun in the past but is still in progress in the present. The French think of such an action as belonging to the present tense rather than to the perfect. Note carefully the examples below.

Depuis quand est-il ici?	How long has he been here?
Il est ici depuis trois heures.	He has been here for three hours.
Combien de temps y a-t-il que vous étudiez le français?	How long have you been studying French?
Il y a cinq ans que je l'étudie.	I have been studying it for five years.
Depuis quand voyagez-vous en France?	How long have you been traveling in France?
Voilà trois mois que nous voyageons en France.	We have been traveling in France for three months.

OBSERVATIONS

(1) When this construction is used, questions are introduced by **depuis quand** or **combien de temps y a-t-il que.**

(2) In the affirmative there are two types of form: (*a*) the **depuis** construction and (*b*) the **voilà . . . que, voici . . . que, il y a . . . que** constructions. The latter are more emphatic.

Note carefully the construction of the sentences below.

Perfect	*Progressive Present Perfect*
Quand est-ce que vous avez regardé cette maison?	**Depuis quand regardez-vous cette maison?**
Je l'ai regardée dix minutes hier.	**Je la regarde depuis dix minutes.**
Il a travaillé sans cesse pendant trois jours.	**Voilà trois jours qu'il travaille sans cesse.**
Elle a fermé sa porte à clef hier soir.	**Combien de temps y a-t-il qu'elle ferme sa porte à clef?**

42. Uses of the Imperfect. This tense (cf. §2), which is sometimes called the past descriptive, is used for expressing the following concepts of time relationship.

(1) What was happening when some other event happened or was happening.

Elle regardait par la fenêtre quand sa mère entra dans le salon.	She was looking out the window when her mother entered the drawing room.
Pendant qu'il lui parlait, Jean pensait à autre chose.	While he was speaking to him, John was thinking about something else.

(2) What was customary or habitual.

Je prenais toujours le petit déjeuner au Dôme.	I always took breakfast at the Café Dome.

(3) What, in a descriptive sense, was the state or condition of the action as it appeared in the past.

Le vieillard n'était pas grand mais il avait l'air robuste.	The old man was not tall but he seemed robust.

(4) In the *if* clause of conditional sentences, what is **not** now true. See also §99.

Si j'étais roi vous seriez ma reine.	If I *were* king you would be my queen.

(5) In indirect quotations, and following a past tense, what was originally stated in the present.

Il m'a demandé comment je m'appelais.	He asked me what my name was.
Elle lui a dit qu'elle ne l'aimait plus.	She told him she no longer loved him.

43. Meaning of Imperfect, Perfect, and Past Definite Compared. In contrast with the imperfect, which, as noted in §42, tells what was happening, what was habitual, or what was, in a descriptive sense, the state or condition of an action, both the perfect and the past definite tell *what happened.* These tenses state the completion or the beginning of the action at or during a given time, or segment of time, in the past. Note below that the English simple past may be used to translate the French imperfect, perfect, and past definite.

French Tenses	Translations *	English Equivalents
Imperfect		
Je montrais.	I showed.	*Simple Past*
	I used to show.	*Habitual Past*
	I would show.	
	I was showing.	*Progressive Past*
Perfect		
J'ai montré.	I showed.	*Simple Past*
	I have shown.	*Perfect*
	I did show.	*Emphatic Past*
Past Definite		
Je montrai.	I showed.	*Simple Past*
	I did show.	*Emphatic Past*

OBSERVATIONS

(1) A French verb is usually reinforced by some such adverb as **bien, fort,** or another, in order to express the *emphatic past* or the *emphatic present*.

(2) Remember that although the perfect and past definite both translate the English simple past, they may not be used interchangeably. The perfect is used in conversation and informal composition, and the past definite is used exclusively in literary style.

Imperfect	*Perfect* or *Past Definite*
Il pleurait quand vous êtes arrivé.	**Il a pleuré quand vous êtes arrivé.**
He was weeping when you arrived. (The thought is that he *was* weeping *before* you arrived.)	He wept when you arrived. (The thought is that he began to weep *after* you arrived.)

* When translating English verb forms into French, ask yourself these questions: Is the thought that of a completed past action or of an uncompleted one? Was the action already existent or in progress, or did it suddenly take place?

Imperfect	*Perfect* or *Past Definite*
Il savait que son ami était parti.	**Il a su (il sut) que son ami était parti.**
He knew (*was informed previously*) that his friend had left.	He learned (*discovered*) that his friend had left.

See the examples based on **pouvoir** and **vouloir** (§136, §137) for additional illustrations of differences in tense meanings.

44. The Imperfect and Pluperfect as *in-progress* concepts of time. (§41). The French view an action begun in the past, but still in progress in the past at the time something else happened, as an imperfect action. Accordingly they use the imperfect tense in place of the pluperfect to express such an action. The sentence types are precisely the same as those of the progressive present perfect. (Cf. §41.)

Pluperfect	*Progressive Pluperfect*
Avait-il étudié quand sa mère est arrivée?	**Depuis quand étudiait-il quand sa mère est arrivée?**
Had he studied when his mother arrived?	How long had he been studying when his mother arrived?
Elles avaient travaillé sans cesse ce jour-là.	**Elles travaillaient sans cesse depuis le matin.**
That day they had worked without stopping.	They had been working without stopping since morning.

45. venir de + an Infinitive. In order to emphasize the recency of a completed action, the French make use of a special verbal construction.

(1) If the action *has just* taken place, it is expressed by the present of **venir + de +** an *infinitive*. (Cf. also §40.) This kind of action may be called an *immediate perfect*.

Perfect	*Immediate Perfect*
J'ai fermé le livre.	**Je viens * de fermer le livre.**
I closed the book.	I have just closed the book.
Elle l'a fini.	**Elle vient de le finir.**
She has finished **it.**	She has just finished **it.**

* Note that the thought is, *I come from closing the book,* and that the French infinitive is translated into English as a past participle.

Perfect	*Immediate Perfect*
Nous sommes sortis. We went out.	**Nous venons de sortir.** We have just gone out.
Ils se sont couchés. They have gone to bed.	**Ils viennent de se coucher.** They have just gone to bed.
Il m'en a donné. He gave me some.	**Il vient de m'en donner.** He has just given me some.

(2) If the action *had just* taken place, it is expressed by the imperfect of **venir** + **de** + an *infinitive.* This kind of action may be called an *immediate pluperfect.* Cf. §32.

Pluperfect	*Immediate Pluperfect*
J'avais fini ma leçon quand Jean est entré. I had finished my lesson when John entered.	**Je venais* de finir ma leçon quand Jean est entré.** I had just finished my lesson when John entered.
Elle s'était lavé les mains. She had washed her hands.	**Elle venait de se laver les mains.** She had just washed her hands.

IDIOMATIC EXPRESSIONS

c'est que the fact is

être au courant de to be informed about, to be posted on

être d'accord to agree

être en avance to be early

être en retard to be late

être en train de to be in the act of

n'y être pour rien to have nothing to do with, not to be involved in

C'est ça! That's right!

Il a manqué de tomber; c'est qu'il marche très mal.

Il est au courant de tout.

Elle est d'accord avec moi.

Il est toujours en avance.

Vous n'êtes jamais en retard.

Il est en train de se lever.

Je n'y suis pour rien.

C'est dommage! That's a pity (shame)!

I

LECTURE

Lisez à haute voix.

La jeune fille descendait lestement. Ses jupes, rasant le sol, avaient des balancements qui me ravissaient. Je la voyais de bas en haut, toute droite, dans sa grâce fière et heureuse. Elle

* The thought is, *I was coming from finishing my lesson when John entered.*

ne me savait point là, derrière les saules; elle marchait d'un pas libre, elle courait sans se soucier du vent qui soulevait un coin de sa robe. Je distinguais ses pieds, trottant vite, vite, et un morceau de ses bas blancs, qui était bien large comme la main, et qui me faisait rougir d'une façon douce et pénible. . . .

Elle causa, ce jour-là, pendant quelques minutes avec les lavandières. Ses rires perlés arrivaient jusqu'à moi, mêlés à la grande voix de la Durance. Puis, elle se baissa pour prendre un peu d'eau dans le creux de sa main; mais la rive était haute, Babet, qui faillit glisser, se retint aux herbes.

Je ne sais quel frisson me glaça le sang. Je me levai brusquement, et, sans honte, sans rougeur, je courus auprès de la jeune fille. Elle me regarda, effarouchée; puis elle se mit à sourire. Moi, je me penchai, au risque de tomber. Je réussis à remplir d'eau ma main droite, dont je serrais les doigts. Et je tendis à Babet cette coupe nouvelle, l'invitant à boire.

Les lavandières riaient. . . .

. . . Elle but, et je sentis le baiser tiède de sa bouche, qui remonta le long de mes bras jusque dans ma poitrine, qu'il emplit de chaleur.

ZOLA: *Les Quatre Journées*

Répondez aux questions suivantes: 1. Décrivez la jeune fille au moment qu'elle descendait à la rivière. 2. Qu'est-ce qui faisait rougir le garçon? 3. Auriez-vous rougi à sa place? 4. Que font les lavandières? 5. Pourquoi s'est-elle approchée de la rivière? 6. A quel moment le garçon s'est-il levé brusquement? 7. Décrivez la coupe qu'il tendait à Babet. 8. Pourquoi a-t-il eu chaud dans sa poitrine? 9. Faites un résumé de cette lecture en vos propres termes.

II

ORAL AND WRITTEN EXERCISES

A. *Pronounce and translate.* 1. Tistet Védène avait depuis longtemps son idée sur la mule du Pape. 2. Tistet Védène apprit que le premier moutardier du Pape venait de mourir subitement. 3. «Tiens! attrape, bandit! voilà sept ans que je te le garde!» 4. Ce coup de pied, la mule du Pape le lui gardait depuis sept ans. 5. Vous avez beau être un modeste, vous aimez bien montrer que vous n'avez pas eu peur. 6. Ils venaient d'assister à une conférence des plus intéressantes. 7. Nous venons de nous rendre compte de vos faiblesses. 8. Vous dites que je viens de trembler, c'est que j'ai peur. 9. A propos, êtes-vous au courant de ce qui se passe chez moi? 10. Je vous assure que votre petit Jacques n'y était pour rien. 11. Il est arrivé trop tard pour avoir pu casser cette vitre. 12. C'est dommage que vous ayez pu le soupçonner! 13. C'est ça! Je suis d'accord avec vous. Alors, adieu!

B. *Use a proper form of each verb in parentheses to translate the italicized verb phrases. Employ the imperfect or past definite.*

Maître Hauchecorne, de Bréauté, *had just arrived* **(venir d'arriver)** à Goderville, et il *was going* **(se diriger)** vers la place, quand il *noticed* **(apercevoir)** par terre un petit bout de ficelle. Maître Hauchecorne, économe en vrai Normand, *thought* [at that moment] **(penser)** que tout *was* **(être)** bon à ramasser qui peut servir, et il *bent over* **(se baisser)** péniblement, car il *suffered* **(souffrir)** de rhumatisme. Il *took* **(prendre)**, par terre, le morceau de corde mince, et il *was getting ready* **(se disposer)** à le rouler avec soin, quand il *observed* **(remarquer)**, sur le seuil de sa porte, maître Malandain, le bourrelier, qui *was looking at him* **(le regarder)**. Ils avaient eu des affaires ensemble au sujet d'un licol, autrefois, et ils *were* **(être)** rancuniers tous deux. Maître Hauchecorne *was seized* [at that moment] **(être pris)** d'une sorte de honte d'être vu ainsi, par son ennemi, cherchant dans la crotte un bout de ficelle. Il *hid* **(cacher)** brusquement sa trouvaille sous sa blouse, puis dans la poche de sa culotte, puis il *pretended* **(faire semblant)** de chercher encore par terre quelque chose qu'il ne trouvait point, et il *went away* **(s'en aller)** vers le marché, la tête en avant, courbé en deux par ses douleurs.

MAUPASSANT: *La Ficelle.*

C. *Reread the above passage, substituting the perfect for the past definite.*

D. ORAL. *Shift the tense of the following statements to the past by prefacing each with* **Il m'a dit que. . . .** *The present, future and perfect will become imperfect, conditional and pluperfect. E.g.,* **Il a trouvé une femme qu'il aime et qu'il épousera. Il m'a dit qu'il avait trouvé une femme qu'il aimait et qu'il épouserait.** 1. Il veut voir le médecin. 2. Il l'attend depuis une heure. 3. Il vient de tomber malade. 4. Il ne comprend pas ce qu'il a. 5. Il va s'évanouir. 6. Il est pauvre. 7. Il dort mal. 8. Il meurt de faim. 9. Il travaille trop. 10. Il a perdu sa femme. 11. Il ira à l'hôpital. 12. Il ne vivra pas longtemps.

E. *Translate the French sentences into English and vice-versa:* 1. Nos amis venaient d'arriver. Our friends have just arrived. 2. Elle s'était lavé les mains. She has just washed her hands. 3. Je viens de lui parler. I had just spoken to him. 4. Depuis quand me cherchiez-vous? How long have you been looking for me? 5. Je suis à Paris depuis huit jours. I had been in Paris a week.

IRREGULAR VERBS

F. *Consult:* **pouvoir** (§136), **vouloir** (§137), **Unit** 5.

(a) *Translate:* 1. Il veut. 2. Il peut. 3. Il voulut. 4. Il put. 5. Je voudrais le faire. 6. J'aurais voulu le faire. 7. J'aurais pu le faire. 8. Il faut que je puisse le faire. 9. Veuillez le faire. 10. Vous pouviez. 11. Vous pourriez. 12. Ils peuvent.

(b) *Write:* 1. We want. 2. We can. 3. They would like to do it. 4. We would have liked to do it. 5. We were able. 6. We would be able. 7. We would have been able. 8. You must be able. 9. You must want it. 10. They want to go there.

III

OPTIONAL

G. *Translate.* 1. I shall never forget my friend Lucien Dupin. 2. We were taking a course in conversation. 3. Dupin didn't study too much; he didn't have time! 4. Usually he was late, but on that day he arrived early. 5. When I entered the classroom he was studying (*two ways*) his lesson. 6. "Are you surprised?" he said.* 7. "Yes! How long have you been here?" 8. "I have been here for an hour. This lesson is not easy. Do you agree with me?" 9. I was going to tell him that I agreed with him when M. Calmette came in. 10. "Monsieur," he said to me **(m'a-t-il dit)**,* "are you responsible for your friend's presence here?" 11. "No, Sir. I have nothing to do with it." 12. "M. Dupin, what do you do with your shirts when they are worn out?" 13. "I throw them away!" 14. "That's a pity! If you do not become more serious, I am going to ask you to leave!" 15. Poor Dupin was afraid and during the entire lesson he was as gentle as a lamb.

H. *Translate, using expressions in* **Example** A. 1. He had had his idea for a long time. 2. He had been keeping it for seven years. 3. No matter how modest you are, you like to show that you are informed of what is going on. 4. They have just realized my weaknesses. 5. I have just attended a lecture. 6. I arrived too late. 7. It is a pity that you have been afraid. 8. You agree with me, don't you?

IV

CONVERSATION 5

1. Où êtes-vous? —Je suis dans la classe de français. Depuis quand y êtes-vous? —J'y suis depuis . . . minutes.

2. Depuis quand étudiez-vous le français? —Je l'étudie depuis . . . mois (ans). Depuis quand suivez-vous ce cours? —Je le suis depuis . . . mois (semaines, jours).

* For inversions in indirect discourse *cf.* §86.

3. Qu'est-ce que vous faisiez (Que faisiez-vous) à minuit, à huit heures du matin, il y a vingt quatre heures, hier à midi, etc.? —Je dormais, étudiais, lisais, écrivais, mangeais, parlais, faisais une promenade, chantais, dansais, me rasais, me brossais les dents, prenais une tasse de café, apprenais un poème, écoutais la radio, regardais la télévision, pensais à mes problèmes, rêvais, m'amusais, attendais le tramway, sortais, rentrais, travaillais, etc.

4. Où étiez-vous à minuit, etc.? —J'étais au lit, à la bibliothèque, au cabaret, dans ma chambre, dans la salle à manger, etc.

5. Qu'est-ce que vous faisiez (Que faisiez-vous) tous les jours quand vous étiez petit? —Quand j'étais petit je jouais à cache-cache, je grimpais dans les arbres, je taquinais les petites filles, j'allais nu-pieds, je barbotais dans la boue, je déchirais mes vêtements, je pleurais beaucoup, je faisait le désespoir (le bonheur) de mes parents, me battais, me plaignais, volais des pommes, faisais dodo, etc.

6. Qu'est-ce que vous voulez être (voir, avoir)? —Je veux être le meilleur étudiant de la classe (le mari d'une jolie femme, la femme d'un brave homme, médecin, ingénieur, général, acteur, champion de boxe, journaliste, etc.); voir la Tour Eiffel, (Notre Dame de Paris, le musée du Louvre, les pyramides, les chutes du Niagara, le Canal de Panama, le Mont Saint-Michel, les Folies-Bergère, etc.); avoir une bonne éducation (un coupé de ville Cadillac, une grande fortune, le Prix Nobel, etc.)

7. Où voulez-vous être (aller, demeurer, travailler)? —Je veux être chez moi (à Paris, etc.); aller au bal (à la campagne, en Europe, etc.); demeurer à New York (au Texas, etc.); travailler dans un bureau (dans une usine, dans un laboratoire, etc.).

8. Pouvez-vous (Peut-on) voir sans ouvrir les yeux (parler sans ouvrir la bouche, apprendre sans étudier, marcher sans mouvoir les pieds)? —Non, je ne peux pas. . . . On ne peut pas. . . .

9. Demandez à quelqu'un où il est, depuis quand il y est, depuis quand il étudie le français, depuis quand il suit ce cours, ce qu'il faisait à minuit, etc., où il était à minuit, ce qu'il faisait quand il était petit, ce qu'il veut être (avoir, voir), où il veut être (aller, demeurer, travailler), s'il peut voir, etc., sans ouvrir les yeux, etc.

10. Ayez la bonté de regarder la fenêtre, etc. Qu'est-ce que vous venez de faire? —Je viens de regarder la fenêtre, etc.

11. Dites à quelqu'un d'avoir la bonté de regarder la fenêtre, etc. Demandez-lui ce qu'il vient de faire.

Sujets de discussion et de conversation:

1. A-t-on raison de condamner les belles-mères?
2. Qu'est-ce que c'est que l'amour?
3. Pourquoi est-ce qu'on s'intéresse plus aux amoureux qu'aux gens mariés?
4. A quel âge doit-on se marier?
5. Qu'est-ce qu'il faut pour être heureux en ménage?

CHAPTER 6

ARTICLES AND NOUNS

GRAMMAR

46. The Definite Article. In French the definite article is either masculine or feminine, singular or plural. When used, it must agree in gender and number with its noun. The various forms of the definite article are set out below.

Singular		*Plural*	
le l' (*m.*) **la l'** (*f.*)	the	**les**	the
le livre	the book	**les livres**	the books
la plume	the pen	**les plumes**	the pens
l'arbre (*m.*)	the tree	**les arbres**	the trees
l'amie (*f.*)	the friend	**les amies**	the friends

47. The Indefinite Article. Like the definite article, the indefinite article in French may be either masculine or feminine in form. When used, it too must agree with its noun in gender.

un (*m.*)	a, an	**un homme**	a man
une (*f.*)	a, an	**une femme**	a woman

48. The Plural of Nouns. The plural of a noun is usually formed by adding an **-s** to the singular. Nouns and their plurals shown below are typical of the vast majority of others.

la chaise	the chair	**les chaises**	the chairs
le champ	the field	**les champs**	the fields
l'enfant (*m.* or *f.*)	the child	**les enfants**	the children
l'église (*f.*)	the church	**les églises**	the churches

49. Some Exceptions in Forming the Plural. By no means do all French nouns form the plural according to the principle set forth in the paragraph above. Other methods of forming plurals are explained below.

(1) Nouns that end in **-s, -x,** or **-z** remain unchanged in the plural.

le fils	the son	**les fils**	the sons
le choix	the choice	**les choix**	the choices
le nez	the nose	**les nez**	the noses

(2) Most nouns that end in **-au** or **-eu,** and seven that end in **-ou,** add an **-x** to form the plural.

le chapeau	the hat	**les chapeaux**	the hats
le neveu	the nephew	**les neveux**	the nephews
le bijou	the jewel	**les bijoux**	the jewels

Other nouns that end in **-ou** which add **-x** to form the plural are these: **le caillou** (pebble), **le chou** (cabbage), **le genou** (knee), **le hibou** (owl), **le joujou** (toy), **le pou** (louse).

(3) Most nouns that end in **-al** change the **l** to **u** and add **-x** to form the plural.

le journal	the newspaper	**les journaux**	the newspapers
le cheval	the horse	**les chevaux**	the horses

BUT: **bal, bals** **chacal, chacals**

OBSERVATION

The plural of **ciel** (sky) is **cieux,** of **œil** (eye) **is yeux,** of **travail** (work) is **travaux.**

50. Contractions of the Definite Article. The prepositions **de** and **à** combine with the definite articles **le** and **les** to produce the contractions shown below.

de + le = du	of the, from the, some, any
de + les = des	of the, from the, some, any
à + le = au	to the, at the
à + les = aux	to the, at the

51. How Possession Is Indicated. Whereas in English possession is usually indicated by means of an apostrophe and an s, ('s), in French possession is indicated by using the preposition **de** + a noun.

le livre du professeur	the teacher's book
le livre de Jean	John's book
le chapeau d'un ami	a friend's hat

52. The Partitive. The English words **some** and **any,** when used as adjectives, are translated into French by means of **de** + the article or by using **de** alone.

(1) The partitive idea is expressed by **de** + the article when the sentence is either affirmative or interrogative.

J'ai	**de la viande.**	I have	some meat.
	de l'argent.		some money.
	du pain.		some bread.
	des livres.		some books.
Ai-je	**de la viande?**	Have I	any meat?
	du pain?		any bread?
	des livres?		any books?

(2) The partitive idea is expressed by **de** alone under circumstances that are exemplified in paragraphs *a, b, c,* and *d* below.

a) In the Negative

Je n'ai pas d'argent.	I haven't any money.
Vous n'avez pas de livres.	You haven't any books.
BUT	
Il n'a vu que des arbres.	He saw only trees.

OBSERVATIONS

(1) The partitive is not always translated into English. The sentence **J'ai de l'argent** may be translated *I have some money* or *I have money.* Often the partitive *cannot* be translated. E.g., **Les chevaux sont des animaux. Nous sommes de bons amis.**

(2) The article is not omitted after **ne . . . que** inasmuch as this construction is restrictive rather than negative.

b) AFTER ADVERBS OF QUANTITY

autant	as much, as many	**trop**	too much, too many
assez	enough	**peu**	few, little
beaucoup	much, many, a great deal	**plus**	more
tant	so many, so much	**combien**	how much, how many
moins	less	**que**	how much, how many

assez de chevaux	enough horses
trop d'argent	too much money
Combien de gâteaux?	How many cakes?
Que de monde ici!	What a lot of people here!

OBSERVATION

The words **la plupart** and **bien** require the article.

La plupart des femmes sont jolies.	Most women are pretty.
Il me l'a dit bien des fois.	He told me so many times.

c) AFTER NOUNS OF QUANTITY

un litre de vin	a liter of wine
une douzaine d'œufs	a dozen eggs
une livre de sucre	a pound of sugar
un verre de vin	a glass of wine
une tasse de café	a cup of coffee

But in **une robe de soie** (a silk dress) and **un homme de talent** (a talented man) the **de** is used to form a noun adjective, not a partitive. Note also **un moulin à vent** (a windmill) and **une montre en or** (a gold watch).

d) WHEN ADJECTIVE PRECEDES NOUN

de jolies robes	(some) pretty dresses
de grands arbres	(some) large trees
de belles femmes	(some) beautiful women
de nouveaux chapeaux	(some) new hats

OBSERVATION

If the adjective is usually associated in meaning with a particular noun, the article is used. *E.g.*, **des jeunes filles, des**

petits pois. For a list of adjectives that precede the noun cf. §58.

(3) After verbs, expressions, and words that require **de** as a preposition when there is no distinctive adjunct, the article is omitted.

Il a besoin d'argent.	He needs money.
Le seau est plein d'eau.	The bucket is full of water.

BUT

Il a besoin de l'argent que vous avez gagné.	He needs the money which you earned.

(4) The definite article is *not* omitted with the partitive when the noun has a distinctive adjunct, as is exemplified by the sentences in paragraphs *a*, *b*, and *c* below.

a) In the Negative

Je ne veux pas du vin dans cette bouteille.	I don't want any of the wine in that bottle.

b) After an Adverb of Quantity

Beaucoup des soldats de ce pays ne sont pas revenus.	Many of the soldiers of that country did not return.

c) After a Negative Interrogation

The definite article is generally not omitted after a negative interrogation because an affirmative answer is usually expected.

N'a-t-il pas des amis et des connaissances?	Does he not have friends and acquaintances?

53. The Required Definite Article. In French the definite article is absolutely required under a number of circumstances where English makes no use of it at all. These various conditions are set forth and exemplified in the paragraphs that follow.

(1) With nouns used in a general sense.

Les chevaux sont utiles.	Horses are useful.
La philosophie enseigne la sagesse.	Philosophy teaches wisdom.

(2) With proper nouns when modified, and with titles.

Le petit Jean nous rendra visite.	Little John will visit us.
Le général de Gaulle n'accepta pas la défaite.	General de Gaulle did not accept defeat.

(3) With masculine names of countries.

Before masculine names of countries, the prepositions *to* and *in* are expressed by **à** contracted with the article. Under like circumstances, the preposition *from* is translated by **de** contracted with the article. The list below includes nearly all the masculine names of countries.

le Mexique * (Mexico)	**au Mexique** (to *or* in Mexico)	**du Mexique** (of *or* from Mexico)
le Japon	**au Japon**	**du Japon**
le Canada	**au Canada**	**du Canada**
le Portugal †	**au Portugal**	**du Portugal**
le Danemark †	**au Danemark**	**du Danemark**
le Brésil	**au Brésil**	**du Brésil**
les Etats-Unis	**aux Etats-Unis**	**des Etats-Unis**

(4) With feminine names of countries.

The definite article must be used with feminine names of countries except after the preposition **en** (*to* or *in*) and **de** (*from*).

La France est un beau pays.	France is a beautiful country.
Nous avons parcouru l'Espagne.	We traveled through Spain.

(5) With names of days of the week.

The definite article must be used with names of days of the week whenever the sentence conveys the notion of habitual or recurring action.

Le samedi (les samedis *or* tous les samedis) elle va au marché.	She goes to market on Saturday (every Saturday *or* Saturdays).

* All other names of countries that end in **-e** are feminine.

† **Portugal** and **Danemark** are the only countries in Europe whose designations are masculine. It is also correct to say **en Portugal** and **en Danemark.**

Il vient toujours le dimanche (les dimanches *or* tous les dimanches).	He always comes on Sunday (Sundays *or* every Sunday).

OBSERVATION

The definite article is regularly omitted if the sentence does not convey the notion of habitual or recurring action.

Il viendra dimanche.	He will come Sunday.

(6) With special expressions.

le mois prochain	next month
vers le soir	towards evening
Il étudie le français.	He studies French.

OBSERVATION

The article is omitted with **parler** if the noun immediately follows the verb.

Il parle français. BUT **Il parle très bien le français.**

54. Omission of the Definite Article. Just as the definite article must be used under certain circumstances, so must it also be omitted in other cases. Several examples of the latter are given below.

(1) After the prepositions **en** and **de** when these occur before the feminine name of a country.

la France (France)	**en France** (to *or* in France)	**de France** (of *or* from France)
l'Angleterre	**en Angleterre**	**d'Angleterre**
la Suisse	**en Suisse**	**de Suisse**
l'Afrique	**en Afrique**	**d'Afrique**

OBSERVATION

If the name of the country is modified, *to* or *in* is expressed by **dans** + the definite article; *from* is expressed by **de** + the definite article. *E.g.,* **dans la Suisse française, de l'Afrique du Nord.**

(2) With titles or modified proper nouns in informal direct address.

Bonjour, petit Jean.	Good day, little John.
Bonsoir, général Duchamp.	Good evening, General Duchamp.

OBSERVATION

In formal direct address one would say: **Bonjour, monsieur le général. Bonne nuit, monsieur le professeur.**

(3) With the names of cities and towns unless the article is part of the name.

à Paris	to (at *or* in) Paris	**de Paris**	from Paris
à Chicago	to (at *or* in) Chicago	**de Chicago**	from Chicago

BUT: **Le Havre, au Havre, du Havre, La Nouvelle-Orléans, à la Nouvelle-Orléans, de la Nouvelle-Orléans.**

55. Idiomatic Use of the Definite Article. The French definite article presents certain idiomatic peculiarities which make it differ notably in usage from the English definite article. Examples given below illustrate some of the more common French usages.

(1) When referring to values, the French definite article used with distributive force replaces the English indefinite article.

Le beurre coûte dix francs la livre.	Butter costs ten francs a pound.

OBSERVATION

The idea of time in a distributive sense is expressed by **par.**

Il ne mange que deux fois par jour.	He eats only twice a day.
Le train part six fois par semaine.	The train leaves six times a week.

(2) For translating the prepositions *on, in,* and *with* in certain expressions.

Nous partirons *le* six juin.	We shall leave *on* June the sixth.
Il vient toujours *le* lundi.	He always comes *on* Monday.
Il travaille *le* matin, *l'*après-midi et *le* soir.	He works *in* the morning, *in* the afternoon, and *in* the evening.
Elle parla *la* main levée.	She spoke *with* her hand raised.

(3) To replace the possessive adjectives when referring to parts of the body or to clothing, and when there is no ambiguity as to the possessor.

Il s'est coupé *le* doigt.	He has cut *his* finger.
Il avait *la* main dans *la* poche.	He had *his* hand in *his* pocket.
Elle avait *les* yeux rouges.	*Her* eyes were red.

56. Elision. Vowel sounds represented by the letters **a, e,** and **i** are elided under the circumstances set out below.

a — The **a** of **la,** both article and pronoun, elides before an initial vowel or **h** mute.
l'élève (the pupil) **Je l'ai vue.** I have seen her.
l'histoire (the story)

e — The **e** of **me, te, se, ne, je, de,** and **le,** of the neuter demonstrative pronoun **ce,** and of **que** alone and in such compounds as **parce que, bien que, quoique,** and others elides before an initial vowel or **h** mute.

i — The **i** of **si** elides only before **il** and **ils.**
s'il and **s'ils** BUT **si elle**

OBSERVATION

Elision does not occur before an aspirate **h.**

la hauteur the height **le héros** the hero

IDIOMATIC EXPRESSIONS

s'agir de	to be about, to be a question of, to be the thing to do	**Il s'agit de mon frère. Il s'agit de le faire.**
s'emparer de	to seize	**Le roi s'empare du pays.**

A la bonne heure	Fine!	**n'importe**	it does not matter
de bonne heure	early	**n'importe où**	anywhere
à peu près	almost	**n'importe qui**	anybody
au loin	in the distance	**n'importe quoi**	anything
de loin	from a distance	**n'importe quel livre**	any book
en bas	downstairs	**ou bien**	or else
en haut	upstairs		

I

LECTURE

Lisez à haute voix.

1. —Je n'ai rien à déclarer, monsieur! 2. —A la bonne heure! Nous allons fouiller un peu vos bagages. Tant mieux, si vous n'avez rien. 3. —Cherchez, monsieur! Cherchez dans n'importe quelle valise, a dit le voyageur, mal à son aise! 4. Au loin on pouvait entendre le sifflet du paquebot qui partait. 5. A peu près cinq cents voyageurs se bousculaient dans la salle. 6. Le sourire aux lèvres, le douanier venait de trouver trois grandes boîtes de cigares. 7. —Monsieur, vous m'aviez bien dit! . . . 8. —En effet, de quoi s'agit-il? 9. —Allons! vous savez très bien de quoi il s'agit! 10. —Vous allez tout gentiment me payer ça ou bien on va s'emparer de tout! 11. —Mais monsieur, je suis professeur de français, je croyais bien! . . . 12. —Bon! très bien! alors vous êtes professeur de français! . . . N'importe! Tout le monde doit acquitter les droits! 13. N'importe où, dans tous les ports d'entrée, il faut les acquitter! 14. —Bon! je payerai n'importe quoi pour rentrer en possession de mes cigares. 15. —C'est ça! Nous allons monter en haut. 16. On ne vous fouille en bas que les bagages, c'est en haut qu'on vous fouille la bourse! 17. Vous apprenez de bonne heure, n'est-ce pas?, qu'on ne voyage pas sans quelques inconvénients! 18. —Si j'avais le courage de M. Perrichon, je vous appellerais «un méchant Gabelou»! 19. —Monsieur le professeur de français, ne vous faites pas de mauvais sang! 20. Tout à l'heure je vais

vous offrir un petit verre et, à propos, je pourrais accepter un de vos fameux cigares!

Répondez aux questions suivantes: 1. Quelle est la fonction des douaniers? 2. Pourquoi le voyageur est-il mal à son aise? 3. Que trouve-t-on dans la valise du voyageur? 4. Que faut-il qu'il fasse pour rentrer en possession de ses cigares? 5. Pourquoi le voyageur explique-t-il au douanier qu'il est professeur de français? 6. Est-ce que le douanier veut bien se faire offrir un cigare? 7. Qui était M. Perrichon? 8. Faites un résumé de cette lecture.

II

ORAL AND WRITTEN EXERCISES

A. *Put the following phrases into the plural.* 1. un arbre, une plume, un livre 2. à l'arbre, au garçon, à la tante 3. de l'ami, de la ville 4. l'auto du médecin, le cahier du professeur, le pied de la vache.

B. *Fill in the blanks with the word for* some *or* any. 1. J'ai ____ amis mais je n'ai pas ____ argent. 2. Elle a ____ frères mais elle n'a pas ____ sœurs. 3. Nous avons ____ souliers mais nous n'avons pas ____ chaussettes. 4. Je mange ____ pain mais je ne mange pas ____ viande. 5. Prenez ____ sucre mais ne prenez pas ____ crême.

C. *Repeat Exercise B, making the first clause negative and the second clause affirmative. E.g.,* Je n'ai pas d'amis mais j'ai de l'argent.

D. *Translate the italicized English words.* 1. Nous ne mangeons pas *enough* légumes. 2. J'ai acheté deux *pounds of* sucre. 3. *How much* lait buvez-vous *a* jour? 4. Avez-vous vu *little* Marie dernièrement? 5. D'habitude, ils viennent *on Thursday.* 6. *Next week* ils vont venir *on Sunday.* 7. Il parle *French* et lit *German.* 8. Etudiez-vous *in the morning* ou *in the evening?* 9. Va-t-il *to New Orleans* ou *to New York?*

E. ORAL

(a) *Model:* **Vous avez des amis mais j'ai plus d'amis que vous.** 1. You have troubles but I have more troubles than you. 2. I have vices but you have more vices than I. 3. They have cars but we have more cars than they. 4. She eats bonbons but he eats more bonbons than she. 5. I buy dresses but you buy more dresses than I.
Repeat, substituting **en.** *Example:* Vous avez des amis mais j'en ai plus que vous. See §67, (2).

(b) *Model:* **Avez-vous des amis? Oui, j'ai de bons amis.** 1. Have you any eggs? Yes, I have some good eggs. 2. Has she any dresses? Yes, she has some pretty dresses. 3. Have they any horses? Yes, they have some beautiful horses. 4. Are there any women here? Yes, there are some beautiful women here. 5. Are there any trees in the yard? Yes, there are some big trees in the yard.
Repeat, substituting **en** *for the noun in each second sentence. Example:* Avez-vous des amis? Oui, j'en ai de bons. I have some good ones. See §67, (2).

F. *Put the following sentences into (1) the imperfect, (2) the future, (3) the conditional, (4) the perfect, (5) the present subjunctive. To the present subjunctive prefix* il doute qu'. 1. Il s'agit de mon frère. 2. Il a raison. 3. Ils aiment beaucoup les cerises.

IRREGULAR VERBS

G. *Consult:* **Devoir** (§138), **Unit** 6.

(a) *Translate:* 1. Il doit partir. 2. Ils doivent de l'argent. 3. Je devrais le faire. 4. J'ai dû le faire. 5. J'aurais dû le faire. 6. Ils durent le faire. 7. Le train devait partir dans dix minutes. 8. Combien vous dois-je? 9. Il me devait la vie.

(b) *Write:* 1. We owe him money. 2. We ought to pay him. 3. He has had to leave. 4. He was to leave. 5. What am I to do? 6. He ought to have left. 7. You must have known. 8. They had had to stay.

III

OPTIONAL

H. *Translate. Consult:* **Lecture** (Chap. 6), **devoir** (§138), *and* **Conversation** 6. 1. He said that he had nothing to declare. 2. So much the better if they find nothing. 3. He had about five hundred cigars in his valise. 4. He would pay anything to get back his cigars. 5. He ought not to have said that he had nothing. 6. That is **(voilà)** why he had to go upstairs. 7. He knew very well what it was all about. 8. We were still good friends. 9. Roses are flowers. 10. They speak English and French in Canada. 11. His father was born in Switzerland but he has not been there. 12. They say that children are treasures. 13. We haven't any Chinese newspapers here. 14. Say anything to anybody. 15. Don't say anything to anyone. 16. When they were in Washington they saw the White House but they did not visit it. 17. Ask him if we are friends. 18. What are elephants?

IV

CONVERSATION 6

1. Quelle langue parle-t-on en Angleterre (au Canada, en France, en Espagne, au Mexique, à l'église, en Chine, en Italie, en Russie, en Allemagne, etc.)? —En Angleterre on parle anglais. On y parle anglais.

2. Avez-vous visité la France, l'Allemagne, le Mexique, etc.? —Oui (Non), je (ne) l'ai (pas) visité(e).

3. Où demeurez-vous? Où êtes-vous né? —Je demeure à Saint-Louis. Je suis né à la Nouvelle-Orléans.

4. Avez-vous un livre (une auto, une maison, un château, de l'argent, de l'argent italien, des enfants, des journaux chinois, des amis russes, des qualités exceptionnelles, des talents, du génie? —Oui, j'ai un . . . , une . . . , de l' . . . , des . . . , du . . . . Non, je n'ai pas de . . . , d' . . . .

5. Est-ce que les chevaux (lions, tigres, chiens, chats, loups, éléphants, chameaux, chacals, mules, ânes, vaches, moutons, chèvres) sont des animaux sauvages ou domestiques? —Les chevaux sont des animaux domestiques.

6. Les marguerites sont des fleurs. Qu'est-ce que c'est que les roses (violettes, pensées, chrysanthèmes, tulipes)?

7. Sommes-nous de bons amis, vous et moi? Demandez à un de vos camarades si vous êtes de bons amis, vous et lui.

8. Est-ce que les femmes (hommes, enfants) sont des anges (diables, monstres, trésors)?

9. Choisissez n'importe qui et dites-lui n'importe quoi.

10. Est-ce que vous avez été (êtes allé) à Paris, à la Nouvelle-Orléans, en Allemagne, en Afrique, en Amérique du Sud,* etc.? —J'ai (Je n'ai pas) été. . . . Je (ne) suis (pas) allé. . . . J'y ai été. Je n'y ai pas été. J'y suis allé. Je n'y suis pas allé.

11. Quand (Lorsque) vous étiez à Paris, etc., avez-vous vu la Tour Eiffel (le tombeau de Napoléon, le tombeau du Président Grant, la Maison Blanche, les ruines, les champs de bataille, l'Alamo, le Vieux Carré, le Mardi Gras, la Seine, le Rhin, le Saint-Laurent, les sœurs Dionne, la reine, les pyramides)? —Quand j'étais à Paris j'ai vu le Moulin Rouge, etc.

12. Où êtes-vous allé et qu'avez-vous vu l'été dernier (pendant les vacances)? —Je suis allé au Canada et j'ai vu la Basilique de Sainte-Anne de Beaupré. Je suis resté chez moi et je n'ai rien vu.

Sujets de discussion et de conversation:

1. Les petits verres se vident-ils plus vite aux Etats-Unis qu'en France? Expliquez!

* This usage has replaced **dans l'Amérique du Sud.**

2. De quelle manière préférez-vous voyager? En bateau? En chemin de fer? En avion? A cheval? A bicyclette? A pied?

3. Expliquez ce proverbe: «Qui a beaucoup vu a beaucoup retenu».

4. Quel voyage projetez-vous pour votre lune de miel?

5. Quand vous serez à Paris, qu'irez-vous voir tout d'abord?

CHAPTER 7

ADJECTIVES AND ADVERBS

GRAMMAR

57. Gender and Number of Adjectives. In general adjectives show agreement in gender and number with the noun they modify. Those that are not irregular form the feminine by adding **-e** to the masculine form, the plural by adding **-s** to either the masculine or the feminine form. Adjectives that end in **-e** have the same form in both the masculine and the feminine. The feminine plural always ends in **-s.**

SINGULAR			PLURAL	
Masculine		*Feminine*	*Masculine*	*Feminine*
petit	small	**petite**	**petits**	**petites**
joli	pretty	**jolie**	**jolis**	**jolies**
brun	brown	**brune**	**bruns**	**brunes**
jeune	young	**jeune**	**jeunes**	**jeunes**
bleu	blue	**bleue**	**bleus**	**bleues**
carré	square	**carrée**	**carrés**	**carrées**

(1) Irregularity in gender and number.

(*a*) Among the adjectives that have an irregular feminine form, the following are of frequent occurrence.

Masculine	*Feminine*		*Masculine*	*Feminine*	
bas	**basse**	low	**épais**	**épaisse**	thick
beau	**belle**	beautiful, fine	**faux**	**fausse**	false, untrue
blanc	**blanche**	white	**fou**	**folle**	crazy
bon	**bonne**	good	**frais**	**fraîche**	fresh
cher	**chère**	dear, expensive	**gentil**	**gentille**	nice
doux	**douce**	sweet, gentle	**gros**	**grosse**	big

Masculine	*Feminine*		*Masculine*	*Feminine*	
heureux	**heureuse**	happy	**nouveau**	**nouvelle**	new
léger	**légère**	light	**sec**	**sèche**	dry
long	**longue**	long	**tout neuf**	**toute neuve**	brand new
mou	**molle**	soft	**vieux**	**vieille**	old
neuf	**neuve**	new			

OBSERVATION

Most adjectives that end in **-eux** have **-euse** in the feminine singular.

joyeux, joyeuse **heureux, heureuse** BUT **vieux, vieille**

(*b*) Adjectives that end in **-au** add **-x** to form the plural. Those that end in **-al** have **-aux** in the plural.

beau, beaux **nouveau, nouveaux** **égal, égaux** **loyal, loyaux**

(*c*) Adjectives that end in **-s** or **-x** remain unchanged in the plural.

un joyeux compagnon a gay companion **le livre épais** the thick book
les joyeux compagnons the gay companions **les livres épais** the thick books

(2) Irregular masculine forms. Certain adjectives have two forms for the masculine singular. Forms that end in **-l** occur before a vowel or a mute **h.** Note, however, that the masculine plural has only one form.

Singular		*Plural*	
beau	**bel**	**beaux**	**le beau jardin**
nouveau	**nouvel**	**nouveaux**	**le bel arbre**
vieux	**vieil**	**vieux**	**les beaux jardins**
mou	**mol**	**mous**	**les beaux arbres**
fou	**fol**	**fous**	**un vieil homme**

OBSERVATION

In present-day French the form **vieux** often occurs before a vowel or mute **h.**

58. The Position of Adjectives. When used in its literal sense, the adjective usually follows the noun. When an adjective has a figurative meaning, however, it usually precedes the noun.

(1) The adjectives listed below usually precede the noun.

beau	**petit**	**jeune**	**gros**
nouveau	**court**	**autre**	**mauvais**
vieux	**cher**	**long**	
grand	**joli**	**bon**	

(2) Many adjectives differ in meaning accordingly as they precede or follow the noun.

cher cousin	dear cousin
un chapeau cher	an expensive hat
mon ancien professeur	my former teacher
l'histoire ancienne	ancient history
la même robe	the same dress
la robe même	the very dress
le brave homme	the good man
l'homme brave	the brave man
une maison propre	a clean house
ma propre maison	my own house
un grand homme	a great man
un homme grand	a tall man
le pauvre homme	the poor (pitiable) man
l'homme pauvre	the poor (destitute) man

OBSERVATION

The adjective **prochain** follows the noun when used for designating time (**la semaine prochaine**), but precedes the noun when it assigns position in a series (**la prochaine chaise**). The adjective **dernier (dernière)** precedes the noun only when it indicates the last in a series. *E.g.*, **le dernier mois de l'année. «La dernière Classe.»**

(3) How **tout** and **tel** are used.

The examples below illustrate the use of the forms **tout, tous, toute, toutes** and **tel, tels, telle, telles.**

tout le livre
the whole (*or* entire) book
tous les livres
all (the) books, every book
toute la maison
the whole (*or* entire) house
toutes les femmes
all (the) women, every woman

un tel homme
such a man
une telle femme
such a woman
de tels journaux
such newspapers
de telles revues
such reviews (periodicals)

59. Comparative Forms of the Adjective. The table below, together with the illustrative sentences that follow it, will make clear how adjectives are compared for inequality and for equality.

1. *Superiority*	**plus (grand) que**	taller than
2. *Inferiority*	**moins (grand) que**	less tall than
3. *Equality* 4. *In the negative,* **si** often replaces **aussi.**	**aussi (grand) que** **n'est pas si (aussi) grand que**	as tall as not so (as) tall as
5. *The word* **de** *replaces* **que** *before numbers.*	**plus de cinq heures** **moins de six livres**	more than five hours less than six books

1. **Sa chaise est plus grande que la mienne.**
2. **Ces champs-ci sont plus verts que ceux-là.**
3. **Ses chiens sont moins petits que les leurs.**
4. **Ce garçon-ci est aussi grand que celui-là.**
5. **Mon cheval n'est pas si beau que le sien.**
6. **Ils ont trouvé plus de vingt dollars.**

The word **ne** occurs without negative force in the second part of comparisons of inequality after **plus, moins,** and **mieux.** This usage is optional except in literary style.

Elle est plus vigoureuse qu'elle ne le paraît.	She is more robust than she seems to be.
Il est moins grand que je ne (le) croyais.	He is less tall than I thought he was.

60. Superlative Forms of the Adjective. The superlative of an adjective is formed by placing the definite article or the possessive adjective before **plus** or **moins**.

le plus joli livre	the prettiest book
mon plus long crayon	my longest pencil
nos arbres les plus verts	our greenest trees
les livres les plus intéressants	the most interesting books

(1) Superlative forms that are used when the adjective precedes the noun.

Voilà les plus belles maisons.
Il portait son plus joli chapeau.

(2) Superlative forms that are used when the adjective follows the noun.

Il préférait sa cravate la plus rouge.
Il ne se fie pas à ses amis les plus loyaux.
Voilà le chien le plus féroce.

OBSERVATION

Adjectives which normally precede the noun may follow it in the superlative. *E.g.,* **les maisons les plus belles**
le garçon le plus jeune

(3) After a superlative the English word **in** is translated by **de.**

Le plus grand garçon de l'école.
Les villes les plus intéressantes du monde.
Le meilleur élève de la classe.

61. Irregular Comparison of Adjectives. Three French adjectives are compared irregularly. Of these three adjectives, two have alternative forms in the comparative and the superlative degree, as shown below.

Positive	*Comparative*	*Superlative*
bon good	**meilleur** better	**le meilleur** the best
mauvais bad	**pire** worse **plus mauvais** worse	**le pire** the worst **le plus mauvais** the worst
petit little	**moindre** less **plus petit** less, smaller	**le moindre** the least **le plus petit** the least, smallest

OBSERVATIONS

(1) The adjective **bon** is the only one in French that does not have a regular comparison. Both **mauvais** and **petit** have regular comparisons; the latter are used more frequently than the irregular forms. The regular forms of **petit** refer to size, the irregular ones to importance. The irregular forms, like most other adjectives, agree in gender and number with the nouns they modify.

sa meilleure leçon	his (her, its) best lesson
les plus mauvais livres	the worst books
la moindre difficulté	the least difficulty
les pires obstacles	the worst obstacles

(2) In contrast with English usage, the comparative has the same form as the superlative when two persons or objects are compared.

Voici les deux femmes: Je regarde la plus belle.

62. The Comparison of Adverbs. Adverbs are compared like adjectives. In the superlative degree the **le** is invariable.

Il parle *plus vite que* moi.	faster than
Il parle *moins vite que* moi.	less fast than
Il parle *aussi vite que* moi.	as fast as
Il *ne* parle *pas si vite que* moi.	not so (as) fast as
Elle parle *le plus vite*.	the fastest

(1) Irregular adverbial forms.

mal	badly	**plus mal**	worse		**le plus mal**	the worst
		pis	worse	(rare)	**le pis**	the worst
bien	well	**mieux**	better		**le mieux**	the best
peu	little	**moins**	less		**le moins**	the least

Elle parle le plus vite possible.	She speaks as fast as possible.
Elle étudie le moins possible.	She studies as little as possible.
Vous parlez mieux que moi.	You speak better than I.
BUT	
Vous êtes un meilleur garçon que Jean.	You are a better boy than John.

63. The Formation of Adverbs. Most adjectives may be changed into adverbs of manner by adding **-ment** to the feminine singular. If the masculine adjective ends in a vowel, however, the feminine **-e** is dropped. The ending **-ment** is equivalent to English **-ly.**

Masculine Adjective	*Feminine Adjective*	*Adverb*	
heureux	**heureuse**	**heureusement**	happily
sec	**sèche**	**sèchement**	dryly, sharply
hardi	**hardie**	**hardiment**	boldly
vrai	**vraie**	**vraiment**	really

OBSERVATION

There are several exceptions to this rule. Note the following irregularities:

gai	**gaiement**	**incessant**	**incessamment**	**prudent**	**prudemment**
gentil	**gentiment**	**profond**	**profondément**	**violent**	**violemment**

64. The Position of Adverbs. In simple tenses an adverb follows the verb immediately. In compound tenses, however, adverbs in **-ment** often follow the past participle. (Cf. §39.)

Vous parlez ***trop.***	**Vous avez** ***trop*** **parlé.**
J'y pense ***souvent.***	**J'y ai** ***souvent*** **pensé.**
Ils l'aimaient ***beaucoup.***	**Ils l'avaient** ***beaucoup*** **aimé.**
Elle s'amuse ***peu.***	**Elle s'est** ***peu*** **amusée.**
Elle répondit ***doucement.***	**Elle a répondu** ***doucement.***

OBSERVATION

Remember that the following common adverbs (cf. Obs. §39) of time and place also stand after the past participle in compound tenses: **aujourd'hui, demain, autrefois, hier, tard, tôt, ici, là.** *E.g.,* **Il est parti hier.** **Elles sont arrivées tard.** When used emphatically these adverbs may stand at the beginning of a sentence. *E.g.,* **Ici on parle français.** **Hier il est parti.**

65. Variable Meaning of Words. For the variable meaning of certain adjectives cf. §58, 2.

Le jour même.	The very day.
Le même jour.	The same day.
Il travaille même.	He even works.
Elle travaille assez.	She works enough.
Il est assez malade.	He is rather ill.
C'est une question très (fort, bien) difficile.	It is a very difficult question.
Il est tout pâle.	He is quite pale.
Elle est toute * pâle.	She is quite pale.
Il a tout lu.	He has read everything.
Il a lu tout le livre.	He has read the whole book.
Il va chez Jean.	He goes to John's house.
Il dîne chez nous.	He dines with us.
Nous autres Français, nous aimons beaucoup faire la cuisine.	We Frenchmen are fond of cooking.

IDIOMATIC EXPRESSIONS

envoyer chercher to send for — **Il envoie chercher son ami.**
jeter un coup d'œil (à, sur) to glance — **Elle nous jette un coup d'œil.**

à la longue in the long run
à merveille wonderfully
à plusieurs reprises on several occasions, repeatedly
à tout prix at any cost
pas du tout not at all
rien du tout nothing at all

* When **tout** is used as an adverb that modifies a feminine adjective beginning with a consonant or an aspirate **h,** it takes the feminine form. BUT **Cette personne est tout heureuse.**

Idiomatic Expressions (cont'd)

tous les trois jours every three days
tout à fait quite, entirely
tout à l'heure* in a little while, a little while ago
tout de même all (just) the same
tout de suite at once, immediately
tous (les) deux both
tout le monde everybody

I

LECTURE

Lisez à haute voix.

1. Ce jour-là, il faisait fort chaud et nous avions tous soif, mais le chef d'équipe ne voulait pas demander de l'eau aux montagnards. 2. Tout à l'heure, disait-il, nous allons trouver une source dans laquelle vous pourrez vous désaltérer à merveille. 3. Vaine espérance! S'étant trompé à plusieurs reprises, le chef s'est enfin décidé à m'envoyer chercher de l'eau à une maison qu'on pouvait voir à travers les arbres. 4. La maison semblait tout à fait abandonnée. 5. Tout de même j'ai frappé à la porte et tout de suite deux montagnardes se sont montrées. 6. Je leur ai fait savoir qu'il me fallait à tout prix un seau d'eau fraîche. 7. Elles m'ont jeté un coup d'œil farouche mais l'aînée m'a prié d'attendre. 8. J'ai attendu dix, vingt, trente minutes! Personne! 9. A la longue je me suis impatienté et je suis retourné à l'endroit où les camarades m'attendaient. 10. Un vieillard aux cheveux blancs, connaissant un peu les lenteurs des montagnards, s'est moqué de mon peu de succès, et a bien voulu me servir de remplaçant. 11. Presque tout de suite il était de retour, le seau d'eau à la main. 12. «C'est très drôle,» dit-il. «En me voyant la bonne femme a fait de grands yeux et m'a demandé si j'étais bien le premier qui s'était présenté. 13. Je lui ai dit que oui. 14. —Je vous croyais plus jeune, monsieur! 15. —En effet, je l'étais, ai-je répondu, mais j'ai vieilli en vous attendant!»

* When used with a present tense or a future tense, this expression means *in a little while.* When used with a past tense, it means *recently.* Do not confuse with **à tout à l'heure** which means *I'll be seeing you! So long!*

Répondez aux questions suivantes: 1. Pourquoi avions-nous tous soif? 2. Pourquoi le chef d'équipe ne voulait-il pas demander de l'eau aux montagnards? 3. Est-ce que les montagnardes m'ont fait bon accueil? 4. Est-ce qu'elles se sont dépêchées d'apporter le seau d'eau? 5. Pourquoi est-ce que je suis retourné chez les camarades? 6. Qui a bien voulu me servir de remplaçant? 7. Pourquoi est-ce que la montagnarde a fait de grands yeux? 8. De quelle manière le vieillard lui a-t-il expliqué pourquoi il avait les cheveux blancs? 9. Racontez cette histoire en vous servant de vos propres termes.

II

ORAL AND WRITTEN EXERCISES

A. *Put the following expressions in the plural.* (NOTE: *The plural of* **un** *is* **des**; *when followed by an adjective it is* **de.**) 1. Un bon petit garçon. 2. Un pauvre vieil homme. 3. Le vieux bâtiment noir. 4. Un mauvais travail. 5. Un général loyal. 6. La vieille amie loyale. 7. Un tel homme. 8. Un gros nez rouge. 9. L'homme heureux. 10. Un bel ami.

B. *Translate.* 1. the fine tree, the poor dog, the same house. 2. the entire town, the clean town, the former town. 3. the last class of the year, last month, next month. 4. the very place, such affairs, the same place. 5. every citizen, some expensive clothes, my own family.

C. *Supply* **plus** *or* **moins.** 1. L'or est —— cher que l'argent. 2. Paris est —— grand que New York. 3. Il fait —— froid au Canada qu'au Mexique. 4. On a —— chaud en hiver qu'au printemps. 5. Les riches sont —— nombreux que les pauvres. 6. Chicago a —— de cinq millions d'habitants. 7. Un homme né en 1740 aurait —— de deux cents ans aujourd'hui. 8. Ceux qui dépensent —— qu'ils (ne) gagnent sont sages. 9. La lune est —— grande que le soleil. 10. Elle est beaucoup —— loin de la terre.

le café est sucré

D. ORAL. *Model:* **Il est bon et elle est bonne.** *Repeat the sentence replacing* **bon** *and* **bonne** *with the proper forms of* **petit, brun, blond, blanc, bas, doux, fou, faux, gros, heureux, léger, mou, sec, vieux, beau, naïf, gris, charmant.**

E. ORAL. *Model:* **Il chante bien mais elle chante mieux que lui.** *Repeat the sentence replacing* **chante** *by the word for* speaks, dances, plays, swims, works, studies, has a good time, writes, reads, sleeps.

IRREGULAR VERBS

F. *Consult:* **faire** (§139) **Unit** 7.

(a) *Translate:* 1. Ils le font. 2. Faites-le. 3. Ils le faisaient. 4. Il faut que je le fasse. 5. Nous le ferons. 6. Je l'avais fait. 7. Le fait-il? 8. Il le fit. 9. Ils le feraient. 10. faisant.

(b) *Write:* 1. Let's do it. 2. I do it. 3. We were doing it. 4. You must do it. 5. You would do it. 6. We would have done it. 7. They did it (*Past Def.*). 8. He will do it. 9. He would do it.

(c) oral. *Model:* **Qu'est-ce qui vous a fait rire?** *Say:* What made you cry? . . . speak? . . . say that? . . . believe it? . . . leave? . . . come back? . . . understand? What hurt you? What gave you pleasure? What did you good?

III

OPTIONAL

G. *Translate. Consult:* **Lecture, Conversation** 7, **Unit** 7. 1. The foreman sent me to get some water. 2. When I saw the mountaineer I became afraid, but just the same I asked for some water. 3. He glanced at me and then went back into the house. 4. Immediately he came out with a bucket in his hand. 5. Sir, at any cost, we need fresh water. Do you have any here? 6. No, but I am going to get some at the spring. I will be back in a little while. 7. On several occasions I have traveled in the mountains, and the mountaineers are quite nice. 8. How is the weather today? 9. It is cold but it is not raining. 10. When I went out this morning it was snowing. 11. I am neither hungry nor thirsty. 12. In my opinion it is Raoul who translates best. 13. What I do best is sing. 14. I draw better than anybody. 15. When are you going to have your hair cut? 16. I had my hair cut last week.

IV

CONVERSATION 7

1. Quel temps fait-il aujourd'hui? —Il fait beau (froid, chaud, du vent, mauvais, un temps de chien). Il pleut (neige).

2. Quel temps faisait-il quand vous vous êtes levé (couché); quand vous êtes rentré hier soir (sorti ce matin, arrivé à la classe); quand vous avez quitté la maison (pris votre petit déjeuner)? —Quand je me suis . . . (je suis . . ., j'ai . . .), il faisait . . . (il pleuvait, neigeait).

3. Etes-vous Américain(e) ou Français(e), blond(e) ou brun(e), petit(e) ou grand(e), jeune ou vieux (vieille), heureux ou malheureux (heureuse ou . . .), sage ou fou (folle), triste ou gai(e), riche ou pauvre, hardi(e) ou timide, faible ou fort(e), travailleur (-euse) ou paresseux (-euse), marié(e) ou célibataire, pessimiste ou optimiste, bon(ne) ou méchant(e), naïf (-ve) ou blasé(e)? —Je suis . . . ; je ne suis pas . . . . Je ne suis ni . . . ni . . . .

4. Avez-vous souvent (toujours, quelquefois, rarement) raison (tort, honte, peur, sommeil, froid, chaud, faim, soif, envie de rire, envie de pleurer)? —J'ai souvent raison. J'ai tort quelquefois. J'ai toujours faim. J'ai rarement soif.

5. Demandez à quelqu'un quel temps il fait, quel temps il faisait quand il s'est levé (est sorti, a quitté la maison), s'il est Américain ou Français, etc., s'il a toujours sommeil, etc.

6. A votre avis, quel est le meilleur élève de la classe? —A mon avis le meilleur élève de la classe c'est. . . .

7. Qui est-ce qui parle (comprend, écrit, prononce, traduit) le mieux? —A mon avis c'est . . . qui parle le mieux.

8. Qu'est-ce que vous faites le mieux (le moins bien)? —Ce que je fais le mieux c'est de jouer du piano (danser, chanter, taper à la machine, parler français, dessiner, patiner, étudier).

9. Quelle est votre classe la plus (moins) intéressante (ennuyeuse)?

10. Est-ce que vous chantez (dansez, parlez français, tapez à la machine, dessinez, jouez du piano, jouez au football) mieux (moins bien, aussi bien) que moi (votre frère, votre sœur, n'importe qui)?

11. Est-ce que vous vous faites couper les cheveux toutes les semaines (tous les quinze jours, tous les mois)? —Je me fais. . . .

12. Quand vous êtes-vous fait couper les cheveux pour la dernière fois? —Je me suis fait couper les cheveux il y a . . . jours.

13. Quand allez-vous vous faire couper les cheveux? —Je vais me faire couper les cheveux cet après-midi (demain, après-demain, la semaine prochaine, d'aujourd'hui en huit).

14. Demandez à quelqu'un s'il chante mieux que vous, s'il se fait couper les cheveux tous les six mois, quand il s'est fait couper les cheveux, quand il va se faire couper les cheveux.

Sujets de discussion et de conversation:

1. Quelle est votre saison préférée?
2. Si vous en aviez le choix, quel climat choisiriez-vous?
3. Le climat exerce-t-il une influence sur le tempérament des hommes?
4. Aimeriez-vous vivre à l'état de nature dans une île des tropiques?
5. Y a-t-il des différences entre les arts du nord et les arts du midi?

CHAPTER 8

I. THE PERSONAL PRONOUNS

GRAMMAR

66. Table of Personal Pronouns. Immediately below, arranged in compact form for purposes of ready reference as well as hasty yet comprehensive review, are all the French personal pronouns complete as to kind, gender, and number. The *disjunctives* are used in cases where the pronoun is stressed. All other pronouns, known as *conjunctives,* are used in cases where the pronoun is unstressed.

Subject		*Direct Object*		*Indirect Object*		*Reflexives*		*Disjunctives*	
je	I	**me**	me	**me**	to, for me	**me**	myself	**moi**	I, me
tu	you	**te**	you	**te**	to, for you	**te**	yourself	**toi**	you
il	he, it	**le**	him, it	**lui**	to, for him	**se**	himself	**lui**	he, him
elle	she, it	**la**	her, it	**lui**	to, for her	**se**	herself	**elle**	she, her
nous	we	**nous**	us	**nous**	to, for us	**nous**	ourselves	**nous**	we, us
vous	you	**vous**	you	**vous**	to, for you	**vous**	yourself(ves)	**vous**	you
ils	they	**les**	them	**leur**	to, for them	**se**	themselves	**eux**	they, them
elles	they	**les**	them	**leur**	to, for them	**se**	themselves	**elles**	they, them

Emphatic pronouns are formed by adding **-même** to the disjunctive pronouns. *E.g.,* **moi-même** *myself*. The other forms are these: **toi-même, lui-même, elle-même, nous-mêmes, vous-même(s), eux-mêmes, elles-mêmes.**

Je l'ai fait moi-même. I did it myself.

67. The Pronouns *y* and *en*. The words **y** and **en,** sometimes called pronominal adverbs, may be better understood, perhaps, by regarding them simply as pronouns that serve various particular purposes under a variety of circumstances. Some characteristic uses of these two pronouns are explained below.

(1) When referring to things — and only seldom to persons — the pronoun **y** replaces a phrase that may be introduced by **à, dans, sur,** or any one of several other prepositions, but never by **de.** According to the context, **y** may mean *there, in it, on it, to them, them, it, about it,* and so on. Whenever **y** means *there,* it refers to a place that has already been mentioned. The word **là,** on the contrary, which also means *there,* usually points out a place that has not been previously mentioned.

Il obéit à mes souhaits.	He obeys (complies with) my wishes.
Il y obéit. (**y** = à mes souhaits)	He obeys (complies with) them.
Elle s'attend à cela.	She is expecting that.
Elle s'y attend. (**y** = à cela)	She is expecting it.
Il est entré dans le salon.	He entered the drawing room.
Il y est entré. (**y** = dans le salon)	He entered it.
Le livre est sur la table.	The book is on the table.
Le livre y est. (**y** = sur la table)	The book is there (on it).
Asseyez-vous là, mon vieux.	Sit down there, old fellow.
Je me fie à vos conseils.	I trust your advice.
Je m'y fie. (**y** = à vos conseils)	I trust it.

OBSERVATION

Note that in the above examples the antecedents are abstractions or objects. When the antecedent is a person, the indirect object is commonly used unless the construction calls for **à** + the disjunctive, as described in §71 below. However, the pronoun **y** does at times refer to persons when a stressed noun or pronoun is the immediate antecedent.

Croyez vous qu'elle pense à lui?	Do you believe that she thinks about him?
Mais oui, elle y pense.	Certainly, she thinks about him.

(2) The pronoun **en** usually replaces a prepositional phrase that is introduced by **de.** Specifically, **en** replaces a noun that is preceded (*a*) by any of the partitive forms, **de, du, de la, des, d'**;

(*b*) by a numeral; (*c*) by an adverb or a noun of quantity that is followed by **de**; (*d*) **en** also replaces a noun preceded by **de** in non-partitive constructions. The word **en** may also stand for **de là** when the latter means *from there.* According to the context, the pronoun **en** may mean *some, any, of it, of them, it, its, from there, them, because of it,* and so on.

(*a*)	**Il a mangé des pommes.**	He ate (some) apples.
	Il en a mangé. (en = des pommes)	He ate some.
(*b*)	**Il choisit trois livres.**	He chooses three books.
	Il en choisit trois. (en = des livres)	He chooses three (of them).
(*c*)	**Alice a beaucoup d'amis.**	Alice has many friends.
	Alice en a beaucoup. (en = d'amis)	Alice has many (of them).
(*d*)	**J'ai parlé de mes leçons.**	I spoke of my lessons.
	J'en ai parlé. (en = de mes leçons)	I spoke of them.
	Je me souviens de ce livre.	I remember that book.
	Je m'en souviens. (en = de ce livre)	I remember it.
	Note also:	
	Nous arrivons de Paris.	We came from Paris.
	Nous en arrivons. (en = de Paris)	We came from there.
	Jean a mangé trop de cerises.	John ate too many cherries.
	Il en est malade. (en = parce qu'il en a **trop** mangé)	He is ill because of it.

OBSERVATION

Note that in examples (*a*) and (*c*) the antecedent is a noun used partitively, and that here **en** can represent either persons or things. But when standing for a noun that is not used partitively and is governed by prepositional **de,** as in example (*d*),

en may refer only to objects or abstractions, unless the person referred to has just been mentioned. In the latter case, **en** may replace **de** + a *disjunctive.*

Je ne me souviens pas d'elle.	I don't remember her.
Il parlait souvent de son fils.	He often spoke of his son.
Il parlait souvent de lui.	He often spoke of him.
BUT	
Henri a fait la connaissance de Jeanne il y a six mois, et il en est tombé amoureux.	Henry met Joan six months ago and fell in love with her.

(3) According to whether the object is governed by the preposition **à** or the preposition **de**, the following verbs differ in meaning.

Il répond à la question.	He answers the question.
Il y répond.	He answers it.
Je réponds de ses idées.	I answer for his ideas.
J'en réponds.	I answer for them.
Ils ont joué aux * cartes.	They played cards.
Ils y ont joué.	They played them.
Elles jouent du * piano.	They play the piano.
Elles en jouent.	They play it.
Jean pense à † ses livres.	John thinks about his books.
Jean y pense.	John thinks about them.
Que pense-t-il de † mon auto?	What does he think of my car?
Qu'en pense-t-il?	What does he think of it?
Il a manqué à ses devoirs.	He failed in his duties.
Il y a manqué.	He failed in them.
Le pauvre manque de pain.	The poor man lacks bread.
Le pauvre en manque.	The poor man lacks it.

But when referring to persons, the disjunctive pronouns are normally used with the verbs **penser** and **répondre de.**

* The expression **jouer à** is used of games, **jouer de** of musical instruments.

† The term **penser à** means to turn one's thoughts towards a person or thing; **penser de** means to have an opinion concerning a person or thing.

Je réponds de Jean.	I answer for John.
Je réponds de lui.	I answer for him.
Il pense à son père.	He is thinking of his father.
Il pense à lui.	He is thinking of him.

68. The Position of Pronouns. In French the personal pronouns, excluding the disjunctives, precede the verb except in the affirmative imperative.

(1) Word order before the verb.

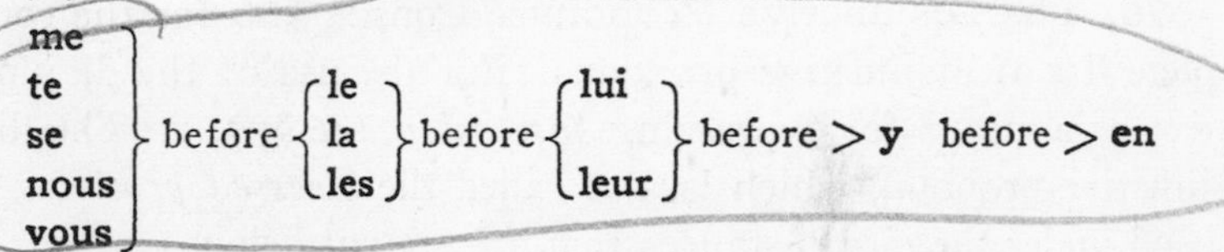

Il les donne à Jean.	He gives them to John.
Il les lui a donnés.	He gave them to him.
Il ne les leur donnera pas.	He will not give them to them.
Lui en avions-nous parlé?	Had we spoken to him about it?
Ils s'y sont bien amusés.	They had a good time there.
Vous les donne-t-elle?	Is she giving them to you?
Il n'y en a pas.	There aren't any.

(2) Word order in the affirmative imperative.

Pronouns in the affirmative imperative follow the verb in the same order as in English. They are joined to the verb and to each other by a hyphen. Unless followed by **en,** the personal pronouns **me** and **te** become **moi** and **toi,** since they are in a stressed position.

DIRECT OBJECT > INDIRECT OBJECT > **y** > **en**

Donnez-moi le livre.	Give me the book.
Donnez-le-moi.	Give it to me.
Lève-toi!	Get up!
Montrons-lui-en.	Let's show him some.
Donnez-m'en.	Give me some.
Allons-y.	Let's go there.
Ne me donnez pas le livre.	Do not give me the book.
Ne me le donnez pas.	Do not give it to me.

69. The Invariable Pronoun *le*. This pronoun, whose antecedent is always an idea that is contained in a previous statement, means *so* when translated at all.

Etes-vous content de lui?—Je le suis.	Are you satisfied with him? I am (so).
Vous dites que je suis libre, mais je ne le suis pas.	You say that I'm free, but I'm not.
Etes-vous reine? —Non, je ne le suis pas.	Are you a queen? No, I am not.

II. DISJUNCTIVE PRONOUNS

70. The Disjunctive Pronouns. Consult §66 for the complete list of disjunctive pronouns. For the use of the disjunctive as a means for expressing *possession,* see §75, 2. The disjunctive pronoun, which is also called the *stressed pronoun,* is used under the circumstances that are set out below.

(1) In an absolute sense; *i.e.,* when the verb is omitted.

Qui frappe à la porte? Moi.	Who is knocking at the door? I (am).

(2) After prepositions.

Il voyage avec elle.	He is traveling with her.
J'y vais sans eux.	I am going there without them.

(3) In comparisons.

Elle est plus grande que lui.	She is taller than he.
Il est moins fort que moi.	He is less strong than I.

(4) After **ce** or **c'** + **être** as predicate nominative, in answer to the question **qui est-ce?**

C'est moi.	It is I.
C'est nous.	It is we.
Ce sont eux.	It is they.

(5) To express emphasis.

Je les vois, eux.	I see *them.*
Moi, je vous le donne.	*I'm* giving it to you.
Je vous parle à vous.	I'm speaking to *you.*
Il se flatte, lui.	*He's* flattering himself.
C'est moi qui le dis.	*I* say it.

OBSERVATION

In this case the conjunctive pronoun, subject or object, as well as the disjunctive, is usually employed. In English the pronoun is emphasized by inflecting the voice.

(6) When the subject or object of the verb is compound.

Lui et moi, nous les aimons.	He and I like them.
Vous et lui, vous travaillez.	You and he are working.
Eux et lui (ils) travaillent.	They and he are working.
Il (les) a cherchés lui et elle.	He looked for him and her.
Il (leur) a parlé à lui et à elle.	He spoke to him and her.

(7) When **aussi** or a similar word intervenes between the subject pronoun and the verb.

Lui, aussi, il me l'a dit.	He too told me so.

71. Disjunctive Pronouns as Verbal Complements. The disjunctive pronoun replaces the unstressed or conjunctive pronoun under the circumstances that are described and exemplified in the paragraphs below.

(1) Following a verb, after the preposition **à** when **à** serves as a synonym for **vers** (*toward*) and stresses direction.

Il vient à moi.	He comes to me.
Elle a couru à eux.	She ran to them.
Nous pensions à vous.	We were thinking about you.
Elle alla à lui.	She went to him.

(2) When the direct object is **me, te, se, nous,** or **vous** the indirect object must be expressed by **à** followed by the disjunctive. To apply this rule to the diagram in §68, we can never combine two pronouns from the same column or from the first and third columns.

Il m'a présenté à son père.	He introduced me to his father.
Il m'a présenté à lui.	He introduced me to him.
Je m'adresse à vous.	I come (address myself) to you.
Il s'en rapporte à eux.	He leaves it up to them.

BUT

Il m'a présenté son père.	He introduced his father to me.
Il me l'a présenté.	He introduced him to me.

III. TROUBLESOME VERBS

72. écouter, attendre, chercher, regarder, payer. The more common English equivalents of these verbs govern their object by means of a preposition. In French, however, all these verbs take a direct object.

Le père écoute son fils.	The father listens *to* his son.
J'ai attendu Jean.	I waited *for* John.
Il cherchait son chapeau.	He was looking *for* his hat.
Elle regarde le jardin.	She is looking *at* the garden.
Qui paye le billet?	Who is paying *for* the ticket?

73. répondre, ressembler, obéir, plaire, entrer. The commoner English equivalents of these verbs take a direct object in English. In French, on the contrary, these verbs require a preposition before the object.

Ils répondent *à* mes lettres.	They answer my letters.
Elle ressemble *à* son père.	She resembles her father.
Le fils obéit *à* sa mère.	The son obeys his mother.
Le concert plaît *à* Jean.	The concert pleases John.
Je suis entré *dans* la maison.	I entered the house.

74. demander, payer, emprunter. Note that one *asks for, pays for,* or *borrows* something (direct object) to (from, for) somebody (indirect object).

Il demande de l'argent.	He asks for money.
Il demande de l'argent à son père.	He asks his father for money.
Il lui en demande.	He asks him for some.
Il demande à son père de lui donner de l'argent.	He asks his father to give him some money.
Il lui demande de lui en donner.	He asks him to give him some.
Je paye les légumes à l'épicier.	I pay the grocer for the vegetables.
Je lui paye les légumes.	I pay him for the vegetables.
Je les lui paye.	I pay him for them.
Ils empruntent des livres à leurs amis.	They borrow some books from their friends.
Ils leur en empruntent.	They borrow some from them.

OBSERVATION

The verb payer may take two direct objects. *E.g.*, **J'ai payé vingt francs ces gants.** I paid twenty francs for these gloves.

IDIOMATIC EXPRESSIONS

s'entendre (avec) to get along (with) — **Il s'entend avec son père.**
se heurter contre to bump into — **Elle s'est heurtée contre la chaise.**
prêter l'oreille to listen attentively — **Ils lui ont prêté l'oreille.**

à cause de on account of
à la fin finally
à son gré to one's liking
au fond at heart, fundamentally
au juste exactly
auprès de with, (next to)
bon marché cheap
d'ailleurs besides, moreover
d'après according to
en outre in addition
faute de for lack of, through want of
malgré in spite of
près de near (not distant from)
quant à as for

I

LECTURE

Lisez à haute voix.

1. —Vous dites qu'il ne s'entend pas avec sa belle-mère? Pourquoi? 2. —Je ne sais pas au juste. 3. Mais on dit qu'elle parle beaucoup et il paraît que le gendre ne l'écoute pas comme il faut. 4. —Ah! Ce pauvre garçon! Je lui disais bien qu'il ne trouverait pas ce mariage à son gré! 5. —Au fond, il s'est perdu faute d'expérience dans les affaires de cœur. 6. —D'après vous, alors, ce n'était pas à cause de son argent . . . 7. —Voilà justement ce qui est drôle! Malgré ce qu'on disait, il paraît que sa femme n'a pas le sou. 8. —Quel désastre! Et maintenant il a auprès de lui la belle-mère! 9. —Où demeure-t-il? 10. Il y a quelques semaines, il cherchait un appartement à meilleur marché. 11. —On m'a dit qu'il a fini par en trouver un. 12. —Vous aimez votre belle-mère, n'est-ce pas? 13. —Oui, je

l'adore. D'ailleurs, nous nous entendons fort bien. 14. —A propos, comment vous êtes-vous fait mal à l'œil gauche? 15. —Je me suis heurté contre la porte hier soir. . . .

Répondez aux questions suivantes: 1. Pourquoi est-il souvent difficile de s'entendre avec les belles-mères? 2. Est-ce qu'on s'entend toujours bien avec les beaux-pères? 3. Pourquoi s'est-il perdu, ce pauvre garçon? 4. S'est-il marié avec une femme riche? 5. Que cherchait-il? 6. A-t-il enfin réussi à trouver ce qu'il cherchait? 7. Doit-on comprendre que celui qui parle aime tendrement sa belle-mère? 8. Peut-on accepter son explication de sa blessure à l'œil gauche? 9. Faites un résumé de cette lecture en vos propres termes.

II

ORAL AND WRITTEN EXERCISES

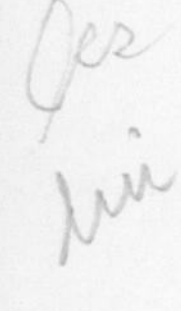

A. *Substitute* **y, en,** *or a disjunctive or personal pronoun for each of the phrases in parentheses.* 1. Ils répondront (aux questions). 2. Avez-vous (des animaux favoris)? 3. J'avais pris trois (billets). 4. Les enfants doivent obéir (à leurs parents). 5. Les mères parlent (de leurs ménages). 6. Les élèves parlaient (de leurs leçons). 7. Le professeur a donné (des devoirs aux élèves). 8. Donnons (du lait au chat). 9. Ne donnez pas (cette bille à cet enfant). 10. Elle a montré (son tablier neuf à sa tante).

B. *Conjugate the following verbs in the present indicative, present subjunctive, future, imperfect, and conditional.* 1. j'obéis 2. j'attends 3. j'écoute 4. je suis 5. j'ai.

C. *Read the following sentences, replacing dashes by prepositions when necessary.* 1. Les enfants doivent obéir —— leurs pères. 2. Ils doivent écouter —— leurs conseils et répondre —— leurs questions. 3. Trop souvent ils ne cherchent que —— leur propre plaisir. 4. Alors ils ressemblent —— des animaux sauvages. 5. Tout le monde regarde —— ces jeunes gens d'un œil irrité et ils ne plaisent —— personne. 6. Elle avait payé six francs —— ses légumes. 7. Il avait demandé de l'argent —— son père. 8. Combien d'argent avait-il emprunté —— son oncle?

D. *Translate the following sentences (1) as they are; (2) substituting* **her** *for* **him**; *(3) substituting* **them** *for* **him**; *(4) in the negative.* 1. Listen to him. 2. Wait for him. 3. Look for him. 4. Look at him. 5. Answer him. 6. Obey him.

E. *Translate.* 1. He introduced me to his father. 2. He introduced me to him. 3. He introduced his brother to me. 4. He introduced him to me. 5. I had asked him for money. 6. He wanted to borrow some eggs from his neighbor. 7. She was thinking of him. 8. The dog was running to them. 9. He had sold them to her. 10. I had bought them from him.

IRREGULAR VERBS

F. *Consult:* **valoir** (§140), **falloir** (§141) in **Unit** 8.
(a) *Translate:* 1. Nos efforts nous ont valu le succès. 2. Il lui faut un mari. 3. Est-ce que cela vaut la peine? 4. Il vaudrait mieux rester à la maison. 5. Il faut que j'aille chez eux. 6. Il faudra beaucoup de temps pour faire ce voyage.

(b) *Write:* 1. My efforts do not always win me success. 2. They need a large house. 3. I doubt that that is worth the trouble. 4. One must not beat a woman, even with a flower. 5. She must go to the store. 6. How much time will it take to do that?

III

OPTIONAL

G. *Translate. Consult:* **Lecture (Chap. 8), Conversation** 8. 1. I do not know exactly whether he gets along with her. 2. It appears that he does not listen to her properly. 3. He has lost his wife for lack of money or because of his mother-in-law. 4. He ought to have looked for a cheaper house. 5. According to his brother he has finally found one to his liking. 6. Guess whom I am thinking about. 7. Speak to someone and ask him what he is thinking about. 8. I asked him what he thought about the situation. 9. Give it back to me. Tell me to give it back to you. 10. Which one of your parents do you resemble? 11. I love my mother but I do not resemble her. 12. I received a letter yesterday but I have not yet answered it. 13. Introduce me to her. 14. Introduce him to me. 15. Introduce us to them. 16. Introduce them to us.

IV

CONVERSATION 8

1. A quoi pensez-vous? —Je pense à la situation internationale (à ma famille, à la crise économique, à mes problèmes personnels, à l'avenir, au passé, aux vacances).

2. Devinez à qui je pense! —Est-ce que c'est un homme ou une femme? Est-il mort ou vivant? Jeune ou vieux? Célèbre ou peu connu? Américain ou Européen? Militaire ou civil?

3. Qu'est-ce que vous pensez de la situation actuelle (de l'art moderne, de la bombe atomique)?

4. Adressez-vous à quelqu'un et demandez-lui à quoi (qui) il pense, ce qu'il pense de la situation, etc.

5. A qui vous êtes-vous adressé? —Je me suis adressé à . . . .

6. Qu'est-ce que vous lui avez demandé? —Je lui ai demandé à quoi il pensait, ce qu'il pensait de la situation, etc.

7. Qu'est-ce qu'il vous a répondu? —Il m'a répondu qu'il pensait à sa jeunesse, que la situation était excellente (dangereuse, affreuse, délicate).

8. Montrez-moi votre livre (stylo, cahier, crayon). Prêtez-le-moi. Merci. Dites-moi de vous le rendre. —Rendez-le-moi.

9. Ayez la bonté de me prêter votre règle. Merci bien. Dites-moi d'avoir la bonté de vous la rendre. —Ayez la bonté de me la rendre.

10. Auquel de vos parents ressemblez-vous? —Je ressemble à mon (ma) . . . .

11. Ressemblez-vous à votre père? —Je (ne) lui ressemble (pas).

12. Avez-vous reçu une lettre hier? Y avez-vous répondu? —J'y ai déjà répondu. Je n'y ai pas encore répondu.

13. Monsieur . . . , voulez-vous que je vous présente à Mlle . . . ? —J'en meurs d'envie. Présentez-moi à elle, je vous en prie.

14. Mademoiselle, voulez-vous que je vous présente M. . . . ? —Mais oui, présentez-le-moi.

15. Mlle Leblanc, je vous présente M. Lebrun, un charmant garçon. —Enchantée (de faire votre connaissance), monsieur. —C'est un honneur, mademoiselle.

16. Connaissez-vous M. Dupont? —Mais oui, monsieur. Je viens de faire sa connaissance. Non, monsieur, je n'ai pas cet honneur.

Sujets de discussion et de conversation.

1. Que veut dire l'expression, «savoir-faire»?
2. Est-ce qu'un homme pauvre doit se marier avec une femme riche ou vice versa?
3. Existe-t-il des classes sociales aux Etats-Unis?
4. Est-il possible de toujours dire la vérité?
5. Les étudiants aiment-ils être reçus chez leurs professeurs?

CHAPTER 9

POSSESSIVE AND DEMONSTRATIVE ADJECTIVES AND PRONOUNS

GRAMMAR

Since the form of the possessive and demonstrative pronouns is determined by the gender and number of the possessive and demonstrative adjectives, both adjectives and pronouns are treated together in the same paragraph.

75. Possessive Adjectives and Pronouns. Carefully observe all the forms set out in the table below. Note that the agreement of both the possessive adjective and the possessive pronoun is with the noun that denotes the thing possessed, and not with the possessor.

Adjectives			*Pronouns*	
mon cheval	my	horse	**le mien**	mine
ma maison		house	**la mienne**	
mes chevaux		horses	**les miens**	
mes maisons		houses	**les miennes**	
ton cheval	your	horse	**le tien**	yours
ta maison		house	**la tienne**	
tes chevaux		horses	**les tiens**	
tes maisons		houses	**les tiennes**	
son cheval	his	horse	**le sien**	his
sa maison	her	house	**la sienne**	hers
ses chevaux	its	horses	**les siens**	its
ses maisons		houses	**les siennes**	
notre cheval	our	horse	**le nôtre**	ours
notre maison		house	**la nôtre**	
nos chevaux		horses	**les nôtres**	
nos maisons		houses	**les nôtres**	

votre cheval	your	horse	**le vôtre**	yours
votre maison		house	**la vôtre**	
vos chevaux		horses	**les vôtres**	
vos maisons		houses	**les vôtres**	
leur cheval	their	horse	**le leur**	theirs
leur maison		house	**la leur**	
leurs chevaux		horses	**les leurs**	
leurs maisons		houses	**les leurs**	

OBSERVATION

The forms **ma, ta, sa** become **mon, ton, son** before vowels and mute **h.**

(1) The preposition **à** or **de** contracts with **le** and **les** of a possessive pronoun.

le mien	mine	**du mien**	of mine	**des miens**	of mine
		au mien	to mine	**aux miens**	to mine

mon cheval	**Il parle du mien.**	He speaks of mine.
	Il parle au mien.	He speaks to mine.
mes chevaux	**Il parle des miens.**	He speaks of mine.

(2) The idea of ownership can be expressed not only by using the proper possessive pronoun but also by employing the preposition **à** with the suitable disjunctive pronoun. The latter construction occurs, however, only after forms of **être.** This usage appears much more often than **le mien, la mienne, les miens, les miennes,** and the other pronouns so formed.

A qui est ce livre?		Whose book is this?	
Ce livre est à (Ces livres sont à)	**moi.**	This book is (These books are)	mine.
	toi.		yours.
	lui.		his.
	elle.		hers.
	nous.		ours.
	vous.		yours.
	eux.		theirs.
	elles.		theirs.

OBSERVATION

Disjunctive pronouns are used to establish ownership, whereas possessive pronouns are used to establish a distinction in ownership. *E.g.,* **Ces disques-ci sont les miens; ceux-là sont les siens. A qui est cette clé? Elle est à moi.**

(3) When referring to parts of the body or to articles of clothing, particularly when there can be no ambiguity as to who the possessor is, the definite article is frequently used instead of the possessive adjective.

Je lui donne *la* main.	I give him *my* hand.
Il avait *les* yeux bleus.	*His* eyes were blue.
Elle se brosse *les* dents.	She brushes *her* teeth.

76. The Demonstratives and Their Use. In French, the demonstratives may be used both as adjectives and as pronouns. Various forms of the demonstrative and some suggestions for properly using them are set out below.

Singular

Adjectival Forms		Pronominal Forms	
ce chien	this *or* that dog	***celui**	
ce chien-ci	this dog	**celui-ci**	this one, the latter
ce chien-là	that dog	**celui-là**	that one, the former
cet arbre	this *or* that tree	***celui**	
cet arbre-ci	this tree	**celui-ci**	this one
cet arbre-là	that tree	**celui-là**	that one
cette femme	this *or* that woman	***celle**	
cette femme-ci	this woman	**celle-ci**	this one, the latter
cette femme-là	that woman	**celle-là**	that one, the former

Plural

ces chiens	these, those dogs	***ceux**	
ces chiens-ci	these dogs	**ceux-ci**	these, the latter
ces chiens-là	those dogs	**ceux-là**	those, the former
ces femmes	these, those women	***celles**	
ces femmes-ci	these women	**celles-ci**	these, the latter
ces femmes-là	those women	**celles-là**	those, the former

OBSERVATIONS

*(1) The forms **celui, celle, ceux,** and **celles** are never used **alone**; they are always followed by **de,** by a relative pronoun, by

ci, or by **là.** Both **ci** (*here*) and **là** (*there*) are omitted after a noun when it is unnecessary to distinguish between proximity and distance.

J'ai mon livre et celui de Jean.	I have my book and John's.
Celui qui entre est Jean.	The one who is entering is John.
J'ai vu Marie ce matin.	I saw Mary this morning.

(2) Note that **ce** becomes **cet** before a vowel or mute **h: ce garçon** BUT **cet oncle, cet homme.** The plural of **ce** and **cet** is **ces.**

77. **Invariable Demonstrative Pronouns.** As should be clear from the adjective that serves to describe these pronouns, they do not include the extensive array of gender and number forms that characterize all other demonstratives. Explanations and examples set out below indicate, however, that they do have a wide variety of uses.

(1) The forms **ceci** (*this*) and **cela** or **ça** (*that*) do not have a specific antecedent. They refer to statements, facts, or objects that have not previously been specified.

Qu'est-ce que c'est que ceci?	What is this?
Cela ne vous regarde pas.	That does not concern you.
C'est ça! Vous avez raison.	That's it! You are right.

(2) The forms **ce** and **c',** which may be variously translated by *that, this, these, those, he, she, it,* or *they,* serve various purposes as explained in the paragraphs that follow.

(*a*) With the forms of **être, ce** or **c'** serves to introduce the logical subject and usually replaces *il, elle, ils,* or *elles.* (*Cf.* §70, 4.)

C'est vrai.	That is true.
C'est lui.	It is he.
C'est Jean.	It is John.
C'est son devoir.	It is his duty.
C'est ma tante.	She is my aunt.
Ce sont mes amis.	They are my friends.
Ce sont là mes frères.	Those are my brothers.

OBSERVATION

If **ce** is used in asking a question, it is also used to introduce the answer.

Qu'est-ce que c'est?	**C'est une pomme.**
Qui est-ce?	**C'est mon frère.**

(*b*) The demonstrative **ce** replaces the pronoun antecedent of a predicate noun that indicates profession, nationality, religion, and the like whenever such predicate nouns are modified. Note when the article is either used or omitted in this kind of construction.

Elle est catholique.	She is a Catholic.
C'est une bonne catholique.	She is a good Catholic.
Il est soldat.	He is a soldier.
C'est un bon soldat.	He is a good soldier.

(*c*) When taken in a neutral sense, **ce** sums up an idea or refers to something that has not previously been mentioned by name.

A-t-il raison? C'est possible.	Is he right? It's (that is) possible.
Il a bien parlé. C'est vrai.	He spoke well. That's true.
Parlez plus haut. C'est beaucoup mieux maintenant.	Speak louder. That's much better now.

78. The English Possessive Noun. Ownership or possession, as indicated in English by the possessive form of a noun, is expressed in French by using the demonstrative pronoun without either **ci** or **là**. Carefully observe the examples below.

Mon étude et *celle* de mon ami.	My study and my friend's.
Leur jardin et *celui* de M. Duval.	Their garden and Mr. Duval's.
Ses cahiers et *ceux* de ses élèves.	His notebooks and his students'.

79. *voici, voilà, il y a.* The word **voici** (*here is, here are*) is compounded of **vois** (*See!*), familiar imperative form of **voir,** and **ici** (*here*). In similar fashion, **voilà** (*there is, there are*) is compounded of **vois** and **là** (*there*). This fact explains why these words can take a direct object. Generally accompanied by a gesture, they are used to point out an object or a person. Because of this function, these two expressions might well be called *verbal demonstratives.* The phrase **il y a** means *there is* or *there are* in a general sense. Unlike **voilà,** the phrase **il y a** may not be used to point out an object or a person.

Voici le vase. Le voici.	Here is the vase. Here it is.
Voilà des pêches. En voilà.	There are some peaches. There are some.
Voilà les belles fleurs.	There are the beautiful flowers.
Il y a de belles fleurs dans mon jardin.	There are some beautiful flowers in my garden.
Où êtes-vous, Marie?—Me voici.	Where are you, Mary? Here I am.
Où sont vos amis?—Les voilà.	Where are your friends? There they are.
Il y a quelqu'un ici.	There is someone here.

OBSERVATION

The pronoun **que** often occurs with **il y a.** *E.g.,* **Qu'est-ce qu'il y a? Il y a que vos amis se moquent de vous.** *What's the matter? (The matter is that) your friends are making fun of you.*

IDIOMATIC EXPRESSIONS

l'échapper belle to have a narrow escape	**Vous l'avez échappé belle.**
prononcer un discours to make a speech	**Il prononce un grand discours.**
se vanter de to boast of (about)	**Il s'est vanté de sa force.**

à côté de	beside	**d'une part**	on the one hand
à la dérobée	on the sly	**de ce côté (de)**	this side of
à cet égard	in this respect		
à mon insu	without my knowledge	**de l'autre côté (de)**	on the other side of
à propos de	about, concerning	**de mon côté**	for my part
au sujet de	about, with respect to	**de tous côtés**	in (from) every direction
chemin faisant	on the way	**du côté de**	in the direction of, toward
d'autre part	on the other hand	**d'un côté**	on the one hand

I

LECTURE

Lisez à haute voix.

1. Mon ami Lucien Dupin était un drôle de type. 2. Par exemple, il aimait prononcer des discours. 3. Il s'arrêtait même dans la rue et se mettait à parler de n'importe quoi. 4. Il se vantait même de ses succès d'orateur ambulant. 5. Un soir nous allions à pied du côté de la Seine. 6. Chemin faisant, je croyais constater qu'il méditait quelque vilain tour, car de temps en temps il me regardait à la dérobée. 7. Il s'est arrêté subitement et à mon insu il a fait comprendre à un gendarme qu'on devait m'arrêter. 8. Voilà le gendarme qui marche à côté de moi et puis, me voilà happé, empoigné. 9. De tous côtés accourent les badauds. 10. De mon côté je pensais à tous mes crimes passés, présents et potentiels! 11. D'une part ma vie me semblait d'une beauté morale exemplaire, mais d'autre part, peut-être avais-je eu tort tout de même de me mêler de certaines petites affaires! . . . 12. Enfin, où était Lucien? 13. Je me retourne et le voilà de l'autre côté de la rue qui rit à gorge déployée. 14. Je m'adresse au gendarme en ces termes: «Monsieur, le vrai criminel est ce type là-bas qui se rit de moi et de vous, c'est-à-dire, de la justice.» 15. Lucien, de son côté, se rendant compte de ce qui se passait, a pris la fuite. 16. Plus tard nous nous sommes rejoints au Café de la Paix et il m'a avoué qu'il l'avait échappé belle. 17. «Rira bien qui rira le dernier».

Répondez aux questions suivantes: 1. Lucien Dupin ressemblait-il à tout le monde? 2. Quand il faisait des discours, de quoi parlait-il? 3. De quoi se vantait-il? 4. Où est la Seine? 5. Lucien qu'a-t-il fait à mon insu? 6. Qu'est-ce qu'un badaud? 7. Ma vie me semblait-elle parfaite en ce moment-là? 8. A ma place qu'auriez-vous fait? 9. Expliquez: «Rira bien qui rira le dernier.» 10. Racontez cette anecdote en vos propres termes.

II

ORAL AND WRITTEN EXERCISES

A. *Translate the italicized English words.* 1. Il avait emprunté mon canif et *his friend's*. 2. *Here are* les livres. *These* sont *mine*; *those* sont *yours*. 3. Je ne savais pas *that*. 4. J'ai fait la connaissance de Charles et de Marie; *the latter* me semble médiocre, *the former* me semble très intéressant. 5. Il est riche, *that* est vrai. 6. *There are* de beaux jardins dans cette ville. 7. Regardez! *There is* un rouge-gorge dans ce vieux chêne! 8. *It* est le dernier jour du mois. 9. Il est *a doctor*; *he* est un bon médecin. 10. Nous parlions de ses études et *of mine*. 11. Le complet de Jean et *his brother's*; la poupée de Jeanne et *her sister's*; ce fauteuil-ci et *that one*. 12. Voilà le train, *there it is*. 13. Voilà Lucie et *here I am*; voilà Henri et *here she is*.

B. *Put the following sentences in the imperfect and translate.* 1. Je sais que c'est lui. 2. Je suis sûr que c'est vrai. 3. C'est lui qui le fait le mieux. 4. Il pense que je le connais. 5. Ce n'est pas joli ce que vous faites là. 6. Il me prend pour celui qu'il connaît. 7. C'est moi qui ai raison. 8. C'est vous qui avez tort. 9. C'est plus sérieux que vous ne pensez. 10. Elle ne sait pas ce que c'est.

C. *Translate.* 1. Did that man borrow your car? 2. No, but he borrowed my father's. 3. This one is your car, isn't it? 4. No, mine is the one which you can see in the garage. 5. Do you like these flowers? 6. No, I prefer those near the house. 7. Your father is always boasting about his roses. 8. I think he is right. His are always beautiful. 9. I like your gloves. 10. Thank you. I bought these two days ago. 11. Whose letter is this? 12. It is mine. 13. He is my cousin. 14. It is she. 15. Our house and theirs are the ones which you can see over there.

IRREGULAR VERBS

D. *Consult:* **savoir** (§142), **connaître** (§143) and **Unit** 9. (a) *Translate:* 1. Je le sais. 2. Je le connais. 3. Il le savait. 4. Il le connaissait. 5. Vous l'avez su. 6. Vous l'aviez connu. 7. Il faut que je le sache. 8. Il faut que nous la connaissions. 9. Nous le saurions. 10. Il les reconnaîtra. 11. Il le sut. 12. Ils le reconnurent.

(b) *Write:* 1. He knows me. 2. They know it. 3. We found it out. 4. They knew you. 5. He would have known it. 6. I have recognized them. 7. They must know it. 8. I must know you. 9. I shall know it. 10. I would know you. 11. They found it out (*Past Def.*). 12. He recognized her. (*Past Def.*)

III

OPTIONAL

E. *Translate. Consult:* **Lecture** (Chap. 9) and **Conversation** 9. 1. I was **(se trouver)** on this side of the river and he was on the other side. 2. Without my knowledge, the policeman was walking beside me. 3. He looked at her on the sly. 4. In this respect he resembled his father. 5. He was always looking for the opportunity to make a speech. 6. On the one hand, he was always boasting about his money; but on the other hand, he was always trying to borrow money from his friends. 7. He went away in the direction of the village. 8. On the way, he talked about everything. 9. He said that he had had a narrow escape in Paris. 10. I often think of Lucien and wonder what has become of him **(ce qu'il est devenu).** 11. Do you know the name of the one who is behind you? 12. He who drives a car is called a chauffeur. 13. Do you know what a savant is? 14. It is one who knows a great deal. 15. Ask him if he knows what a chanteuse is? 16. Do you prefer my necktie or Paul's?

IV

CONVERSATION 9

1. Veuillez avoir la bonté de me dire si vous savez comment s'appelle la jolie jeune fille qui est assise à votre gauche. —Pardon?

2. Vous n'avez pas compris? —Non, monsieur, je n'ai pas compris. Répétez, s'il vous plaît. —Avec plaisir. Qui est cette jeune fille-là? —C'est Mlle Leblanc. —Qui est celle-ci? —C'est Mlle Dupuis. —Qui est ce jeune homme? —C'est M. Martin.

3. Comment s'appelle celle (celui) qui est (assise, assis) à votre droite (à votre gauche, devant vous, derrière vous, à la droite de M. Lebrun, etc.)? —Celle (celui) qui est (assise, assis) à ma droite s'appelle Mlle Fournier (M. Poirier).

4. Savez-vous comment s'appelle celui (celle) qui est assis(e) devant vous? —Je ne sais pas comment s'appelle celui (celle) qui est assis(e) devant moi. —Demandez-lui comment il (elle) s'appelle. —Comment vous appelez-vous, monsieur (mademoiselle)? —Je m'appelle Jean (Marie) Broussard. —Enchanté, monsieur (mademoiselle).

5. Comment s'appelle celui qui conduit une auto (guérit des malades, tue quelqu'un, vole, vend, chante, enseigne, écrit des pièces, écrit des poèmes, écrit pour un journal, tape à la machine, fait des discours, sait beaucoup, ne sait rien, peint des tableaux)? —Celui qui conduit une auto, etc., s'appelle un chauffeur (médecin, assassin, voleur, vendeur, chanteur, professeur ou instituteur, dramaturge, poète, journaliste, dactylo, orateur, savant, ignorant, artiste).

6. Comment s'appelle celle qui soigne les malades (enseigne, vend, chante, fait des chapeaux, fait des robes, s'occupe des cheveux, fait des massages, joue des rôles au théâtre, fait la cuisine, nettoie la maison)? —Celle qui soigne les malades, etc., s'appelle une infirmière (institutrice ou *un* professeur, vendeuse, chanteuse ou cantatrice, modiste, couturière, coiffeuse, masseuse, actrice, cuisinière, bonne).

7. Qu'est-ce que c'est qu'un chauffeur, etc. (une infirmière, etc.)? —C'est celui (celle) qui conduit une auto, etc. (soigne des malades, etc.).

8. Savez-vous ce que c'est qu'un médecin? —Non, je ne sais pas ce que c'est (qu'un médecin). Expliquez-moi ce que c'est (qu'un médecin).

9. M. Mouton ne sait pas ce que c'est qu'un médecin. Expliquez-lui ce que c'est. Demandez à Mlle Boudreau (si elle sait) ce que c'est qu'un assassin.

10. Voici mon nez (ma bouche, mes yeux, mes dents). Montrez-moi le (la, les) vôtre(s). —Voici le (la, les) mien(ne)(s).

11. Préférez-vous ma cravate ou la vôtre (celle de M. Dupont)? —Je préfère la vôtre (la mienne, la sienne).

12. Mon crayon est jaune. De quelle couleur est le vôtre? —Le mien est bleu (rouge, noir, vert, blanc, brun, jaune aussi).

13. Je n'ai pas de crayon (livre, règle). Prêtez-moi le (la) vôtre. Merci beaucoup. A qui est ce crayon? A qui est celui-ci? —Il est à moi (vous, lui, elle).

Sujets de discussion et de conversation.

1. Quel est votre cours préféré?
2. Devrait-on abolir les examens?
3. Pourrait-on dire que la plupart des étudiants américains ne font pas d'études sérieuses au collège?
4. Quelles sont les qualités requises d'un bon professeur?
5. Quelles sont les qualités requises d'un bon étudiant?

CHAPTER 10

RELATIVE PRONOUNS

GRAMMAR

80. The Relative Pronouns. Just as in English, so too in French, relative pronouns appear in the complex sentence. By means of the relative pronoun one can express in a single statement what otherwise would require two or more sentences. A relative pronoun stands for its antecedent in the main clause and at the same time fulfills a grammatical function in the subordinate clause.

(1) Most important of the relative pronouns are **qui,** which serves as the subject of a subordinate clause, and **que,** which serves as an object. The function of the relative pronoun as subject or object becomes clearer when one breaks up a sentence into independent clauses.

> **The man *who saw you* is my friend.**
> **The man saw you. The man is my friend.**
> **L'homme *qui vous a vu* est mon ami.**
>
> **The book *that is on the table* is mine.**
> **The book is on the table. The book is mine.**
> **Le livre *qui est sur la table* est à moi.**
>
> **The man *whom I saw* is my best friend.**
> **I saw the man. He is my best friend.**
> **L'homme *que j'ai vu* est mon meilleur ami.**

The distinction between **qui** (subject) and **que** (object) must be sharply borne in mind when translating from French into English. Since the subject follows the verb in an inverted relative clause, the student must be careful not to confuse the subject with the object in these cases. Remember that **que** becomes

qu' before any vowel. The form **qui**, on the contrary, is invariable. Cf. §56.

Les personnes qu'avait vues mon frère.	**The persons my brother had seen.**
	NOT
	The persons who had seen my brother.

OBSERVATION

In English the relative pronoun is often omitted. In French, however, it must always be expressed.

(2) The form **qui** is used as the object of a preposition when referring to persons, whereas **lequel, laquelle, lesquels,** and **lesquelles** are used with prepositions when referring to things. In determining the correct use of relative pronouns with prepositions, we may rely upon the English use of *whom* and *which.* Thus, *with whom* and *by whom* are **avec qui** and **par qui**; *with which* and *by which,* when referring to a masculine singular antecedent, are **avec lequel** and **par lequel.** Remember that in English the words *who* and *whom* refer to persons, and that the word *which* refers only to things.

The forms of **lequel** contract with **de** and **à** in conformity with the rules that govern the use of the article. *E.g.,* **duquel, de laquelle, desquels, desquelles, auquel, à laquelle, auxquels, auxquelles.**

Les amis avec qui je parlais.	The friends with whom I was talking.
Le bateau dans lequel il s'assit.	The boat in which he sat down.
Le crayon avec lequel il écrivait.	The pencil with which he was writing.

(3) The form **dont,** meaning *of whom, of which, whose,* refers to both persons and things, and normally is used in place of **de qui** (persons) or **duquel,** *etc.* (persons or things). The word **dont** stands immediately before the subject of the subordinate clause. For this reason, translating English sentences often

involves rearranging the word order. Thus, *The house whose roof I saw* must be rethought to read, *The house of which I saw the roof. E.g.,* **La maison dont j'ai vu le toit.** Note, also, the following examples:

Le garçon dont le frère vous a parlé est malade.	The boy whose brother spoke to you is ill.
Le garçon dont vous avez vu le frère est malade.	The boy whose brother you saw is ill.

OBSERVATION

The word **dont** cannot be used when it is dependent on a noun that is governed by a preposition. Compare the following sentences. Note that in the second sentence **de qui** (or **duquel**) is used instead of **dont.**

Le garçon dont je vous ai parlé est malade.	The boy of whom I spoke to you is ill.
BUT	
Le garçon au frère de qui (duquel) vous avez parlé est malade.	The boy to whose brother you spoke is ill.

(4) The phrases *in which, at which, on which, i.e.,* a preposition of place plus a relative, may be expressed by **dans lequel, auquel, sur lequel** or by the single word **où.**

La ville où (dans laquelle) il demeure.	The city in which he lives.
Au moment où je l'ai vu.	At the moment at which (when) I saw him.
Le pays d'où il est venu.	The country from where (whence) he came.

(5) When it occurs after a preposition, the English word *what* is translated into French by **quoi.** For *what* expressed by relative pronouns combined with demonstratives, cf. §81, 1, 2.

Dites-moi à quoi vous pensez.	Tell me what you are thinking about.
Il a de quoi vivre.	He has the means to live.
Il n'y a pas de quoi.	You are welcome.

(6) The following summary of forms and meanings of the two types of relative pronoun may be used for reference or for hasty review.

INVARIABLE RELATIVE PRONOUNS

qui (subject) who, which, that
qui (object of a preposition) whom
que (direct object) whom, which, that
dont of whom, of which, whose, from whom, from which, about whom, etc.
où where, in which, at which, to which, on which
d'où from where, from which, whence
quoi (object of preposition) what

VARIABLE RELATIVE PRONOUNS

lequel **laquelle** **lesquels** **lesquelles**	who which whom	As a rule these forms are used as the object of a preposition when referring to things, or as subject or object in order to avoid ambiguity.

Observe and explain the use of the relative pronouns in the sentences below.

Voilà la femme que nous avons rencontrée hier.	There is the woman we met yesterday.
Elle a des yeux qui brillent.	She has eyes that shine.
Avez-vous remarqué la maison de laquelle (d'où) elle est sortie?	Did you notice the house she came out of?
L'homme dans la maison duquel je suis entré.	The man whose house I entered.
Oui, voilà une conversation dont je me souviens très bien.	Yes, that is a conversation which I remember very well.
Mais savez-vous de quoi je me souviendrai toujours?	But do you know what I shall remember always?
Je n'oublierai jamais les yeux de ces femmes, lesquels paraissaient des étoiles.	I shall never forget the eyes of those women, which resembled stars.

OBSERVATION

In the last sentence, **lesquels** is used instead of **qui** to show clearly that the antecedent is **yeux**, not **femmes**.

81. Relatives Combined with Demonstrative Pronouns. The relative pronouns **qui** and **que** combine with certain demonstrative pronouns to produce the forms set out below.

celui qui (*as subject of a subordinate verb*) the one who, he who, the one which
celui que (*as object of a subordinate verb*) the one whom, he whom, the one which
celle qui the one who, she who, the one which
celle que the one whom, she whom, the one which
ceux qui those who, the ones who, the ones which (*masculine*)
celles qui those who, the ones who, the ones which (*feminine*)
ce qui (*as subject*) that which, what
ce que (*as object*) that which, what

(1) The forms **celui qui** and **celui que** can be used as subject, as indirect object, or as direct object when referring to a person or to some definite thing that has been mentioned. The forms **ce qui** and **ce que,** on the other hand, refer to no definite object. If English *what* can be changed to *that which,* use **ce qui** or **ce que.**

Donnez-moi celui que vous avez.	Give me the one you have.
Donnez-moi ce que vous avez.	Give me what you have.
Celui qui a dit cela mentait.	The one who said that was lying.
Ce qui m'amuse c'est sa manière de parler.	What amuses me is his manner of speaking.

(2) The English phrases *that of which* and *of what* are translated by either **ce dont** or **de quoi.** Verbs that require **de** take one of these forms when translating *what.* The verb **penser** requires **à.**

Je sais de quoi il parlait.	I know what he was talking about.
C'est ce dont je me suis servi.	That is what I used.
Voilà de quoi je me souviens le mieux.	That is what I remember best.
Savez-vous de quoi je me rends compte?	Do you know what I realize?
Savez-vous à quoi je pense?	Do you know what I am thinking about?

OBSERVATION

Note that in the above examples the use of **ce dont, de quoi,** or **à quoi** is necessary because the verb in the subordinate clause takes **de** or **à.** If the verb in the main clause takes **de,** then **ce qui** or **ce que** is preceded by **de.** *E.g.,* **Il parlait de ce qui l'intéressait.** *He was speaking of what interested him.* If the verbs of both clauses should require **de,** as would be the case in such a sentence as *I remember what he talked about,* the translation would be, **Je me souviens de ce dont il a parlé.** So as to avoid this repetitious **de ce dont,** the sentence should be rearranged to read, *I remember what he said.* **Je me souviens de ce qu'il a dit.**

IDIOMATIC EXPRESSIONS

tirer to pull, to draw — **Le cheval tire la charrue.**

se tirer d'affaire to get along, to get out of difficulties — **Il se tire d'affaire.**

s'en tirer to get along, to manage — **Il s'en tire toujours.**

à la mode	fashionable, in style	**d'autant plus que**	all the more because, so much the more that
à l'écart	aside	**sur-le-champ**	immediately
à part	to one side, aside	**tant bien que mal**	rather poorly
autour de	around		
de la sorte	in this way		
ainsi que	as, as well as		

I

LECTURE

Lisez à haute voix.

1. Ah, mon vieux, les femmes! 2. C'est mon ami Amiel qui me tire à part et me met au courant de ses déboires domestiques. 3. Ce soi-disant sexe faible, dit-il, est bien fort, ainsi que je vais vous le montrer tout à l'heure. 4. Ainsi que vous le savez, ma femme tient à être toujours à la mode. 5. Bon! hier à midi elle

me dit, presque sans y faire attention: «Chéri, il me faut une robe rouge. Je vais faire le tour des Galeries Lafayette cet après-midi.» 6. Sur-le-champ je décide de l'accompagner dans l'espoir de pouvoir mettre un frein à ses manies dispendieuses. 7. Comme on a tort de croire que les femmes ne savent pas s'entendre! 8. J'affirme qu'il y a entente instinctive chez elles toutes les fois qu'il s'agit de la bourse du mari. 9. A peine dans le magasin, voilà qu'un groupe de beautés se rangent autour de moi. 10. Des sourires, des gazouillements, des roucoulements, rien de plus, et flatté, enchanté, je ne pense plus au budget. 11. On me tire à l'écart et pendant que je fais le vieux galant tant bien que mal les vendeuses enthousiastes s'occupent de ma pauvre femme. 12. Coup de théâtre! Ma femme sort d'un petit boudoir faisant des révérences, se dandinant, élégante, portant une robe rouge magnifique. 13. «Voyez, monsieur! qu'elle est mignonne, votre petite femme! Comme c'est chic, comme cette robe lui va à merveille!» 14. Comment s'en tirer quand de belles femmes s'y prennent de la sorte? 15. J'ai vidé ma bourse sur-le-champ et voilà pourquoi je ne serai pas des vôtres ce soir. 16. Ah, mon vieux, les femmes!

Répondez aux questions suivantes: 1. Que dit mon ami Amiel? 2. Quelle manie a sa femme? 3. Qu'est-ce qu'elle lui dit? 4. Pourquoi Amiel décide-t-il de l'accompagner? 5. Les femmes savent-elles s'entendre parfois? 6. Que font les beautés qui se rangent autour d'Amiel? 7. De quelle manière sa femme sort-elle d'un petit boudoir? 8. Pourquoi Amiel n'était-il pas des nôtres ce soir-là? 9. Faites un résumé de cette lecture.

II

ORAL AND WRITTEN EXERCISES

A. *Translate the English words that are in italics.* 1. Je sais *that* il est rentré. 2. Voici l'ami *who* vous cherchait. 3. C'est le musicien *of whom* je vous ai parlé. 4. Le stylo avec *which* il écrit est à moi. 5. Connaissez-vous celui *whom* nous venons de voir? 6. Les amis *of whom* je pense sont en France. 7. Le professeur distrait oublie *what* il veut faire. 8. *What* nous amuse n'est pas *what* vous croyez. 9. La maison *whose roof* est jaune est *the one which* nous avons visitée hier. 10. Je parlais avec Jean *whose brother* aime tant les sports. 11. *The one who* ressemble à son père est *the one whom* vous connaissez.

B. *Make complex sentences of the simple sentences by using appropriate relative pronouns. E.g.,* **J'ai vu une femme. Elle m'a parlé,** *or* **La femme que j'ai vue m'a parlé.** 1. Elle demeure dans une villa. Cette villa est belle. 2. Son mari cultive un champ. Il l'a hérité de son père. 3. Son père est mort il y a dix ans. Il était venu de Suisse. 4. Il n'approuvait pas le mariage de son fils avec cette femme. Je vous ai déjà parlé d'elle.

C. *Pronounce and translate, then change the verbs to their corresponding compound tenses. E.g.,* **Il se plaint de tout. Il s'est plaint de tout. Le porteur s'occupera de vos bagages. Le porteur se sera occupé de vos bagages.** 1. Nous nous en passons. 2. Il se douterait de quelque chose. 3. Ils se plaindront de vous. 4. Il ne nous plaignait jamais. 5. Ils se rient de vous. 6. Je me souviendrai de vos efforts.

D. *Translate the French sentences and the italicized English clauses.* 1. Il se passe de café. *The coffee which he does without* . . . 2. Je savais que vous aviez besoin de mes conseils. *My advice which you needed* . . . 3. Les soldats se moquaient de l'ennemi. *The enemy whom the soldiers made fun of* . . . 4. On se sert d'un couteau pour couper. *The knife one uses for cutting the meat.* 5. Il faut que vous vous serviez de mon auto. *My car which you must use* . . .

E. *Translate.* 1. Tell me that you have understood. 2. Tell me what you have understood. 3. I told you that I understood everything. 4. I told you what I understood. 5. Tell me what amuses you. 6. I will tell you what amuses me. 7. What amuses me is **(c'est)** your nose. 8. What makes me cry does not concern you. 9. All you do concerns me. 10. Remember what I have done for you.

IRREGULAR VERBS

F. *Consult:* **écrire** (§144), **dire** (§145), **lire** (§146), and **Unit** 10.

(a) *Translate:* 1. Il écrit. 2. Il écrivit. 3. Il lit. 4. Il lut. 5. Ils diront. 6. Ils dirent. 7. J'écrivais. 8. J'écrirais. 9. Nous disons. 10. Nous dirons. 11. Ne me le dites pas. 12. Il faut que je lise, que je dise, que j'écrive.

(b) *Write:* 1. They write. 2. They wrote (*P. Def.*) 3. They have read. 4. I had written. 5. He would have said. 6. They were writing. 7. They would write. 8. We were reading. 9. We would read. 10. Let's write it. 11. You must read. 12. We must write.

III

OPTIONAL

G. *Translate. Consult:* **Lecture** (Chap. 10), **Conversation** 10. 1. The saleswoman who pulled me aside was dressed fashionably **(bien mise)**. 2. The girls made fun of me and I must admit **(dois avouer)** that I got along rather poorly in the store. 3. The saleswoman affirmed that the red dress was wonderfully becoming to her, for in this way she knew she could **(pourrait)** flatter me. 4. She knew what I was thinking about when I came into the store. 5. Those who say that women do not know how to get along with each other do not know what they are saying. 6. It is true that Amiel's wife always wants to be in style, but does he always remember what he spends to play golf and poker? 7. Personally we always side with **(se ranger du côté de)** the women and defend them! 8. The woman I love is prettier than the one who loves me. 9. What do you want me to read? 10.

What is the name of one whose job it is to drive a car? 11. Does he know who wrote *Les Misérables*? 12. Did she understand the sentence that they read? 13. Open the newspaper and read just any sentence.

IV

CONVERSATION 10

1. Choisissez quelqu'un. . . . Comment s'appelle celui (celle) que vous avez choisi(e)? . . . qui vous a choisi(e)? —Celui (Celle) que j'ai choisi(e) s'appelle. . . . Celui (Celle) qui m'a choisi(e) s'appelle. . . .

2. Posez une question à quelqu'un. . . . Comment s'appelle celui (celle) à qui vous avez posé une question? . . . celui (celle) qui vous a posé une question? —Celui (Celle) à qui j'ai posé une question. . . . Celui (Celle) qui m'a posé une question. . . .

3. Est-ce que vous pensez (écrivez) souvent à celle (celui) qui vous aime? . . . que vous aimez? —Je (ne) pense (pas) souvent à celle (celui) qui m'aime. . . . que j'aime.

4. Est-ce que celle (celui) qui vous aime est aussi belle (beau) que celle (celui) que vous aimez?

5. Comment s'appelle celui (celle) dont le métier est de conduire une auto, etc. —Celui dont le métier est de conduire une auto s'appelle un chauffeur.

6. Qu'est-ce que c'est qu'un chauffeur, médecin, etc.? —C'est celui dont le métier est de. . . .

7. Est-ce que vous lisez (écrivez) le français mieux (aussi facilement) que l'anglais (l'espagnol, le latin, etc.)?

8. Demandez à M. Gomez (Luigi, Schmidt, Strowski) s'il lit (écrit) le français aussi bien que l'espagnol (l'italien, l'allemand, le polonais).

9. Savez-vous qui a écrit *Les Misérables, Les Fleurs du Mal, Candide, Le Misanthrope, Les Trois Mousquetaires?* —C'est . . . qui a écrit . . .

10. Savez-vous ce qu'a écrit Alexandre Dumas (Victor Hugo, Voltaire, Molière, Baudelaire, Flaubert, etc.)? Qu'est-ce que vous avez lu de Victor Hugo, etc.?

11. Voulez-vous faire quelque chose pour moi? —Avec plaisir. Que voulez-vous que je fasse? —Je veux que vous lisiez quelque chose. —Que voulez-vous que je lise? —Ouvrez votre livre et lisez n'importe quelle phrase (une phrase quelconque).

12. Avez-vous compris la phrase qu'il a lue (ce qu'il a lu)? —Oui (Non), je (ne) l'ai (pas) compris(e)? —Dites-lui d'avoir la bonté de répéter la phrase qu'il (ce qu'il) vient de lire. —Ayez la bonté de répéter la phrase que vous venez de lire (ce que vous venez de lire).

Sujets de discussion et de conversation:

1. Avez-vous de la sympathie pour le pauvre Amiel?
2. Est-il vrai que les femmes gaspillent l'argent de leurs maris?
3. S'il s'agissait de choisir entre une carrière et un mari, que feriez-vous, mesdames?
4. De nos jours aux Etats-Unis, les femmes s'intéressent-elles plus à l'étude des humanités que les hommes?
5. Est-ce que les femmes du Sud des Etats-Unis savent mieux toucher le cœur des hommes que celles du Nord?

CHAPTER 11

INTERROGATION AND WORD ORDER

GRAMMAR

82. Interrogation. In spoken French, a question may be indicated by (1) the tone of one's voice, (2) using special words or phrases, or (3) word arrangement of the sentence. The various interrogatory devices are explained below.

(1) By the tone of voice.

Vous savez cela?	You know that?
Il vous a dit mon nom?	He told you my name?

(2) By placing **n'est-ce pas?** after an affirmative statement.

Vous me croyez, n'est-ce pas?	You believe me, don't you?
Vous l'avez fait, n'est-ce pas?	You did it, didn't you?
Ils l'ont fini, n'est-ce pas?	They finished it, didn't they?

(3) By inversion, when the subject is a pronoun.

En êtes-vous sûr?	Are you sure of it?
Travaille-t-il?	Is he working?

(4) By inversion, when the subject is a noun. In this case the noun subject is duplicated by its pronoun. The word order is *noun* + *verb* + *pronoun.*

Les hommes sont-ils ici?	Are the men here?
Les femmes ont-elles vendu des fleurs?	Did the women sell some flowers?

(5) After **où?, quand?, comment?, combien?,** the preferable and informal word order in simple tenses is *interrogative adverb* + *verb* + *noun.* The formal word order is *interrogative adverb* + *noun* + *verb* + *pronoun.*

Quand arrive le train? OR **Quand le train arrive-t-il?**	When does the train arrive?
Où demeuraient vos amis? OR **Où vos amis demeuraient-ils?**	Where did your friends live?

OBSERVATION

If the verb has a direct object or is in a compound tense, the word order is *interrogative adverb + noun + verb + pronoun.* This is always the word order after **pourquoi.**

Quand votre mère sert-elle le dîner?	When does your mother serve dinner?
Quand vos amis ont-ils quitté New York?	When did your friends leave New York?
Pourquoi Jean désire-t-il vendre son chien?	Why does John wish to sell his dog?

(6) By using **est-ce que.** This must be placed immediately before any affirmative statement or immediately after an interrogative word. (Cf. §9.)

Inversion	Est-ce que?
Travaille-t-il?	**Est-ce qu'il travaille?**
Les hommes sont-ils ici?	**Est-ce que les hommes sont ici?**
Quand votre mère sert-elle le dîner?	**Quand est-ce que votre mère sert le dîner?**
Pourquoi Jean désire-t-il vendre son chien?	**Pourquoi est-ce que Jean désire vendre son chien?**

83. The Interrogative Pronouns. In French, as in English, certain relative pronouns also function grammatically as interrogatives. The explanations below indicate the principal distinctions.

(1) Table of interrogative and relative pronouns, together with their English equivalents and explanations of their proper use.

Interrogatives		Relatives	
qui?	who? whom? *(Subject, object, or object of a preposition. Always a person.)*	**qui**	who, which, that *(Subject. Person or thing.)* whom *(Object of a preposition.)*
que?	what? *(Object. Always a thing. Never used alone or after a preposition.)*	**que**	whom, which, that *(Object. Person or thing. Never used after a preposition.)*
quoi?	what? *(Used alone or after a preposition.)*	**quoi**	what *(Used after a preposition, especially in indirect questions.)*
lequel? which one? **lesquels?** which ones? **laquelle?** which one? **lesquelles?** which ones? **auquel?** to which one? **duquel?** of which one?	*(Person or thing. Subject of a verb or object of a preposition.)*	**lequel**, **lesquels**, **laquelle**, **lesquelles**	who, whom, which *(Chiefly as object of a preposition when the antecedent is a thing. Subject or object to avoid ambiguity when referring to either persons or things.)*
dont	*Never an interrogative.*	**dont**	whose, of which, of whom
ce qui	*Never an interrogative.*	**ce qui**	that which, what *(Subject of a subordinate verb.)*
ce que	*Never an interrogative.*	**ce que**	that which, what *(Object of a subordinate verb.)*

(2) To avoid inversions, particularly in conversation, **est-ce que?** is placed after the pronoun. (Cf. §9, §82, 6.) Note carefully the alternative forms of the interrogative pronouns below.

qui? *or* **qui est-ce qui?**	who?	*(Used as subject.)*
qui? *or* **qui est-ce que?**	whom?	*(Used as object.)*
qu'est-ce qui?	what?	*(Used as subject.)*
que? *or* **qu'est-ce que?**	what?	*(Used as object.)*
de qui? *or* **de qui est-ce que?**	of whom?	*(Or any other preposition.)*
de quoi *or* **de quoi est-ce que?**	of what?	*(Or any other preposition.)*

Qui avez-vous vu? **Qui est-ce que vous avez vu?**	Whom did you see?
Qu'avez-vous vu? **Qu'est-ce que vous avez vu?**	What did you see?
Qui vous a fait rire? **Qui est-ce qui vous a fait rire?**	Who made you laugh?
Qu'est-ce qui vous a fait rire?	What made you laugh?
De qui avez-vous besoin? **De qui est-ce que vous avez besoin?**	Whom do you need?
De quoi avez-vous besoin? **De quoi est-ce que vous avez besoin?**	What do you need?

OBSERVATION

Inversion takes place after the short forms, not after the long forms.

(3) When the word *whose?* establishes possession it is translated by **à qui?** When it expresses relationship, by **de qui?**

A qui est cette maison?	Whose house is that?
De qui êtes-vous le fils?	Whose son are you?

84. The Interrogative Adjectives. When *which?* or *what?* is used as an adjective, it is translated by **quel?**, **quels?**, **quelle?**, or **quelles?** In the table below, note the relationship between the interrogative adjectives and the **lequel** forms of the interrogative pronouns.

Adjectives			Pronouns	
quel	**livre?**	which, what book?	**lequel?**	which one?
quelle	**femme?**	which, what woman?	**laquelle?**	which one?
quels	**livres?**	which, what books?	**lesquels?**	which ones?
quelles	**femmes?**	which, what women?	**lesquelles?**	which ones?
de quel	**ami?**	of which friend?	**duquel?**	of which one?
à quel	**ami?**	to which friend?	**auquel?**	to which one?

(1) The phrase *which of* is translated by **lequel de.**

Lequel de ces livres préférez-vous?	Which of these books do you prefer?

(2) When asking for identification, the phrase *what is?* is translated by **quel est?** or **quelle est?**

Quel est ce livre?	What is this book?

(3) When asking for a definition, the phrase *what is?* is translated by **qu'est-ce que c'est qu'un(e).**

Qu'est-ce que c'est qu'un crayon? What is a pencil?
Un crayon c'est un objet dont on se sert pour écrire.

(4) The phrase *who is?* can be translated by either **qui est?** or **quel (quelle) est?**

Qui est cet homme?	Who is that man?
Quelle est cette dame?	Who is that lady?
Quelles sont ces gens?	Who (what) are those people?

OBSERVATION

A form of **quel** is preferable to **qui** when the subject is feminine or plural.

Qu'est-ce que c'est? **Qu'est-ce?**	} What is it?
Qu'est-ce que c'est que cela (ça)?	What is that?
Qu'est-ce que c'est qu'un taxi?	What is a taxi?
Savez-vous ce que c'est qu'un taxi?	Do you know what a taxi is?
Je sais ce que c'est.	I know what it is.

(5) The expression *what a!* is only one word in French. It is translated by either **quel** or **quelle.**

Quel homme! Quelle femme!	What a man! What a woman!
Quels enfants!	What children!

85. Peculiarities of Word Order in Exclamations. Certain characteristics of word order distinguish French exclamatory sentences. The manner of expression differs notably from English, as the explanations and examples below make clear.

(1) The word **que** is often used redundantly for the purpose of achieving emphasis.

Quelle vie *que* la mienne!	What a life is mine!
C'est un scélérat *que* cet homme!	That man is a scoundrel!
C'est une belle ville *que* Paris!	Paris is a beautiful city!

(2) A French exclamatory sentence that begins with **comme, que,** or **combien** has a normal word order. The translation of any of these words is transposed in the English sentence in order that the adjective or adverb may stand immediately after *how*.

Comme la vie est dure!	How hard life is!
Que vous êtes bien!	How nice looking you are!
Qu'elle chante bien!	How well she sings!
Combien je regrette le temps perdu!	How I regret the lost time!

86. Rhetorical Inversion. The student must distinguish carefully between inversions that are made for the purpose of interrogation and those that are employed merely for stylistic effect.

(1) Inversion for stylistic effect occurs when any of the following words and phrases is placed at the beginning of a sentence or clause: **bientôt, peut-être, à peine, au moins, du moins, en vain, encore, toujours, aussi, ainsi,** and some others that are less common.

Peut-être votre père a-t-il raison.	Perhaps your father is right.
A peine m'eut-il aperçu qu'il se sauva.	Scarcely had he seen me when he ran away.
Du moins vous a-t-il salué.	At least he greeted you.
En vain ai-je cherché un moyen de m'échapper.	In vain I sought a means of escape.
Il a tort; aussi doit-il se taire.	He is wrong; hence he should keep quiet.

(2) A parenthetical expression after a direct quotation is always inverted. The commonest verbs used in parenthetical expressions are these: **dire, répondre, demander, crier, faire** (to say), **reprendre** (to resume, to continue), **s'écrier** (to exclaim).

—Bonjour, dit-il.	"Good day," he said (said he).
—Hélas, m'a-t-elle répondu, ma mère est morte.	"Alas," she answered, "my mother is dead."
—Qu'est-ce que c'est? demanda-t-il.	"What is it?" he asked.
—Plaignez-nous, fit-il.	"Pity us," he said.

IDIOMATIC EXPRESSIONS

attendre	to wait for	**Mon père m'attend.**
s'attendre à	to expect	**Mon père s'attend à me trouver chez moi.**
chercher	to look for	**Ils me cherchent.**
chercher à	to seek, to endeavor	**Ils cherchent à m'amuser.**
arriver	to arrive	**Jean est arrivé de bonne heure.**
arriver à	to succeed (in)	**Jean arriva à franchir le fleuve.**

Qu'est-ce qui arrive à Jean? What is happening to John?

à la recherche de	in search of	**au reste** / **du reste**	however, furthermore
à sa recherche	in search of (it, him, her)	**en attendant**	meanwhile
Allons donc!	Come! Nonsense!	**Soit!**	So be it! Granted!
à peine	hardly, scarcely	**Tiens!**	Well! Is that so!
		Voyons!	See here!

I

LECTURE

Lisez à haute voix.

1. Cet incident se passa dans la rue Maltache à Paris. 2. Je me promenais par un beau jour de printemps un peu à l'aventure dans cette belle ville qui fait les délices de tout esprit libre épris de la beauté et de l'humanité. 3. J'aperçois un gamin qui paraît chercher quelque chose par terre. 4. Je m'arrête en bon camarade, pensant l'aider. 5. J'attends un moment et puisqu'il n'arrive pas à trouver ce qu'il cherche je m'adresse à lui. 6. «Qu'y a-t-il?» 7. Fort étonné le gosse lève la tête: «Allons donc! Qu'est-ce que cela veut dire? «Qu'y a-t-il?»» 8. «Est-ce que vous * cherchiez une *quille?* Soit! je vais vous aider.» 9. «Je cherche une *quille?*» fit-il. «Qu'est-ce que c'est qu'une *quille?*» 10. «Une *quille*, c'est un petit caillou rond comme un œil-de-bœuf.» 11. «Tiens! Qui êtes-vous?» Et le gamin tournant vite l'index près

* Naturellement on dit *tu* en s'adressant à un enfant, mais dans ce cas le narrateur, qui parle mal le français, emploie le *vous* et par conséquent ne fait que déconcerter le gosse.

de la tempe, s'en est allé à reculons. 12. Il a dû s'en aller à la recherche de son papa car à peine est-il parti, que le voilà de retour accompagné d'un homme extrêmement menaçant. 13. «Voyons! Qu'y a-t-il?» m'a-t-il dit. «Laissez donc tranquille ce garçon ou je ferai venir la police! Du reste, qu'on ne vous voie plus ici!» 14. Et maintenant c'est moi qui prends la fuite ne sachant trop à quoi m'attendre. 15. De retour chez moi je consulte le dictionnaire et tout s'éclaircit: *quille* ne veut pas dire *bille!*

Répondez aux questions suivantes: 1. Où cet incident s'est-il passé? 2. Quel temps faisait-il? 3. Qu'est-ce qui fait les délices de tout esprit libre épris de la beauté et de l'humanité? 4. Que faisait le gamin que j'ai aperçu? 5. Pourquoi est-ce que je me suis arrêté? 6. Est-ce que je lui parle tout de suite? 7. Qu'est-ce que je lui dis? 8. Que répond le gosse? 9. Le gamin veut-il savoir ce que c'est qu'une *quille*? 10. D'après moi, qu'est-ce que c'est qu'une *quille*? 11. Comment le gamin s'en va-t-il? 12. Qui est-il allé chercher? 13. Qu'est-ce qu'il me dit? 14. Expliquez la différence entre *quille* et *bille.* 15. Faites un résumé de cette lecture.

II

ORAL AND WRITTEN EXERCISES

A. *Translate the italicized English words.* 1. *What* fait-il? 2. *What* est la leçon? 3. *Where* vous allez? 4. *Of whom* parlait-elle? 5. *Which* des deux est votre sœur? 6. *What* ils font? 7. *How* allez-vous? 8. *When* votre petit frère arrive-t-il? 9. *From where* vient-il? 10. *Why* va-t-il là-bas? 11. *Who* vous cherche? 12. *Whom* cherchez-vous? 13. *What* se passe là-dedans? 14. *Who* sont ces demoiselles? 15. *Which* champs labourent-ils? 16. *What* dit l'auteur? 17. *On which* chaise est-il assis? 18. *Of what* parlait-il? 19. *What* a-t-il dit? 20. *How* les trouvez-vous?

B. ORAL. *Model:* **Je sais ce que c'est qu'un médecin.** 1. I know what an animal is. 2. Do you know what a café is? 3. Tell me what the cancan is. 4. Can you tell me what a ballet is? 5. Ask someone what lingerie is. 6. I would like to know what roulette is. 7. Will you please tell us what a limousine is? 8. Explain to me what a coupé de ville is.

C. ORAL. *Model:* **Qu'est-ce qui arrive à Jean?** 1. What is happening to you? 2. What happened to you? 3. What has happened to me? 4. What amuses you? 5. What interests him? 6. What bores her? 7. What hurts you? 8. What has given you that idea? 9. What has frightened you? 10. What made you laugh?

D. ORAL. *Model:* **A quoi vous attendez-vous?** 1. What were you expecting? 2. What are you interested in? 3. What do you trust in? 4. What are you thinking about? 5. What do you resemble? 6. What are you playing at? (*N.B. The verbs of 4, 5, and 6 are not reflexive.*)

E. ORAL. *Model:* **De quoi vous êtes-vous servi?** 1. What did you complain of? 2. What did you make fun of? 3. What did you laugh at? 4. What did you remember? 5. What have you recovered from? 6. What did you do without?

F. ORAL. *Model:* **Voici la brosse dont je me suis servi.** 1. Here is the situation which I complained of. 2. Here is the picture that I made fun of. 3. You know the story that I laughed about. 4. I will tell you the words which I have remembered. 5. The illness from which I have recovered was not grave. 6. The things which I have done without were not worth much.

G. ORAL. *Model:* **C'est ce qui lui est arrivé.** 1. That is what happened to them. 2. Here is what amuses me. 3. Tell me what bores you. 4. I know what interests him. 5. That is what makes me laugh. 6. That is what hurts him the most. 7. Do you know what has given me that idea? 8. Ask him what frightened him.

H. *Rewrite the following sentences substituting a possessive, demonstrative, or interrogative pronoun for the italicized words. E.g.,* Quelle *maison* préférez-vous, la *maison* de Paul ou ma *maison*? Laquelle préférez-vous, celle de Paul ou la mienne? 1. Je plains votre femme et vous plaignez ma *femme.* 2. Nous plaignons tous les deux la *femme* de Théophile. 3. La *femme* que j'aime ne m'aime pas. 4. J'attends le train de midi. Quel *train* attendez-vous? 5. Je me sers de ma main droite. De quelle *main* vous servez-vous? 6. Il aimait son enfant et les *enfants* de son frère. 7. Il a écrit son nom et elle a écrit son *nom.* 8. L'*individu* qui a commis le crime est un monstre. 9. Dieu aime les *gens* qui s'aiment. 10. Ces souliers ne me vont pas. Montrez-moi ces *souliers*-là. —Quels *souliers*? —Les *souliers* qui ressemblent un peu à vos *souliers.* 11. Donnez-moi votre cahier et le *cahier* de votre camarade. 12. A qui sont ces *cahiers*-là? 13. Ils sont aux *élèves* qui sont absents.

IRREGULAR VERBS

I. *Consult:* **craindre** (§147), **rire** (§148), **Unit** 11.
(a) *Translate:* 1. Je le crains. 2. Plaignez-moi. 3. Il faut que je le peigne. 4. Il éteindra. 5. Ils rirent. 6. Ils riront. 7. Ils rient. 8. Il le peignit. 9. Vous riiez. 10. Je l'ai rejoint.
(b) *Write:* 1. He pities him. 2. Do not fear me. 3. You must extinguish. 4. He would paint. 5. He smiled (*P. Def.*) 6. He will laugh. 7. He is smiling. 8. He extinguished (*P. Def.*) 9. We were smiling. 10. Have you painted?

III

OPTIONAL

J. *Translate. Consult:* **Lecture** (Chap. 11) and **Conversation** 11. 1. How long have you been waiting for me? 2. Whom was he expecting to see? 3. Do you love me, he asked, and she blushed. 4. Well, at least she loves me, he said. 5. Nonsense! She loves *me.* 6. See here! Let's endeavor to solve this problem.

7. He will never succeed in making her love him. 8. You say she doesn't love me yet? Granted! But meanwhile I am going to do my best to win her love. 9. "Moreover," he said, "leave right now!" **(et plus vite que ça).** 10. How nice the weather is this evening! 11. He must have gone to look for his father. 12. He ran away, not knowing what to expect. 13. Which of your hands do you use to scratch your head? 14. What interests me most is art. 15. What interests her? 16. What happened in 1918? 17. Who chose you? 18. Whom did you choose? 19. Which of your courses is the most boring? 20. What is the country whose capital is Madrid?

IV

CONVERSATION 11

1. Lequel des états des Etats-Unis est le plus grand (petit, populeux, avancé)? —C'est . . . qui est le plus grand des états des Etats-Unis.

2. Laquelle de vos deux mains est la plus utile?

3. De quelle main vous servez-vous pour écrire (lancer une balle, tenir une fourchette, couper la viande, vous gratter la tête)? —Je me sers de ma main droite (gauche) pour. . . .

4. Laquelle de vos classes (Lequel de vos cours) est la (le) plus facile (difficile, intéressant(e), ennuyeux(euse))?

5. Qu'est-ce qui vous intéresse le plus? —Ce qui m'intéresse le plus c'est la littérature (l'art, la science, les sports, l'étude, le commerce, la musique, le théâtre, la politique, etc.)

6. Montrez-moi la main avec laquelle vous écrivez, etc. —Voici celle avec laquelle j'écris (je lance une balle, je tiens une fourchette, etc.).

7. Qu'est-ce qui est arrivé en mil quatre cent quatre-vingt-douze? en mil sept cent quatre-vingt-neuf? en mil huit cent trois? en mil huit cent quinze? en mil neuf cent quatorze? en mil neuf cent quarante-cinq?

8. Savez-vous en quelle année la Première Guerre Mondiale a commencé? . . . la Seconde Guerre Mondiale a fini? . . .

Christophe Colomb a découvert l'Amérique? . . . Napoléon nous a vendu la Louisiane? . . . Napoléon a perdu la bataille de Waterloo? . . . la Révolution Française a commencé?

9. Choisissez quelqu'un. . . . Qui est-ce qui vous a choisi? Qui est-ce que vous avez choisi? —C'est . . . qui m'a choisi. C'est . . . que j'ai choisi.

10. Demandez à celui qu'on a choisi qui l'a choisi.

11. Demandez à quelqu'un quelle main est la plus utile, laquelle de ses classes est la plus intéressante, ce qui l'intéresse le plus, ce qui est arrivé en mil huit cent trois, ce qu'il fait avec les yeux, s'il sait ce que c'est qu'un chauffeur, avec quoi il entend, à quoi il pense, combien de mains il a, ce qu'il a vu quand il était à New York, ce qu'il faisait quand il était petit, ce qu'il va faire demain.

12. Quelle est la capitale de la France, des Etats-Unis, de la Grande Bretagne, de la Russie, de l'Italie, du Canada, de la Belgique, d'Haïti, de la Suisse, de l'Espagne, de l'Egypte, de la Louisiane, de l'Iowa, de la province de Québec?

13. Quel est le pays (l'état) dont la capitale est Londres (Paris, Washington, le Caire, Rome, Moscou, Ottowa, Québec, Bruxelles, Berne, Port-au-Prince, Bâton Rouge, Des Moines, Madrid)? —Le pays dont la capitale est Londres est la Grande-Bretagne.

Sujets de discussion et de conversation:

1. Quel est votre sport préféré?

2. Les bons athlètes donnent-ils souvent plus de prestige aux universités que les professeurs?

3. Le grand public s'intéresse-t-il autant qu'autrefois aux sports dans les petits collèges?

4. Si vous aviez un fils, l'encourageriez-vous à pratiquer le sport? à jouer au football?

5. Devrait-on prendre de l'exercice tous les jours?

VOCABULAIRE: **l'équipe** *f.* team; **la partie** game; **faire du ski** to ski; **une rencontre sportive** athletic meet; **jouer au tennis** to play tennis; **le canotage** boating; **la natation** swimming; **l'aviron** *m.* rowing; **le match** match.

CHAPTER 12

NEGATIONS : INDEFINITE ADJECTIVES AND PRONOUNS

GRAMMAR

87. Forms of Negation. When negation is used in a sentence, it consists of **ne** and some other word. Some of these combined negative forms function as *correlative expressions.*

(1) The principal negative forms that are most commonly used are set out below.

ne . . . pas	not
ne . . . point	not (*More emphatic than* **pas.**)
ne . . . guère	hardly
ne . . . nullement	not at all
ne . . . plus	no longer, any more
ne . . . jamais *	never
ne . . . rien	nothing, anything
ne . . . que (Cf. §52, Obs.)	only, nothing . . . except, but
ne . . . ni . . . ni	neither . . . nor
ne . . . personne	nobody, not anybody
ne . . . aucun(e)	no, none, not any
ne . . . nul(le)	no, no one

(2) In compound tenses, **pas, point, guère, nullement, plus, jamais, rien,** precede the past participle; **que** and **personne** follow it. The word **ne** precedes the verb or auxiliary. (Cf. §39.)

Il ne me parle point.	He does not speak to me.
Votre ami ne vient plus nous voir.	Your friend no longer comes to see us.
Il ne m'avait rien emprunté.	He had borrowed nothing from me.
Je n'ai vu qu'elle.	I saw only her.

* Used with a verb but without **ne,** the word **jamais** means *ever. E.g.,* **Vous a-t-il jamais vu?** *Did he ever see you?*

(3) The words **personne, rien, aucun** and **nul** may function as either subject or object.

Personne ne l'a vu.	Nobody saw him.
Il n'a vu personne.	He saw nobody.
Nul n'est prophète en son pays.	No one is a prophet in his own country.
Je n'ai rien dit à personne.	I said nothing to anyone.

(4) The expression **ne . . . ni . . . ni** does not take the partitive. The words *nor . . . either,* when used alone, are translated by **(ni) . . . non plus.** The expression *neither of the two* is translated by **aucun des deux** or by **ni l'un ni l'autre.**

Je n'ai ni argent ni amis.	I have neither money nor friends.
Aucun des deux (*or* ni l'un ni l'autre) ne m'intéresse.	Neither of the two interests me.
Ni moi non plus.	Nor I either.

(5) The expression **ne . . . que** means *only*, but when used with other negatives its translation varies.

Il n'a gagné que deux francs.	He earned only two francs.
Je n'ai plus qu'un désir.	I have but one desire.
Il ne doit en avoir guère que deux.	He must scarcely have more than two.
Cela me dégoûte rien qu'à le voir.	It disgusts me just to see it.
Elle n'avait fait que chanter.	She had done nothing but sing.

(6) The double negative, although used infrequently, does occur. Cf. §120, (1) for negative word order before the infinitive.

Je ne peux pas ne pas le faire.	I cannot (but do it) help doing it.
Il ne pouvait pas ne point vous regarder.	He could not help looking at you.

(7) The word **ne** cannot be used alone. In mild contradictions *not* is translated by **non.**

(Non) pas moi mais vous.	Not I but you.

88. *ne* : Real and False Negatives. Under certain circumstances the word **ne**, when used alone with a verb, suffices to express the negative form *not.* In other situations **ne** has no negative force at all. These usages are explained below.

(1) The verbs **savoir, pouvoir, oser,** and **cesser** can be made negative by **ne** alone, although **pas** may also be used with them. In the expression **je ne saurais** + infinitive (*I cannot*), and in the expression **un je ne sais quoi** (*an indefinable something*), **pas** is always omitted. The word **ne** also stands alone in dependent clauses when the main clause is negative.

Je n'ose (pas) vous le dire.	I dare not tell you.
Je ne sais (pas) si je dois le dire.	I don't know whether I should say it.
Elle a un je ne sais quoi de chic.	There is something stylish about her.
Il n'y a rien qu'il ne mange.	There is nothing that he doesn't eat.

(2) After certain expressions the so-called *pleonastic* **ne** is used, but the following verb is not made negative unless **pas** also is used. Among these expressions are **craindre, avoir peur, empêcher, éviter, depuis que,** and comparisons. (Cf. §64 and §105.)

Je crains qu'il ne le fasse.	I am afraid he will do it.
Evitez qu'elle ne sache la vérité.	Avoid her learning the truth.
Il a beaucoup changé depuis que je ne l'ai vu.	He has changed a lot since I saw him.
Il est plus riche que ne l'est son frère.	He is richer than his brother (is).
BUT	
Je crains qu'il ne le fasse pas.	I am afraid he will not do it.

89. Indefinite Adjectives. The words **quelque(s)** and **chaque** are used only as adjectives. Observe their use in the sentences below.

J'ai quelque argent et quelques amis.	I have some (a little) money and some (a few) friends.
Je le vois chaque jour.	I see him every (each) day.
Il l'a perdu quelque part.	He lost it somewhere.

90. Indefinite Pronouns. The following words, which are sometimes called *indefinites,* are used only as pronouns.

quelqu'un(e)	somebody, some one	**on** (Cf. §126.)	one, we, they, people
quelques-un(e)s	some, a few	**personne** (Cf. §87.)	nobody, no one
quelque chose	something		
chacun(e)	each, each one	**rien** (Cf. §87.)	nothing

Avez-vous vu quelqu'un?	Did you see someone (anyone)?
Quelques-uns de ces livres sont très jolis.	Some of these books are very pretty.
Chacun fait ce qu'il peut.	Each does what he can.
On a volé ma valise.	They have (someone has) stolen my valise.
Personne n'a rien trouvé.	No one has found anything.
N'avez-vous rien à faire?	Have you nothing to do?
Y a-t-il quelque chose de bon à boire?	Is there anything good to drink?

OBSERVATION

The indefinites **quelqu'un, quelque chose, personne,** and **rien** require **de** before an adjective and **à** before an infinitive.

Avez-vous quelque chose d'intéressant à lire?	Do you have something interesting to read?
N'avez-vous rien à dire?	Have you nothing to say?

91. Indefinite Adjectives and Pronouns. The indefinites that are set out below are used both as adjectives and as pronouns.

ne . . . aucun(e) (Cf. §87.)	not a, not one, none, no
ne . . . nul, nulle (Cf. §87.)	not a, not one, none, no
autre, autres	other, others
tel, telle, tels, telles (Cf. §58, 3.)	such
plusieurs	several
tout, toute, tous, toutes (Cf. §58, 3.)	every, all, the whole
Je ne trouve aucune chaise. Aucune.	I find no chair. None.
Nous avons une autre leçon.	We have another lesson.
Il a d'autres projets.	He has other plans.
Il est tombé plusieurs fois.	He fell several times.

OBSERVATIONS

(1) Note the various translations of *any* in the sentences below.

Avez-vous quelque espoir?	Do you have any (*just a little*) hope?
Avez-vous de l'espoir?	Have you any (*some*) hope?
Donnez-moi n'importe quel livre.	Give me any (*just any*) book.
Y a-t-il quelque chose de bon ici?	Is there anything (*something*) good here?
L'as-tu vu quelque part?	Have you seen him anywhere?
J'irais n'importe où et je ferais n'importe quoi.	I would go (*just*) anywhere and do anything.

(2) Learn the pairs of opposites that are set out below.

quelqu'un	somebody	**quelque part**	somewhere
personne	nobody	**nulle part**	nowhere
quelque chose	something	**chacun**	each, each one
rien	nothing	**aucun**	not a, none
quelquefois	sometimes	**déjà**	already
jamais	never	**pas encore**	not yet
souvent	often	**la même chose**	the same thing
rarement	rarely	**autre chose**	something else

(3) Learn the following correlating conjunctions:

ou . . . ou	either . . . or
ne . . . ni . . . ni	neither . . . nor
et . . . et	both . . . and
soit . . . soit	whether . . . or
soit que . . . soit que *or* **ou que**	whether . . . or (*Followed by the subjunctive.*)
non seulement . . . mais encore	not only . . . but also
tantôt . . . tantôt	sometimes . . . sometimes, now . . . now

IDIOMATIC EXPRESSIONS

au fur et à mesure que	in proportion as, gradually as
en face de	opposite
vis-à-vis	opposite
ni moi non plus	nor I either, nor I

I

LECTURE

Lisez à haute voix.

La cigale et la fourmi

La cigale, ayant chanté
  Tout l'été,
Se trouva fort dépourvue
Quand la bise fut venue:
Pas un seul petit morceau
De mouche ou de vermisseau.
Elle alla crier famine
Chez la fourmi sa voisine,
La priant de lui prêter
Quelque grain pour subsister
Jusqu'à la saison nouvelle.
Je vous paierai, lui dit-elle,
Avant l'août, foi d'animal,
Intérêt et principal.
La fourmi n'est pas prêteuse:
C'est là son moindre défaut.
Que faisiez-vous au temps chaud?
Dit-elle à cette emprunteuse.
—Nuit et jour à tout venant
Je chantais, ne vous déplaise.
—Vous chantiez? j'en suis fort aise:
Eh bien! dansez maintenant.

La Fontaine

Répondez aux questions suivantes:

1. Qui avait chanté? 2. Combien de temps avait-elle chanté? 3. Qu'est-ce que la cigale avait fait? 4. Comment s'est-elle trouvée quand la bise est venue? 5. Quand s'est-elle trouvée

dépourvue? 6. Combien de morceaux de mouche ou de vermisseau avait-elle? 7. De quoi n'avait-elle pas un seul petit morceau? 8. Chez qui la cigale est-elle allée crier famine? 9. De qui la fourmi était-elle la voisine? 10. Qu'a-t-elle prié la fourmi de faire? 11. Quand a-t-elle promis de payer? 12. La fourmi est-elle prêteuse? 13. Qui était l'emprunteuse? 14. Qu'est-ce que la cigale avait fait pendant la saison chaude? 15. Qu'est-ce que la fourmi lui a conseillé de faire alors. 16. Faites un résumé de cette fable en vos propres termes.

II

ORAL AND WRITTEN EXERCISES

A. *Translate.* 1. Non seulement ma famille mais encore mes amis m'ont abandonné. 2. Nous n'avons que faire de l'argent que vous pourriez nous prêter. 3. L'homme n'est ni bon ni méchant. 4. «Nulle part le bonheur ne m'attend.» (Lamartine) 5. Nous ne pouvons pas ne pas accepter ce travail, vu l'état de nos finances. 6. On dit qu'un homme amoureux ne veut ni manger ni dormir. 7. On ne pouvait guère voir qu'un morceau de ciel bleu. 8. Et le grand public et les savants honorent cet homme de science.

B. *Make the sentences negative by using the negative forms in parentheses. E.g.,* **(ne . . . pas) Il a travaillé. Il n'a pas travaillé.** 1. (ne . . . jamais) Il vous le vendra. 2. (ne . . . ni . . . ni) Il avait des amis et de l'argent. 3. (ne . . . plus) Elle voulait nous en parler. 4. (ne . . . rien) Ils avaient cherché dans la cuisine. 5. (ne . . . que) Ils avaient acheté des bonbons.

C. *Translate the italicized English words.* 1. Il n'a vu *nobody.* 2. *Nobody* ne l'a vu. 3. Avait-il rencontré *someone*? 4. Nous n'avions jamais parlé *to anyone.* 5. Font-ils *something*? 6. Non. Ils ne font *anything.* 7. Le bonheur doit exister *somewhere* ici bas. 8. Le bonheur parfait n'existe *nowhere.* 9. *Each* fait ce qu'il peut. 10. *None* ne fait tout son possible. 11. *Each* homme voudrait faire de son mieux. 12. Avez-vous *a few* journaux? 13. Oui, j'en ai *a few*. 14. Avaient-ils trouvé *something good*? 15. *Nobody interesting* ne se trouvait à la conférence.

D. *Change the simple tenses to their corresponding compound tenses. E.g.,* **Personne ne parle. Personne n'a parlé. Personne ne parlait. Personne n'avait parlé.** 1. Je n'aimais que Jeanne. 2. Il ne s'intéresse à rien. 3. Elle ne vous verrait plus. 4. Gaston ne fait jamais rien. 5. Il ne dira rien à personne.

E. ORAL. *Complete each sentence with a contrasting expression.* 1. Il a bu quelque chose de chaud mais elle n'a . . . bu du tout. 2. Il a vu quelqu'un mais elle n'a vu. . . . 3. Il veut toujours faire la même chose mais elle préfère faire . . . de temps en temps. 4. Il se plaint toujours de quelque chose mais elle ne se plaint . . . de. . . . 5. Il l'aimait toujours mais déjà elle ne l'aimait. . . .

IRREGULAR VERBS

F. *Consult:* **boire** (§149), **voir** (§150), and **Unit** 12.
(a) *Translate:* 1. Je le vois. 2. Il en boit. 3. Nous le voyons. 4. Vous en buvez. 5. Nous l'avons vue. 6. Vous aviez bu. 7. Vous boirez. 8. Nous verrions. 9. Il but. 10. Ils virent.

(b) *Write:* 1. He sees me. 2. I drink it. 3. You see us. 4. I was drinking. 5. I haven't drunk any. 6. You used to see. 7. We would see. 8. I must see you. 9. I must drink it. 10. He saw them (*P. Def.*).

III

OPTIONAL

G. *Translate. Consult:* **Lecture** (Chap. 12) and **Conversation** 12. 1. They did not see each other until the next day. 2. Try as she may, she will never get accustomed to your way of living. 3. He has a grudge against everybody. 4. He will never realize anything. 5. I never drink any water. 6. He is only fifteen years old. 7. We didn't go anywhere last night. 8. They go there only very rarely. 9. He said that he had neither uncles nor aunts. 10. They asked him what he did when he had nothing to do. 11. No one had come to see us. 12. We have only five of them. 13. Are you hot or cold? —Neither one. 14. You say that you have done nothing interesting? I (haven't) either. 15. She found herself destitute when the north wind had come. 16. She went to her neighbor's, begging her to lend her some grain. 17. That is her least fault. 18. I am very glad of it, said she to her.

IV

CONVERSATION 12

1. Etes-vous allé quelque part hier soir? —Je suis allé au cinéma, etc. —Je ne suis allé nulle part.

2. Est-ce que quelqu'un est venu vous voir? —Un de mes amis est venu me voir. Personne n'est venu me voir.

3. Qu'est-ce que vous avez fait (d'intéressant)? —J'ai vu un film remarquable, etc. Je n'ai rien fait (d'intéressant).

4. Combien de livres avez-vous perdus cette année? —J'en ai perdu. . . . Je n'en ai perdu aucun.

5. Avez-vous vingt-deux ans? —Non, je n'ai que vingt et un ans.

6. Avez-vous deux bouches (trois mains, deux nez, onze doigts)? —Non, je n'en ai qu'une (que deux, qu'un, que dix).

7. Allez-vous souvent au cabaret? —Non, je n'y vais que très rarement. Je n'y vais jamais.

8. Etes-vous déjà allé en France? —Je n'y suis pas encore allé.

9. Avez-vous bu beaucoup de champagne? —Je n'en ai bu que très peu. Je n'en ai jamais bu.

10. Avez-vous des frères et des sœurs? —J'ai des frères mais je n'ai qu'une sœur. Je n'ai qu'un frère et une sœur. J'ai un frère mais je n'ai pas de sœur. Je n'ai ni frère ni sœur.

11. Avez-vous faim ou soif? —Je n'ai ni faim ni soif. —Et vous? —(Ni) moi non plus.

12. Etes-vous très riche ou très pauvre? —Je ne suis ni l'un ni l'autre. —Et vous? —(Ni) moi non plus.

13. Qu'est-ce que vous faites (dites, mangez, buvez) quand vous n'avez rien à faire (dire, manger, boire)? —Quand je n'ai rien à faire je ne fais rien.

14. Demandez à quelqu'un s'il est allé quelque part hier soir, si quelqu'un est venu le voir, ce qu'il a fait d'intéressant, combien de livres il a perdus, s'il a vingt-deux ans, s'il a deux bouches, s'il va souvent au cabaret, s'il est déjà allé en France, s'il a bu beaucoup de champagne, s'il a des frères et des sœurs, s'il a faim ou soif, ce qu'il fait quand il n'a rien à faire.

15. Qu'est-ce qu'on vous a demandé? —On m'a demandé si j'étais allé quelque part hier soir, si quelqu'un était venu me voir, ce que j'avais fait . . . , combien de livres j'avais . . . , si j'avais . . . , si j'allais . . . , si j'étais déjà allé . . . , si j'avais bu . . . , si j'avais des . . . , si j'avais faim . . . , ce que je faisais quand . . . .

16. Qu'est-ce que vous avez répondu? —J'ai répondu que je n'étais allé nulle part, que personne n'était venu me voir, que je n'avais rien fait . . . , que je n'en avais perdu aucun, etc.

Sujets de discussion et de conversation:

1. Qu'est-ce que c'est qu'une fable?

2. Quel genre de littérature préférez-vous? Expliquez votre choix.

3. Si vous écriviez un livre, serait-ce un roman, une pièce, une étude scientifique ou un recueil de vers? Pensez-vous écrire un livre quelque jour?

4. Pourquoi le grand public exige-t-il que le héros triomphe et que le scélérat soit puni?

5. Quel est le meilleur roman que vous ayez jamais lu? Faites-en le résumé.

CHAPTER 13

FUTURE AND CONDITIONAL TENSES

GRAMMAR

92. The Future. The future tense of regular verbs is formed by adding **-ai, -as, -a, -ons, -ez, -ont** to the infinitive, the **-e** of **-re** verbs being dropped. (Cf. §3, §14, §23.) Remember that verbs like **mener** and **appeler,** which acquire an accent, as in *je mène, etc.,* or which double the final consonant of the stem, as in *j'appelle, etc.,* also make these changes in all forms of the future and the conditional. Verbs that have **é** in the stem, however, keep that **é** in the future and the conditional. Verbs that end in **-yer** become *-ierai, etc.,* in the future and the conditional. (Cf.§ 11, 3.) This latter change is optional with verbs that end in **-ayer.** Examples of some of these verb forms are shown below.

achèterai, achèverai, gèlerai, lèverai, mènerai, promènerai
appellerai, jetterai, rappellerai
céderai, compléterai, espérerai, préférerai, répéterai, révélerai
ennuierai, essaierai *or* **essayerai, nettoierai, paierai or payerai**

Note and learn the irregular future forms below.

irai	(aller)	**faudra**	(falloir)	**vaudrai**	(valoir)
courrai	(courir)	**mourrai**	(mourir)	**verrai**	(voir)
devrai	(devoir)	**pourrai**	(pouvoir)	**voudrai**	(vouloir)
enverrai	(envoyer)	**saurai**	(savoir)	**aurai**	(avoir)
ferai	(faire)	**tiendrai**	(tenir)	**serai**	(être)

93. The Future Perfect. The future perfect = the *future* of **avoir** or **être** + a *past participle.* (Cf. §33.)

Il n'aura rien perdu.	He will have lost nothing.
Il se sera douté de quelque chose.	He will have (has probably) suspected something.
A cette heure-là nous serons partis.	By that time we shall have left.

OBSERVATION

The future perfect tense is used more frequently in French than in English. The average Frenchman would nearly always translate *when you finish* as **quand vous aurez fini.**

94. The Conditional. The conditional tense is formed by adding the imperfect endings **-ais, -ais, -ait, -ions, -iez, -aient** to the future stem. (Cf. §4, §15, §24.) This tense is used for the purposes set out below.

(1) To express futurity in relation to past time, whence the term *past future* which is also sometimes employed to designate the conditional tense.

Il m'a dit qu'il reviendrait tout de suite.	He told me he would return immediately.

(2) To express what *would happen* or what *would be* true, now or in the future, if something else *should happen* or *were* true, now or in the future.

Je serais content, si vous étiez content.	I would be happy if you were happy.
Je le ferais, si vous le faisiez.	I would do it if you did it.
Si j'étais (de) vous, je le ferais.	If I were you, I would do it.

95. The Conditional Perfect. The conditional perfect = the *conditional* of **avoir** or **être** + a *past participle*. (Cf. §34.) It is used to express the relationships set out below.

(1) Completed futurity in relation to a past time.

Il croyait qu'à cette heure-là nous serions partis.	He thought that by that time we would have left.

(2) What *would have happened* or what *would have been* true, in the past, if something else *had happened* or *had been* true, in the past.

J'aurais été content si vous aviez été content.	I would have been happy if you had been happy.
Je l'aurais fait si vous l'aviez fait.	I would have done it if you had done it.
Si j'avais été (de) vous, je l'aurais fait.	If I had been you I would have done it.

96. The Immediate Future. Just as in English we may say either *I shall do it* or *I am going to do it,* so in French we may say either **Je le ferai** or **Je vais le faire.** In other words, the present of **aller** + the *infinitive* is equivalent to the future, with the further implication that the action in question is to take place quite soon. Likewise, **aller,** followed by an infinitive, may be used in the imperfect tense, in which case the construction replaces one use of the conditional. This use of **aller** in the present and imperfect is extremely frequent. In ordinary conversation it almost entirely replaces the regular future construction.

Je pense qu'il va le faire = Je pense qu'il le fera.
Je pensais qu'il allait le faire = Je pensais qu'il le ferait.

97. Special Uses of Future and Conditional Tenses. After **quand, lorsque** (*when*), **dès que, aussitôt que** (*as soon as*), **pendant que** (*while*), futurity, if implied, must be expressed in French.

Quand il arrivera je lui parlerai.	When he arrives (*literally,* will arrive), I shall talk to him.
Dès qu'elle sera partie je vous le dirai.	As soon as she has left (*literally,* will have left), I'll tell you.
Il promit de le faire lorsque j'aurais fini mon travail.	He promised to do it when I had finished [*literally* should (would) have finished] my work.

OBSERVATION

Neither the future nor the conditional is used after **si** (*if*), though futurity may usually appear to be implied unless **si** has the meaning of *whether.*

Savez-vous s'il viendra?	Do you know whether he will come?

98. Probability or Supposition with Future and Conditional. The future and the conditional, as also their compounds, often express probability or supposition.

Jean sera malade aujourd'hui.	John is probably (*or* must be) ill today.
Est-ce que vous seriez l'homme?	Are you by any chance the man?
Ils seront déjà partis.	They have probably already left.
Vous seriez-vous fait mal?	Can you have hurt yourself? Is it possible that you have hurt yourself?

99. Tense Sequence and Translation of Conditional Sentences. Note carefully the tense sequence of the following sentences, and the various possible translations of the *if* clause.

PRESENT —— FUTURE

S'il travaille,	If he works, / If he will work,
il gagnera de l'argent.	**he will earn money.**

IMPERFECT —— CONDITIONAL

S'il travaillait,	If he worked, / If he were to work, / Should he work, / Were he to work,
il gagnerait de l'argent.	he would **earn money.**

PLUPERFECT —— CONDITIONAL PERFECT

S'il avait travaillé,	If he had worked, / Had he worked,
il aurait gagné de l'argent.	he would have earned money.
Si elle était rentrée,	If she had returned, / Had she returned,
il serait parti.	he would have left.

OBSERVATION

(1) In the pluperfect —— conditional perfect sequence, the pluperfect subjunctive is used in both the *if* clause and the result clause, but only in extremely literary style.

S'il nous eût dit la vérité, nous n'eussions pas tant souffert.

OR

Nous eût-il dit la vérité, nous n'eussions pas tant souffert.

(2) The student must carefully analyze any English sentence, particularly one that contains an *if* clause or a *result* clause in which *should, would,* or *could* occurs. Note the translation into French of the following sentences *when:*

Should expresses (*a*) the conditional, (*b*) supposition, (*c*) obligation.

(*a*) I should (would) break my neck if I fell.	**Je me casserais le cou si je tombais.**
(*b*) Should he (were he to) go there tonight, he would find them.	**S'il y allait ce soir, il les trouverait.**
(*c*) You should (ought to) accompany them.	**Vous devriez les accompagner.**

In careful English usage, *should* is the past tense of *shall.* In current usage the common tendency is to replace *shall* and *should* by *will* and *would.* In fact many grammarians and English scholars no longer insist on the distinction between *shall* and *will.*

Would expresses (*a*) the conditional, (*b*) habitual action, (*c*) to be willing *or* please.

(*a*) He would do it if he had time.	**Il le ferait s'il avait le temps.**
(*b*) She would (used to) get up at six o'clock when she lived in the country.	**Elle se levait à six heures quand elle demeurait à la campagne.**
(*c*) If you would (were willing to) buy me a hat, I would wear it.	**Si vous vouliez m'acheter un chapeau, je le porterais.**
Would you (please) show me that book?	**Voudriez-vous me montrer ce livre-là?**

Note that in the last two sentences *would* is translated by forms of **vouloir.** Remember that *will you,* a form of politeness, is expressed in French by the present tense of **vouloir** + an *infinitive. E.g.,* **Voulez-vous me montrer le chapeau?** *Will you show me the hat?*

Could means (*a*) was able, (*b*) would *or* should be able, (*c*) could have (would *or* should have been able).

(*a*) If they could (were able to) study, they would learn it.	**S'ils pouvaient étudier, ils l'apprendraient.**
(*b*) They could (would be able to) learn it if they would study.	**Ils pourraient l'apprendre s'ils étudiaient.**
(*c*) He could have learned it (would have been able to learn it) if he had studied.	**Il aurait pu l'apprendre s'il avait étudié.**

100. The Conditional in Clauses of Concession. After **quand** or **quand même,** or with **que,** the conditional may express concession. Sentences that include these expressions are given below.

Quand (même) vous me le donneriez, je ne l'accepterais pas. OR **Vous me le donneriez que je ne l'accepterais pas.** BUT **Même si vous me le donniez je ne l'accepterais pas.**	Even if you gave it to me, I would not accept it. OR Should you give it to me, I would not accept it.
Quand (même) on m'aurait tué, je n'aurais pas crié. OR **On m'aurait tué que je n'aurais pas crié.** OR **On m'eût tué que je n'eusse pas crié.** (Cf. §99, Obs. 1.)	Though they had killed me, I would not have cried out.

IDIOMATIC EXPRESSIONS

douter de to doubt

Je doute de cela.
Je doute de tout le monde.
Je n'en ai pas douté.
J'en doute.

se douter de	to suspect	**Je m'en suis douté.** **Je m'en doutais bien.** **Il ne se doutera de rien.**

à l'avenir	in the future	**sans doute**	no doubt, doubtlessly
bien entendu	of course, certainly	**sans aucun doute**	without a doubt
Bien sûr!	Yes indeed! Certainly!	**bref**	in short, in brief
		en un mot	in a word, in short
évidemment	obviously	**somme toute**	all in all, in short
de plus en plus	more and more	**tout compte fait**	everything considered, in short
quand même	just the same, even if		

I

LECTURE

Lisez à haute voix:

Je n'avais pas vu mon vieux camarade Vital Herbelot depuis vingt-cinq ans. Je le trouvais tout différent de celui dont j'avais gardé le souvenir. Il avait dans toute sa personne quelque chose d'aisé, de décidé, qui ne sentait en rien le fonctionnaire.

—N'es-tu plus dans l'administration?

—Non, mon ami, répondit-il, je suis cultivateur. J'ai donné ma démission pour deux pêches. Je te dirai tout cela.

Après le café mon ami Vital commença son récit.

—Je faisais mon chemin dans l'administration où ma famille m'avait placé et, sans l'affaire des pêches, sans doute serais-je devenu un jour chef de bureau. A cette époque-là ma femme qui était très souffrante dut garder la maison lors d'une réception chez mon directeur. Comme je sortais elle me dit: «On parle de pêches qui ont coûté trois francs la pièce. . . . Si tu étais gentil, tu m'en rapporterais une. . . . Tu en choisiras une comme si c'était pour toi et tu la dissimuleras adroitement . . .» Comment peut-on opposer un refus catégorique à une jeune femme qu'on aime?

C'était un très beau bal. Bon! j'ai réussi à glisser deux belles pêches dans mon chapeau haut de forme et étais en train de traverser le salon lorsque la fille de mon directeur, qui avait besoin d'un chapeau pour le cotillon, s'écria:

«Un chapeau! Il nous manque un chapeau!» A ce moment elle m'a vu. «Vite, monsieur Herbelot, votre chapeau!»

Tu vois d'ici le tableau. Les pêches roulèrent sur le parquet, les danseuses riaient. J'aurais voulu m'enfoncer sous le parquet et disparaître.

D'une voix ironique la jeune fille me dit: «Monsieur Herbelot, ramassez donc vos pêches!»

Dans mon bureau, on me disait: «Herbelot, ramassez vos pêches!» Je pouvais entendre dire dans la rue: «C'est le monsieur aux pêches!»

La place n'était plus tenable, et huit jours après j'ai donné ma démission.

D'après *Les Pêches* par André Theuriet

Vocabulaire: **quelque chose d'aisé** something prosperous (carefree); **sentir le fonctionnaire** to smack of; **cultivateur** *m.* farmer; **démission** *f.* resignation; **pêche** *f.* peach; **récit** *m.* story; **faire son chemin** to get along, to advance; **chef de bureau** *m.* senior clerk; **lors** at the time of; **directeur** *m.* manager, director; **dissimuler** to hide; **glisser** to slip; **chapeau haut de forme** *m.* top hat; **parquet** *m.* floor; **s'enfoncer** to sink.

Répondez aux questions suivantes: 1. Herbelot avait-il beaucoup changé en vingt-cinq ans? 2. Est-il toujours dans l'administration? 3. Pourquoi sa femme n'assistait-elle pas à la réception? 4. Que désire la femme d'Herbelot? 5. Pourquoi a-t-il consenti à sa prière? 6. Y auriez-vous consenti, messieurs? 7. Où a-t-il mis les pêches? 8. Qui avait besoin d'un chapeau? 9. Qu'est-ce qui est arrivé quand elle a pris le chapeau d'Herbelot? 10. Qu'a-t-elle dit à Herbelot? 11. Qu'est-ce qu'on disait dans le bureau? Dans la rue? 12. A sa place auriez-vous donné votre démission? 13. Faites un résumé de cette lecture.

II

ORAL AND WRITTEN EXERCISES

A. *Translate.* 1. Doutez-vous toujours de ma sincérité? 2. Oui, monsieur, j'en doute toujours. 3. Il se rendra de plus en plus compte de vos faiblesses. 4. Sans doute le feriez-vous si l'occasion se présentait. 5. A l'avenir, dit-il, vous devriez vous conduire en homme de bien. 6. Quand (même) vous me le donneriez, je ne l'accepterais pas.

B. *Put the following present indicative verb forms in the future and conditional. E.g.,* **Il mène. Il mènera. Il mènerait.** 1. Nous menons. 2. J'appelle. 3. Nous appelons. 4. Vous achetez. 5. Il espère. 6. Ils essuient. 7. Je paye. 8. Vous jetez. 9. Vous possédez. 10. Il se rappelle. 11. Tu préfères.

C. *Translate the immediate future forms, then replace them with future and imperfect forms, and translate the latter. E.g.,* **Il va partir. Il partira. Il allait partir.** *He is going to leave. He will leave. He was going to leave.* 1. Ils vont venir. 2. Je vais vous le montrer. 3. Tu vas faire ta malle. 4. Il va me présenter à elle. 5. Elle va me le présenter. 6. Je vais le lui demander.

D. *Translate the italicized English words.* 1. Venez nous voir quand vous *are* à Lyon. 2. Je vous le donnerai aussitôt qu'ils *have gone.* 3. Savent-ils *whether* leurs amis le permettront? 4. J'allais étudier pendant que Jean *slept* et vice versa. 5. Jean *is probably ill.* 6. Je ne fumerais pas la pipe *if I didn't like tobacco.* 7. Vous l'apprendrez *if you study.* 8. Vous auriez réussi *if you had worked.* 9. Nous vous entendrions *if you talked louder.* 10. Je le verrais *if he were to come.* 11. S'ils étaient arrivés plus tôt, *we would have left on time.* 12. *He could have done it* s'il s'était appliqué.

IRREGULAR VERBS

E. *Consult:* **asseoir** (§151), **courir** (§152), and **Unit** 13.

(a) *Translate:* 1. Je m'assieds. 2. Asseyons-nous. 3. Il s'asseyera. 4. Elle s'est assise. 5. Elle est assise. 6. Elle s'assit. 7. Il court. 8. Il courut. 9. Il courait. 10. Il courrait.

(b) *Write:* 1. He sits down. 2. Sit down. 3. We shall sit down. 4. I sat down. 5. I was seated. 6. They sat down (*P. Def.*). 7. I run. 8. I ran (*P. Def.*). 9. We were running. 10. He will run. 11. I would have run.

III

OPTIONAL

F. *Translate. Consult:* **Idiomatic Expressions** (Chap. 13) and **Conversation** 13. 1. We would (used to) get up early when we lived in the country. 2. Were he to offer me a fortune, he could not buy my caresses. 3. Should you leave today, you would arrive in Chicago tomorrow morning. 4. If she had loved him, she would have married him. 5. He was going to leave at ten but he missed the train. 6. You say he is going to do without his coffee? 7. He doesn't doubt anyone. 8. In short, he no longer has a cent. 9. I suspected it. 10. What would you like to be? 11. I would like to be a ballerina. 12. If I were to go to France I would go by plane. 13. If I had lived at the time of the French Revolution I would not have sent Marie-Antoinette to the guillotine. 14. If I were a nurse I would take care of sick people. 15. Would you be happier if you knew how to type? 16. If I had five cents I would buy a cup of coffee. 17. If you could be just anything, what would you be? 18. If he were dictator, what would he do?

IV

CONVERSATION 13

1. Qu'est-ce que vous êtes? —Pardon? —Je voudrais savoir quel est votre métier. —Ah, j'y suis. Je suis étudiant(e). —Et qu'est-ce que vous voudriez être? —Je voudrais être médecin (ingénieur, dentiste, avocat, modiste, militaire, prêtre, pasteur, journaliste, professeur, acteur, artiste, écrivain, cultivateur, éleveur, géologue, photographe, chimiste, mécanicien, banquier, propriétaire, commerçant, industriel, administrateur, policier, pompier, plombier, maçon, charpentier, épicier, garagiste, caissier, rentier, patron).

2. Si vous n'étiez pas Américain qu'est-ce que vous voudriez être? —Si je n'étais pas Américain je voudrais être Canadien (Anglais, Français, Irlandais, Italien, Allemand, Russe, Suédois, Danois, Norvégien, Espagnol, Suisse, Belge, Hollandais, Grec, Turc, etc.)

3. Si vous pouviez être n'importe quoi, qu'est-ce que vous seriez? —Si je pouvais être n'importe quoi je serais poète, etc.

4. Si vous alliez en ville (à Montréal, au Brésil, en France), comment iriez-vous? —Si j'allais en ville j'irais à pied (en auto, à bicyclette, en chemin de fer, en bateau, en avion).

5. Si vous aviez cinq sous (vingt sous, un dollar, cent dollars, mille dollars, etc.) qu'est-ce que vous achèteriez? —Si j'avais cinq sous j'achèterais une tasse de café, etc.

6. Si vous aviez vécu à l'époque de la Révolution Française auriez-vous envoyé Marie-Antoinette à la guillotine? Si vous aviez connu Napoléon (Pasteur, Voltaire, Louis XIV, Verlaine, Jeanne d'Arc, Mme Curie) l'auriez-vous admiré(e)? Si vous étiez né en mil neuf cent dix quel âge auriez-vous aujourd'hui? Si vous étiez dictateur que feriez-vous? Si vous étiez plus vieux seriez-vous plus sage? Si vous étiez plus riche seriez-vous plus heureux?

7. Si vous étiez chauffeur (médecin, professeur, infirmière, etc.) que feriez-vous? —Si j'étais chauffeur je conduirais une auto.

8. Savez-vous taper à la machine (parler russe, nager, patiner, piloter un avion, conduire une auto, jouer au bridge, jouer de la flûte, etc.)? —Je (ne) sais (pas). . . .

9. Connaissez-vous le président des Etats-Unis (la reine d'Angleterre, le doyen de notre université, le gouverneur de l'état, Charles Boyer)? —Je (ne) le (la) connais (pas).

10. Savez-vous qui est le président des Etats-Unis (le président de la République Française, le roi des Belges, etc.) —Je (ne) sais (pas) qui c'est.

11. Seriez-vous plus heureux si vous saviez taper à la machine, etc.? . . . si vous connaissiez la reine d'Angleterre, etc.? —Je (ne) serais (pas) plus heureux si je savais . . . si je connaissais. . . .

Sujets de discussion et de conversation:

1. Les cultivateurs sont-ils plus indépendants que les employés de bureau?
2. La vie d'un fermier est-elle moins dure qu'autrefois?
3. Aimeriez-vous vivre à la campagne?
4. Pourrait-on dire que la nature est l'ennemi de l'homme?
5. Pouvez-vous imaginer une situation plus embarrassante que celle d'Herbelot?

CHAPTER 14

PRESENT AND PERFECT SUBJUNCTIVE

GRAMMAR

101. The Subjunctive Mood. For conjugation of the present and perfect tenses of the subjunctive mood cf. §6, §17, §26, and §36. Since verbs in the subjunctive mood are practically never used in present-day English, it is therefore impossible to offer any universally applicable translation for a given tense of the French subjunctive. It is seldom translated by *may,* which is best rendered into French by **il se peut que.** Rather, the French subjunctive is generally translated by the English indicative. Whereas **il ira** can always be translated as *he will go,* and **il alla** as *he went,* the present subjunctive form, by itself, means nothing at all. Use of the subjunctive in the sentence determines whether it is to be translated by the English present, future, or infinitive.

The singular stem and the third person plural stem of the present subjunctive of irregular verbs may be derived from the third person plural of the present indicative. The first and second persons plural, however, are derived from the *first* person plural of the present indicative. The only irregular verbs that do not form their present subjunctive according to this rule are these: **être** (§36), **avoir** (§36), **aller** (§127), **faire** (§139), **falloir** (§141), **pleuvoir** (§153), **pouvoir** (§136), **savoir** (§142), **valoir** (§140), and **vouloir** (§137).

102. Use of the Subjunctive. This mood, which is usually introduced by **que,** is generally used in a subordinate clause whose subject differs from that of the main clause. The subjunctive is used when the main clause contains any of the words or expressions that are set out below.

(1) A verb or an expression of emotion. *E.g.,* **regretter, craindre; être content, heureux, désolé, enchanté, fâché; avoir peur**; and such. BUT: **espérer,** in the affirmative, takes the indicative mood.

Je regrette qu'il le fasse.	I am sorry he does it.
Je suis content qu'il l'ait fait.	I am glad he did it.
BUT	
J'espère qu'il le fera.	I hope he will do it.

(2) A verb of wishing, wanting, commanding, or ordering. *E.g.,* **désirer, vouloir, souhaiter, ordonner,** and such.

Voulez-vous que je le finisse?	Do you want me to finish it?
BUT	
Voulez-vous le finir?	Do you want to finish it?

(3) An expression of necessity. *E.g.,* **il faut, il est nécessaire, il convient** (*it is fitting*), and such.

Il faut que vous y soyez.	You must be there.
BUT	
Il faut y être.	One must be there.

(4) A verb or an expression of doubt or denial. *E.g.,* **nier** (*to deny*), **douter; il est douteux**; and such.

Je doute qu'il y en ait.	I doubt that there are any.

(5) An impersonal expression which implies uncertainty or expresses an opinion. *E.g.,* **Il est possible, il est rare, il est bon, il est temps, il semble, il se peut, il est important,** and such.

Il est possible qu'il soit parti.	It is possible he has left.
BUT	
Il est certain qu'il est parti.	It is certain he has left.
Il me semble qu'il a raison.	It seems to me that he is right.

(6) A verb or an expression of believing, thinking, declaring, or hoping, used either negatively or interrogatively. *E.g.*, **penser, croire, dire, espérer; être sûr, être certain**; and such.

Je ne crois pas que ce soit vrai.	I do not believe it is true.
Etes-vous certain qu'il ait tort?	Are you sure he is wrong?
BUT	
Je crois que c'est vrai.	I believe it is true.

OBSERVATION

Even when used negatively or interrogatively the verbs or expressions listed under (6) do not absolutely require the subjunctive. They may be followed by the indicative if no doubt or uncertainty is implied.

Il n'a pas dit qu'il partait.	He did not say he was leaving.
Pensez-vous qu'il viendra?	Do you think he will come?
Il ne croyait pas qu'ils viendraient.	He did not believe that they would come.

103. Tense Sequence : Translation of Present and Perfect Subjunctive. If the verb of the principal clause is in the present or future tense, the present or perfect subjunctive is used in the subordinate clause. The choice between present and perfect subjunctive is determined as follows:

(1) If the action of the subordinate verb takes place at *the same time as* or *subsequent to* that of the main verb, use the present subjunctive.

(2) If the action of the subordinate verb takes place *before* that of the main verb, use the *perfect subjunctive.* Carefully observe the sentences below and note the various ways of translating the subjunctive.

PRESENT SUBJUNCTIVE

Je regrette	**qu'il finisse.**	I am sorry	he is finishing, finishes, will finish.
	qu'il arrive.		he is arriving, arrives, will arrive.

PERFECT SUBJUNCTIVE

Je regrette	**qu'il ait fini.** **qu'il soit arrivé.**	I am sorry	he finished, has finished, will have finished. he arrived, has arrived, will have arrived.

104. Infinitive Constructions in Place of Subjunctive. Under the circumstances described below, a construction that makes use of the infinitive may be substituted for one using the subjunctive.

(1) If the subject of the subordinate verb is the same as that of the main verb, an infinitive construction is used instead of the subjunctive.

Infinitive	*Subjunctive*
Il désire nous le donner.	**Je désire qu'il nous le donne.**
Je veux m'en passer.	**Je veux que vous vous en passiez.**
Il est content de venir.	**Il est content que vous veniez.**
Il travaille pour acheter ce qu'il désire.	**Il travaille pour qu'elle achète ce qu'elle désire.**

OBSERVATION

Note that the first two of the above subjunctive constructions are best translated by the English infinitive. *E.g., I want him to give it to us. I want you to do without it.*

(2) Such verbs as **permettre, défendre** (*to forbid*), **empêcher** (*to prevent*), and **ordonner** may take the subjunctive, but an infinitive construction is preferable even with a change of subject. With **il faut**, however, the reverse is true.

Possible	*Preferable*	
Empêchez qu'il ne sorte.	**Empêchez-le de sortir.**	Prevent him from leaving.
Permettez que je vous baise la main.	Permettez-moi de vous baiser la main.	Let me kiss your hand.
Il me faut partir.	Il faut que je parte.	I must leave.

105. Pleonastic *ne* with the Subjunctive. The verbs **empêcher, éviter,** and **craindre,** as also the conjunctions **avant que** and **à moins que,** usually take a pleonastic **ne** before a verb in the subordinate clause. (Cf. §88, 2.)

Je crains qu'il ne soit blessé.	I am afraid he is wounded.
Parlez-lui avant qu'il ne sorte.	Speak to him before he goes out.

106. The Subjunctive Imperative. The present indicative, as explained in §10, §20, §29, and §68, 2, provides imperative forms only for the second person singular **(tu),** for the second person plural **(vous),** and for the first person plural. The present subjunctive is used for expressing the imperative in the first person singular and in the third person singular and plural, under the circumstances described below.

(1) The present subjunctive is normally used in an independent clause, usually after **que,** to express a wish or a command. Such clauses are not really independent because they always presuppose an unexpressed main clause.

Qu'on ne dise pas que j'ai menti.	Let it not be said that I have lied.
Qu'elle entre tout de suite.	Let her (may she, have her) come in at once.
Que je meure si je mens.	May I die if I am lying.
Que personne ne sorte!	Let no one go out!

(2) Note the examples below where **que** is not used.

Vive l'Amérique!	(Long) live America!
Vivent nos soldats!	(Long) live our soldiers!
A Dieu ne plaise!	God forbid!
Dieu vous bénisse!	God bless you!
Vogue la galère!	Come what may!
Ainsi soit-il.	So may it be.
Soit!	Granted! (So be it!)
Plût à Dieu que ce fût vrai! (*Imperfect subjunctive*)	Would to God it were true!

IDIOMATIC EXPRESSIONS

manquer	to miss	**J'ai manqué le train.**	I missed the train.
manquer à	to be missed by, lacking to	***Marie manque à Jean.**	John misses Mary.
		†Vous me manquez, ma mère.	I miss you, mother.
		‡Je vous manquerai, mon fils.	You will miss me, my son.
manquer à	to fail	**Il manque à son devoir.**	He fails in his duty.
manquer de	to lack	**Ils manquent d'argent.**	They lack money.
manquer de	+ infinitive to be near, almost; (in negative) not to fail to	**Ils ont manqué de tomber.**	They almost fell.

à coup sûr	certainly	**coup sur coup**	in rapid succession
coup d'état	coup d'état (*overthrow of a government*)	**coup de théâtre**	unexpected turn of events
coup de fusil	shot; exorbitant price (*in a restaurant*)		
coup de grâce	coup de grâce (*finishing blow*)	**du même coup**	at the same time
coup de main	helping hand, (*in military parlance*) sudden attack	**d'un seul coup**	at one blow (swoop)
		tout à coup	all of a sudden
coup de maître	master stroke	**tout d'un coup**	at once, all at once
coup d'œil	glance		

* The thought is, *Mary is lacking to John.*
† *You are lacking to me.*
‡ *I will be lacking to you, son.*

I

LECTURE

Lisez à haute voix.

—Tiens! vous avez ce livre, demande une jeune femme à son amie, en voyant un roman célèbre dans le salon de cette dernière. Est-il bien, ce roman? Voulez-vous me le prêter?

—Ma chère amie, je ne prête jamais mes livres, car quand je les prête on ne me les rend pas; mais si vous voulez lire ce roman, venez le lire chez moi.

Quelques jours après, cette amie méfiante a besoin d'un aspirateur pour nettoyer son appartement. Elle va trouver son amie, et lui demande de vouloir bien lui prêter le sien.

—Ma chère, lui répond-elle, je l'ai déjà prêté une fois à quelqu'un qui a oublié de me le rapporter et j'ai eu toutes les peines du monde à rentrer en possession de mon aspirateur. Aussi, je ne le prête plus jamais. Mais pour vous montrer toute ma bonne volonté de vous obliger, si vous voulez vous en servir, venez vous en servir chez moi.

Répondez aux questions suivantes: 1. Que voit la jeune femme dans le salon de son amie? 2. Que demande-t-elle à son amie? 3. Qu'est-ce qu'elle ne prête jamais? 4. Où lui faudra-t-il lire le roman? 5. De quoi cette amie méfiante a-t-elle besoin plus tard? 6. Qui va-t-elle trouver? 7. Pourquoi ne prête-t-elle plus son aspirateur? 8. De quelle manière veut-elle bien montrer sa bonne volonté? 9. Cette histoire fait-elle penser au proverbe «Rira bien qui rira le dernier»? Pourquoi? 10. Faites un résumé de cette lecture.

II

ORAL AND WRITTEN EXERCISES

A. *Translate.* 1. Que le diable m'emporte, s'écria le conspirateur, j'ai manqué le premier ministre! 2. Je crains que ce coup de fusil ne nous ait trahis, et que notre coup d'état ne soit manqué. 3. La prochaine fois je veux que tu me donnes un coup de main. 4. Je ne crois pas que tu manques de courage. 5. Aussi faut-il que tu sois là pour donner le coup de grâce. 6. Que tu vives ou que tu meures, tu ne manqueras pas à la patrie. 7. Il se peut qu'un jour les passants jettent un coup d'œil reconnaissant à ton tombeau.

B. *Note the following verbs whose present indicative and subjunctive are identical in the third person plural. Reread the sentences changing* **ils** *to* **il.** 1. Ils comprennent parce qu'il faut qu'ils comprennent. 2. Ils choisissent ce qu'on veut qu'ils choisissent. 3. Ils travaillent quand il faut qu'ils travaillent. 4. Quoiqu'ils rient ils ne rient pas assez. 5. Ils la vendent mais je crains qu'ils ne la vendent trop bon marché. 6. Ils partent mais je préfère qu'ils restent. 7. Ils restent mais je préfère qu'ils partent. 8. Ils dorment parce qu'il faut qu'ils dorment. 9. Je ne veux pas qu'ils boivent le vin qu'ils boivent.
Repeat, changing **ils** *to* **vous.**

C. *Note the following verbs whose present indicative and subjunctive are not identical in the third person plural. Reread the sentences changing* **il** *to* **ils.** 1. Il est là parce qu'il faut qu'il soit là. 2. Il a du courage parce qu'il faut qu'il en ait. 3. Il fait ce que je veux qu'il fasse. 4. Il y va parce qu'on veut qu'il y aille. 5. Je veux qu'il sache plus qu'il ne sait. 6. Je doute qu'il vaille autant qu'on dit qu'il vaut. 7. Il le veut mais je regrette qu'il le veuille.
Repeat, changing **il** *to* **vous.**

D. *Translate the clauses in the second column and precede each by each of the clauses in the first column.*

(*a*) **Je sais que**	1. You are right.
(*b*) **Je doute que**	2. You are happy.
(*c*) **On dit que**	3. You are doing your duty.
(*d*) **Je regrette que**	4. You are succeeding.
	5. You have forgotten me.
	6. You have gone there.
	7. You have hurt yourself.
	8. You are following me.

(a) *Repeat the above exercise, substituting* **he** *for* **you.**

E. *Translate the italicized English words.* 1. Il veut le voir, *and he wants you to see him.* 2. Nous voulons le faire, *and we want him to do it.* 3. Ils vont assister à sa conférence, *and we want you to attend it also.* 4. Elle est contente d'être ici, *and she is glad you are here.* 5. Il vend son auto, *and he wants me to sell mine.* 6. *I want to do without it,* et je veux qu'il s'en passe aussi. 7. Nous désirons lui rendre visite, *and we want her to call on us.* 8. Ils aiment chanter, *and they like you to sing also.*

IRREGULAR VERBS

F. *Consult:* **pleuvoir** (§153), **suivre** (§154), and **Unit** 14. (a) *Translate:* 1. Je suis mon maître. 2. Suivez-moi. 3. Je vous suivrai. 4. Il faut qu'il me suive. 5. Il m'a suivi. 6. Il me suivit. 7. Il me suivait. 8. Il faut qu'il pleuve. 9. Il avait plu. 10. Il pleuvait.

(b) *Write:* 1. He follows him. 2. They follow me. 3. I would follow her. 4. I must follow them. 5. I have followed her. 6. He followed him (*P. Def.*). 7. You were following her. 8. I want it to rain. 9. It rained (*P. Def.*). 10. It would rain.

III

OPTIONAL

G. *Translate. Consult:* **Exercise A** (Chap. 14), **Lecture, Conversation** 14. 1. I am afraid this shot has betrayed us. 2. Therefore you must not lack courage. 3. I shall not fail to cast a grateful glance at your tomb. 4. Whether I live or die no one will miss me. 5. They never give them back to me. 6. If she wants to use it she can use it at her friend's house. 7. I want you to choose the one who talks the best. 8. Please tell us what you have just done. 9. If you want me to go there I will go there. 10. If you want me to erase what I have drawn I will erase it. 11. If you want me to be nice I will be nice. 12. If you do not want me to know the truth I shall not know it. 13. He wants to sell it to you. 14. He wants me to sell it to you. 15. He almost **(manquer de)** killed himself. 16. If you want to use it come to use it at my home.

IV

CONVERSATION 14

1. Voulez-vous faire quelque chose pour moi? —Mais avec plaisir. (Tout ce que vous voudrez.) Que voulez-vous que je fasse? —Je veux que vous choisissiez quelqu'un. —Qui voulez-vous que je choisisse? —Choisissez n'importe qui (un élève quelconque, celui que vous voudrez, le meilleur élève de la classe, celui qui parle le mieux, celle qui demeure à la Nouvelle-Orléans, celui qui travaille dans la bibliothèque, celle qui est arrivée en retard).

2. Je choisis M. Durand. —Vous me choisissez? —Oui, je vous choisis. —Que voulez-vous que je fasse? —Je veux que vous vous leviez. —Si vous voulez que je me lève, je me lèverai. —Levez-vous donc. —Avec plaisir. (Durand se lève.) Que voulez-vous que je fasse maintenant? —Je veux que vous me disiez ce que vous venez de faire. —Je viens de me lever. —Voulez-vous faire encore quelque chose pour moi? etc.

3. Je veux que vous alliez au tableau noir (preniez un morceau de craie, écriviez votre nom, l'effaciez, dessiniez quelque chose, effaciez ce que vous avez dessiné, posiez la craie, retourniez à votre place, vous asseyiez). —Allez-y. Prenez-le. Ecrivez-le. Effacez-le. Dessinez-le. Posez-la. Retournez-y. Asseyez-vous.

4. (En faisant chaque action) Avec plaisir. Que voulez-vous que je fasse maintenant? —Je veux que vous me disiez ce que vous venez de faire. —Je viens d'aller au tableau (de prendre un morceau de craie, d'écrire mon nom, de l'effacer, de dessiner quelque chose, de poser la craie, de retourner à ma place, de m'asseoir).

5. Choisissez quelqu'un et dites-lui que vous voulez qu'il lève la main (écrive une phrase, pose une question à quelqu'un, ouvre

la porte, ferme la fenêtre, travaille mieux, étudie beaucoup, ait de la patience, soit gentil, vienne vous voir, dorme bien, sache la vérité, arrive à l'heure, finisse son travail).

6. Je veux que vous leviez la main (écriviez une phrase, posiez . . . , ouvriez . . . , fermiez . . . , travailliez mieux . . . , étudiiez . . . , ayez . . . , soyez . . . , veniez . . . , dormiez . . . , sachiez . . . , arriviez . . . , finissiez . . . .

7. Si vous voulez que je lève la main (écrive . . . , pose . . . , ouvre . . . , ferme . . . , travaille . . . , étudie . . . , aie . . . , sois . . . , vienne . . . , dorme . . . , sache . . . , arrive . . . , finisse . . .) je la lèverai (écrirai . . . , poserai . . . , ouvrirai . . . , fermerai . . . , travaillerai . . . , étudierai . . . , aurai . . . , serai . . . , viendrai . . . , dormirai . . . , saurai . . . , arriverai . . . , finirai . . . .

Sujets de discussion et de conversation:

1. On trouve cette phrase dans les *Pensées* de Montesquieu: «L'étude a été pour moi le souverain remède contre les dégoûts de la vie, n'ayant jamais eu de chagrin qu'une heure de lecture ne m'ait ôté.» Que veut-il dire?

2. De nos jours est-il plus difficile de faire des lectures sérieuses qu'au temps de nos pères?

3. Faut-il des talents particuliers pour écrire un roman?

4. Si l'on ne vous permettait qu'un seul livre, quel livre choisiriez-vous?

5. Est-ce que tout le monde au collège devrait être obligé de suivre «un cours d'Humanités»?

CHAPTER 15

IMPERFECT AND PLUPERFECT SUBJUNCTIVE
OTHER USES OF THE SUBJUNCTIVE

GRAMMAR

107. The Imperfect and Pluperfect Subjunctive. For the conjugation of these tenses cf. §7, §18, §27 and §37. Rules that govern the use of the present subjunctive and perfect subjunctive in the subordinate clause, whenever certain ideas are expressed in the principal clause, apply equally to the imperfect subjunctive and the pluperfect subjunctive. The use of these tenses, which is rare in modern French except in very careful or academic literary style and even then usually only in the third person singular and plural, is contingent upon the tense of the principal clause. (Cf. §108.)

(1) As observed above, the imperfect and pluperfect subjunctive are used sparingly in modern French. In conversation and familiar writing, the present subjunctive replaces the imperfect, and the perfect subjunctive replaces the pluperfect.

Literary Style	*Conversation and Familiar Writing*
Elle craignit qu'il la vendît.	**Elle a craint qu'il la vende.**

She was afraid he would sell it.

J'avais peur qu'il ne fût arrivé.	**J'avais peur qu'il ne soit arrivé.**

I was afraid he had arrived.

(2) Use of the subjunctive may often be avoided entirely by using the infinitive or some other construction.

The Subjunctive Used	*The Subjunctive Avoided*
Il est possible qu'elle vienne.	**Peut-être qu'elle viendra.**
Ecrivez-lui qu'il vienne.	**Ecrivez-lui de venir.**
Il nie que Jean soit ici.	**Il affirme que Jean n'est pas ici.**
J'étais heureux qu'il fût arrivé.	**J'étais heureux de son arrivée.**
Bien qu'elle fût malade, elle voulut sortir.	**Tout en étant malade, elle a voulu sortir.**
Il sortit sans qu'elle le sût.	**Il est sorti à son insu (sans le lui dire).**

108. Tense Sequence : Translation of Imperfect and Pluperfect Subjunctive. If the verb of the principal clause is in any past tense, the imperfect or pluperfect subjunctive will be used in the subordinate clause. The choice between the imperfect and the pluperfect subjunctive is determined according to the principles set out below.

If the action of the subordinate verb takes place at the same time as, or subsequent to, that of the main verb, the imperfect subjunctive is used.

If the action of the subordinate verb takes place before that of the main verb, the pluperfect subjunctive is used. (Cf. §103.) Observe the sentences below and note the various ways of translating the subjunctive.

Je regrettais / **Je regrettai** / **J'ai regretté** } **qu'il finît.**	I was sorry { that he was finishing. / that he would finish. / that he finished.
J'avais peur qu'il n'arrivât.	I was afraid he would arrive.
Quoiqu'il fût malade il était venu.	Although he was ill he had come.
Il était important qu'il réussît.	{ It was important for him to succeed. / It was important that he succeed. / It was important that he should succeed.
Ils furent contents qu'il fût sorti.	They were glad he had gone out.

109. The Subjunctive in Adjectival Clauses. As the explanations and examples set out below should make clear, the subjunctive is used in certain clauses that are invariably introduced by a relative pronoun, **qui, que, dont, où,** and the like. The relative pronoun must *never* be omitted.

(1) The subjunctive is used in an adjectival clause whenever the clause expresses some qualification which one desires the antecedent of the relative pronoun to possess.

Il me faut un ami à qui je puisse parler franchement.	I need a friend to whom I can speak frankly.
Je cherche une femme qui me comprenne.	I am looking for a woman who understands me.
Ils voulaient une bonne qu'on pût laisser seule à la maison.	They wanted a maid whom one could leave alone in the house.

OBSERVATION

If the antecedent of the relative pronoun is definite, then the indicative mood is used.

J'ai un ami à qui je peux parler franchement.

(2) The subjunctive is used in an adjectival clause whenever the antecedent of the relative is modified by **premier, dernier, seul,** or a superlative, or whenever the existence of the antecedent is either doubted or denied.

Voilà la plus jolie femme que j'aie jamais vue.	There is the prettiest woman I ever saw.
Il n'y a que lui qui puisse le faire.	He is the only one who can do it.
Y a-t-il un pays au monde où l'on soit vraiment libre?	Is there any land in the world where one is really free?

OBSERVATION

After a superlative that expresses certainty in the mind of the speaker, the indicative is used.

C'est le seul livre que j'ai lu cette semaine.	It is the only book I read this week.

110. The Subjunctive after Conjunctions. The subjunctive is used in adverbial clauses after conjunctions, particularly after those that express purpose, condition, concession, or negative value.

(1) The conjunctions below require the subjunctive. They should be thoroughly memorized.

afin que	in order that	**bien que**	although
pour que	in order that	**quoique**	although
avant que (ne)	before	**à moins que (ne)**	unless
jusqu'à ce que	until	**de crainte que (ne)**	for fear that
en attendant que	until	**de peur que (ne)**	for fear that
pourvu que	provided	**malgré que**	in spite of the fact that
au cas que	provided	**sans que**	without
supposé que	assuming, supposing that		

OBSERVATION

Frequently **attendre que** is used instead of **attendre jusqu'à ce que.**

J'attendais (jusqu'à ce) qu'il arrivât.	I was waiting until he should arrive.

(2) Whenever the subject of the verbs in the principal and the subordinate clauses is the same, the construction is *preposition + infinitive.*

Corrigez-vous avant de corriger les autres.	Correct yourself before correcting others.
BUT	
Corrigez-vous avant qu'il ne soit trop tard.	Reform before it is too late.
Il le fit sans le savoir.	He did it without knowing it.
BUT	
Il le fit sans qu'ils le sussent.	He did it without their knowing it.

OBSERVATION

Similarly, in constructions like those above, the prepositions **afin de, pour, de peur de,** and **à moins de** replace the conjunctions **afin que, pour que, de peur que,** and **à moins que.**

(3) The subjunctive is used after a number of expressions such as *whatever, however,* and such.

Quelque grand qu'il soit, je ne le crains pas.	However large he may be, I do not fear him.
Quelles que soient vos raisons, je ne vous pardonne pas.	Whatever may be your reasons, I do not forgive you.
Quoi que vous fassiez, vous ne faites rien qui vaille.	Whatever you do, you do nothing worth while.
Qui que vous soyez, et quoi que vous disiez, on ne vous croira pas.	Whoever you are, and whatever you say, you will not be believed.

IDIOMATIC EXPRESSIONS

se passer	to happen	**Qu'est-ce qui se passe?** **Il ne se passe rien.**
se passer de	to do without	**Je me passe de café.** **Je m'en suis toujours passé.**
A quoi bon?	What's the use?	**A quoi bon travailler?**
à bas!	down with	
au-dessous de	below	
au-dessus de	above	

I

LECTURE

Lisez à haute voix.

SONNET

Mon âme a son secret, ma vie a son mystère:
Un amour éternel en un moment conçu.
Le mal est sans espoir, aussi j'ai dû le taire,
Et celle qui l'a fait n'en a jamais rien su.

Hélas! j'aurai passé près d'elle inaperçu,
Toujours à ses côtés, et pourtant solitaire,
Et j'aurai jusqu'au bout fait mon temps sur la terre,
N'osant rien demander et n'ayant rien reçu.

Pour elle, quoique Dieu l'ait faite douce et tendre,
Elle ira son chemin, distraite, et sans entendre
Ce murmure d'amour élevé sur ses pas;

A l'austère devoir pieusement fidèle,
Elle dira, lisant ces vers tout remplis d'elle:
"Quelle est donc cette femme?" et ne comprendra pas.

FÉLIX ARVERS (1806–1850)

Répondez aux questions suivantes:

1. Quel est le secret du poète? 2. S'agit-il d'un amour passager? 3. Combien de temps lui a-t-il fallu pour tomber amoureux de celle qu'il aime. 4. Pourquoi a-t-il dû taire son amour? 5. Est-ce que la personne en question connaît le poète? 6. Sait-elle qu'il l'aime? 7. Qu'est-ce qu'il osera demander? 8. Qu'est-ce qu'il aura reçu? 9. Quant à elle, comment Dieu l'a-t-il faite? 10. Comment ira-t-elle son chemin? 11. Qu'est-ce qu'elle n'entendra pas? 12. A quoi sera-t-elle toujours fidèle? 13. S'il lui arrivait de lire ce sonnet, que dirait-elle? 14. Croyez-vous qu'elle eût pu lire le poème sans comprendre de qui il s'agissait? 15. Combien de vers y a-t-il dans un sonnet? 16. Combien de syllabes y a-t-il dans chaque vers du poème? 17. Priez votre professeur de vous expliquer ce que c'est qu'un *alexandrin.*

II

ORAL AND WRITTEN EXERCISES

A. *Translate.* 1. Celui qui croit pouvoir trouver en soi-même de quoi se passer de tout le monde se trompe fort; mais celui qui croit qu'on ne peut se passer de lui se trompe encore davantage. (La Rochefoucauld) 2. Quelque rare que soit le véritable amour, il l'est encore moins que la véritable amitié. (La Rochefoucauld) 3. Je suis un bon citoyen, mais dans quelque pays que je fusse né je l'aurais été tout de même. (Montesquieu) 4. Si je savais quelque chose qui me fût utile et qui fût préjudiciable à ma famille, je le rejetterais de mon esprit. Si je savais quelque chose qui fût utile à ma famille, et qui ne le fût pas à ma patrie, je chercherais à l'oublier. Si je savais quelque chose utile à ma patrie et qui fût préjudiciable à l'Europe et au genre humain, je le regarderais comme un crime. (Montesquieu) 5. Quelque bien qu'on dise de nous, on ne nous apprend rien de nouveau. (La Rochefoucauld)

B. *Replace the italicized infinitive by the correct form of the subjunctive.* 1. Il craint que son père n'*avoir* manqué le train. 2. Bien qu'elle *savoir* la réponse, elle ne voulut pas répondre. 3. J'étais heureux qu'il *descendre* à mon hôtel. 4. Je l'aimerai pourvu qu'il vous *rendre* heureux. 5. Bien qu'il lui *écrire* tous les jours, elle ne lit guère ses lettres. 6. Je cherche un étudiant qui ne *faire* jamais de mauvais tours. 7. Il avait peur qu'elle ne l'*abandonner*. 8. Il fallait qu'ils se *passer de* café. 9. Quoi que vous lui *dire,* vous n'arriverez pas à l'en convaincre. 10. Il n'y a qu'elle qui *pouvoir* dompter ce célibataire farouche. 11. Nous doutions qu'ils *être* arrivés. 12. Ils n'apprendront rien à moins que vous n'y *faire* attention.

Wherever possible, rearrange the above sentences so as to avoid using the imperfect and pluperfect subjunctive or the past definite and past anterior. (Cf. §107, 2.)

C. *Translate the italicized English words.* 1. Il partit *without seeing us.* 2. Elle partit *without his knowing it.* 3. Il a changé de place *so that he can sit beside her.* 4. Je ne fais rien *for fear of disturbing you.* 5. Je ne fais rien *for fear my friends may disturb you.* 6. La cuisinière avait lavé la vaisselle *before going to bed.* 7. Lave-toi *before your mother returns.* 8. Ils feront tout *in order to succeed.* 9. La mère fit tout *in order that her son might win the prize.*

D. *Complete the following sentences by using the italicized verbs in the tenses indicated:* 1. (Imperf. Subj.) Il fallait qu'il le *vendre, ramasser, choisir, pendre.* 2. (Perf. Subj.) Je regrette que vous les *perdre, connaître, éviter, choisir.* 3. (Fut.) Je sais qu'ils *venir, s'en aller, courir, regarder.* 4. (Pres. Subj.) Je doute qu'ils *venir, s'en aller, courir, regarder.* 5. (Pluperf. Subj.) Nous craignions qu'elle ne *sortir, pleurer, l'attendre, finir.* 6. (Pres. Subj.) Elle regrette que je *m'en servir, m'en souvenir, m'en plaindre, m'en passer.* 7. (Perf. Ind.) Il dit qu'ils *s'en servir, s'en souvenir, s'en plaindre.*

E. *Translate.* 1. I know you are right. 2. I knew you were right. 3. I doubt that you are right. 4. I doubt that you were right. 5. He thinks we are happy. 6. He thought we were happy. 7. He is glad we are happy. 8. He is glad we were happy. 9. I tell you that it is true. 10. I told you it was true. 11. I want it to be true. 12. He is certain that you have seen him. 13. He was certain that you had seen him. 14. He is not certain that you have seen him. 15. I hope he will go home. 16. What is the use of staying here?

IRREGULAR VERBS

F. *Consult:* **recevoir** (§155), **croire** (§156), **Unit** 15.

(a) *Translate:* 1. Je reçois. 2. Je recevais. 3. Je recevrais. 4. Il faut que je le reçoive. 5. Nous croyons. 6. Nous croirons. 7. Il m'a déçu. 8. Vous auriez cru. 9. Il m'aperçut. 10. Ils me crurent.

(b) *Write:* 1. He deceives me. 2. He was perceiving it. 3. They would receive us. 4. You must receive me. 5. You used to believe. 6. He would believe it. 7. We have received them. 8. You must believe me. 9. They disappointed me (*P. Def.*). 10. He believed it (*P. Def.*).

III

OPTIONAL

G. *Translate. Consult:* **Exercises A, B** (Chap. 15), **Lecture, Unit** 15, **Conversation** 15. 1. He is mistaken if he believes that he can do without everybody. 2. In whatever country he might have been born he would have been a good citizen. 3. However useful you may be, you are less so than I. 4. I have conceived an eternal love but she will never know it. 5. His trouble is hopeless, so he has had to keep quiet about it. 6. If I dare ask for nothing I shall receive nothing. 7. Although God has made her sweet and tender she will never understand the secret of my soul. 8. I have been getting along pretty well for a week. 9. I had just noticed it. 10. Are you sorry that it is bad weather? 11. I am glad that it rained yesterday. 12. I am afraid people will think I am too serious. 13. I am looking for a husband whom I can trust. 14. I believe that Gaston knows how to drive a car but I doubt that he knows how to buy one. 15. I believe that there are good students in this class but I do not think that there are any geniuses.

IV

CONVERSATION 15

1. Quel temps fait-il? Etes-vous content (Regrettez-vous) qu'il fasse froid, mauvais, etc.? . . . qu'il pleuve (neige)?

2. Quel temps a-t-il fait hier? —Il a fait chaud, etc. Il a neigé (plu). —Regrettez-vous (Etes-vous content) qu'il ait plu (neigé, fait chaud, etc.)?

3. De quoi avez-vous peur? (Qu'est-ce que vous craignez?) —J'ai peur (Je crains) de tomber malade, d'avoir un accident, de mourir trop jeune, de ne pas réussir, d'être pauvre, de perdre mes amis . . . que mes amis ne m'abandonnent, que mes professeurs ne me grondent, que mes parents ne tombent malades,

qu'on ne me comprenne pas, qu'on ne me croie trop frivole (sérieux), que la guerre n'éclate, qu'un serpent (chien enragé) ne me morde.

4. Permettez-vous que je vous fasse un compliment (une petite observation) ? —Mais certainement. —Votre robe (cravate, blouse, chapeau, coiffure, etc.) est très chic (ravissant(e), charmant(e), mignon(ne), très bien). Votre prononciation laisse à désirer (est incorrecte, abominable, affreuse). —Vous êtes trop aimable. J'en suis désolé.

5. Quelle sorte de mari (femme, ami) cherchez-vous? —Je cherche un mari qui soit gentil (aimable, riche, ambitieux), qui ait bon caractère (beaucoup d'argent, de beaux yeux), qui sache me comprendre (piloter un avion, bien danser, bien jouer au bridge, faire son chemin, faire la cuisine), à qui je puisse me fier (raconter tous mes chagrins).

6. Croyez-vous que je suis (sois) votre ami (ennemi) ? —Je crois que vous êtes mon ami. Je ne crois pas que vous soyez mon ennemi.

7. Croyez-vous que je suis (sois) plus vieux (jeune) que vous? —Je crois que vous êtes . . . Je ne crois pas que vous soyez . . . Je doute que vous soyez. . . .

8. Croyez-vous que . . . soit (est) le meilleur élève de la classe? —Je (ne) crois (pas) qu'il l'est (le soit). Je doute qu'il le soit.

9. Croyez-vous que . . . ait (a) toujours raison (tort, soif, faim, sommeil) ? —Je (ne) crois (pas) qu'il a (ait) toujours raison. Je doute qu'il ait toujours tort.

10. Croyez-vous que . . . sait parler anglais (conduire une auto, nager, jouer au tennis, le présent du verbe *être,* mon nom) ? —Je crois qu'il sait. . . . Je suis sûr qu'il sait. . . .

11. Croyez-vous que . . . sache parler chinois (piloter un avion, écrire un sonnet, faire un discours en japonais, tous les verbes de la langue française) ? —Je ne crois pas qu'il sache. . . . Je doute qu'il sache. . . . Je suis sûr qu'il ne sait pas. . . .

12. Croyez-vous être plus (moins, aussi) intelligent (riche, heureux, sérieux) que . . . ? —Je (ne) crois (pas) être plus intelligent que lui (qu'elle).

13. Croyez-vous qu'il y ait (a) des idiots (des hommes de génie, des apaches, des as, des poètes, des existentialistes) dans cette classe. —Je (ne) crois (pas) qu'il y a (ait). . . .

14. Croyez-vous que j'aie fait un voyage dans la lune? . . . que je sois allé au pôle nord? . . . que je me sois levé à quatre heures du matin?

Sujets de discussion et de conversation:

1. Est-ce que tout le monde aime la poésie?
2. Savez-vous par cœur quelques poèmes français?
3. Quelles sont des chansons françaises que tout le monde chante ou connaît?
4. Que symbolise *la Marseillaise* dans la civilisation française et mondiale?
5. Aimeriez-vous faire le tour de la France à bicyclette, à cheval, en auto, en chemin de fer, ou en avion? Expliquez votre préférence.

CHAPTER 16

NUMBERS : FRACTIONS : TIME OF DAY

GRAMMAR

111. Cardinal and Ordinal Numbers. An ordinal number is formed by adding **-ième** to its corresponding cardinal. If the cardinal number ends in **-e,** the **-e** is dropped before adding the ordinal ending. When reading through the list of ordinal numbers below, note carefully the peculiarity of *first, fifth, ninth, twenty-first,* and others.

THE CARDINAL NUMBERS

1 **un, une**	21 **vingt et un**	70 **soixante-dix**
2 **deux**	22 **vingt-deux**	71 **soixante et onze**
3 **trois**	23 **vingt-trois**	76 **soixante-seize**
4 **quatre**	30 **trente**	80 **quatre-vingts**
5 **cinq**	31 **trente et un**	(*From this point to* **100,** *repeat* **quatre-vingt** *and count to* **19.**) (Cf. Obs. 6.)
6 **six**	34 **trente-quatre**	
7 **sept**	35 **trente-cinq**	
8 **huit**	40 **quarante**	81 **quatre-vingt-un**
9 **neuf**	41 **quarante et un**	85 **quatre-vingt-cinq**
10 **dix**	46 **quarante-six**	90 **quatre-vingt-dix**
11 **onze**	50 **cinquante**	91 **quatre-vingt-onze**
12 **douze**	51 **cinquante et un**	100 **cent**
13 **treize**	57 **cinquante-sept**	101 **cent un**
14 **quatorze**	58 **cinquante-huit**	200 **deux cents**
15 **quinze**	60 **soixante**	201 **deux cent un**
16 **seize**	(*From this point to* **80,** *repeat* **soixante** *and count to* **19.**)	1000 **mille**
17 **dix-sept**		1001 **mille un**
18 **dix-huit**		2000 **deux mille**
19 **dix-neuf**	61 **soixante et un**	1,000,000 **un million**
20 **vingt**	69 **soixante-neuf**	1947 **mil neuf cent quarante-sept** *or* (more common) **dix-neuf cent quarante-sept**

The Ordinal Numbers

1st	**premier, -ière**	9th	**neuvième**
2nd	**second(e), deuxième**	10th	**dixième**
3rd	**troisième**	11th	**onzième**
4th	**quatrième**	21st	**vingt et unième**
5th	**cinquième**	71st	**soixante et onzième**
6th	**sixième**	101st	**cent unième**
7th	**septième**	1000th	**millième**
8th	**huitième**	1001st	**mille unième**

OBSERVATIONS

(1) The final consonant of **cinq, six, sept, huit, neuf, dix, dix-sept, dix-huit,** and **dix-neuf** is silent before a word that begins with a consonant or an aspirate **h** if the latter word is to be multiplied by any of the numbers just mentioned. Otherwise the final consonant of the cardinal is pronounced. Neither elision nor liaison occurs before **huit** and **onze.**

(2) The ordinal **second(e)** is used for designating the second of only two items. The word **deuxième** designates the second in a longer series of items.

(3) Cardinal and ordinal numbers precede the noun. Except for **un, premier,** and **second,** all are invariable.

(4) The conjunction **et** is omitted in **quatre-vingt-un** and **quatre-vingt-onze.**

(5) The **-t** of **vingt** is pronounced in **vingt et un, vingt-deux, vingt-trois, vingt-quatre, vingt-cinq, vingt-six, vingt-sept, vingt-huit, vingt-neuf.**

(6) The numbers **quatre-vingt** and **cent** take an **-s** when not followed by another numeral. *E.g.,* **quatre-vingts** but **quatre-vingt-cinq; deux cents** but **deux cent sept.**

(7) Contrary to English usage, **un** is never used with **cent** or **mille.** *E.g.,* **cent oiseaux** **mille ennemis**

(8) The cardinal number **mil** is used exclusively in dates. Dates are commonly expressed by hundreds, however, as in English. *E.g., in 1789* = **en mil sept cent quatre-vingt-neuf** *or* **en dix-sept cent quatre-vingt-neuf.**

(9) The cardinal numbers **million** and **milliard** (1,000,000,000) require **un** and are followed by **de** before a noun. *E.g.*, **un million de soldats,** *a million soldiers.*

(10) The ending **-aine** added to numerals forms the following feminine nouns: **une huitaine,** a week; **une douzaine,** a dozen; **une quinzaine,** a fortnight. When added to any number other than those just given, **-aine** indicates an approximation. *E.g.*, **une quarantaine,** about forty; **une centaine d'hommes,** about a hundred men.

(11) Both the order of succession of rulers and the numbers of the days of the month are expressed by cardinal numbers. The numerals **premier** and **première** are exceptions to this rule.

François Ier	Francis the First
François II	Francis the Second
Le premier juin *or* **le 1er juin**	June (the) first
Le deux juin *or* **le 2 juin**	June (the) second

112. Fractions. The numerator of a fraction is regularly denoted by a cardinal number, and the denominator by an ordinal, as in English. *E.g.*, **les cinq septièmes,** *five sevenths.* Note, however, the following special forms: **un demi,** *one half*; **un tiers,** *one third*; **les trois quarts,** *three fourths.*

OBSERVATIONS

(1) The word **demi** is invariable when it precedes the noun it modifies; it is joined to the noun by a hyphen. When **demi** follows its noun it is variable.

une demi-livre	a half pound	**une livre et demie**	a pound and a half

(2) Used as a noun, the word *half* is usually expressed by **la moitié** or **une moitié.**

Je vous ai donné la moitié de ce que je vous dois.	I have given you half of what I owe you.

(3) Learn the following sentences by heart. These illustrate methods of doing addition, multiplication, subtraction, and division.

Deux et deux font quatre.	Two and two are four.
Deux fois quatre font huit.	Two times four are eight.
Deux moins deux égale zéro.	Two minus two equals zero.
Deux divisé par deux égale un.	Two divided by two equals one.
Le quart de deux est un demi.	One fourth of two is one half.
Le tiers de deux est deux tiers.	One third of two is two thirds.

113. The Time of Day. To express the time of day, the French begin with the nearest hour and add the minutes. After the half hour they subtract the minutes from the nearest hour. The following examples illustrate how the time of day is expressed.

Quelle heure est-il?	What time is it?
Il est une heure.	It is one o'clock.
Il est deux heures.	It is two o'clock.
Il est trois heures (et un)* quart.	It is a quarter past three.
Il est quatre heures et demie.	It is four thirty.
Il est cinq heures moins un (*or* le) quart.	It is a quarter to five.
Il est six heures dix (minutes).	It is six ten.
Il est sept heures moins vingt.	It is twenty minutes to seven.
Il est minuit et quart.	It is 12:15 A.M.
Il est midi et demi.	It is 12:30 P.M.
Il est onze heures du matin.	It is 11:00 A.M.
Il est une heure de l'après-midi.	It is one P.M.
à six heures du soir.	at six P.M.
A quelle heure?	At what time?
à sept heures précises	at exactly seven o'clock, *or* at seven sharp
une demi-heure	a half hour
dans trois quarts d'heure	in three quarters of an hour

IDIOMATIC EXPRESSIONS AND VOCABULARY

Quel jour du mois est-ce aujourd'hui?	What day of the month is it today?
C'est aujourd'hui le vingt.	Today is the twentieth.
Ce sera demain le dix.	Tomorrow will be the tenth.
D'aujourd'hui en huit.	A week from today.
Il y a huit jours.	A week ago.

* Both **et** and **un** may be omitted in such expressions as this.

Il y a deux heures.	Two hours ago.
Quel âge avez-vous?	How old are you?
J'ai vingt ans.	I am twenty.

en été	in summer	**au bout de**	at the end of
en automne	in autumn	**de nos jours**	in our time
en hiver	in winter	**d'ordinaire**	ordinarily
au printemps	in spring	**d'habitude**	customarily, usually
à partir de	from . . . on	**jusqu'à**	until
dès	from . . . on	**lors de**	at the time of

MONTHS OF THE YEAR *

janvier	January
février	February
mars	March
avril	April
mai	May
juin	June
juillet	July
août	August
septembre	September
octobre	October
novembre	November
décembre	December

DAYS OF THE WEEK *

lundi	Monday
mardi	Tuesday
mercredi	Wednesday
jeudi	Thursday
vendredi	Friday
samedi	Saturday
dimanche	Sunday

I

LECTURE

Lisez à haute voix.

1. Mme Couzin me traitait comme un fils. 2. Elle avait perdu ses quatre fils pendant la Grande Guerre, et par conséquent elle s'intéressait à moi d'une façon maternelle. 3. Elle ne perdait jamais l'occasion de me faire parler français. 4. En me servant le petit déjeuner, c'était toujours toute une série de questions, de corrections, et d'observations grammaticales. 5. Par exemple: *Elle:* Quel jour du mois est-ce aujourd'hui, monsieur? 6. *Moi:* Je ne sais pas comment il faut répondre à cette question. 7.

* Note that the names of the months and of the days of the week are not capitalized in French. These words are always masculine, as are the names of the four seasons.

Elle: Il faut répondre, c'est aujourd'hui le douze avril. Quand est-ce que vous êtes arrivé à Toulouse? 8. *Moi:* Je suis arrivé il y a deux semaines. 9. *Elle:* Et vous allez rester jusqu'au printemps prochain? 10. *Moi:* Non, madame, il faut que je retourne dans mon pays au bout de six mois. 11. *Elle:* Mais vous devriez rester plus longtemps. A propos (elle indique une photo) qui est cette jeune personne? 12. *Moi:* C'est ma fille. 13. *Elle:* Votre fille? Quel âge avez-vous? 14. *Moi:* J'ai dix-huit ans. 15. *Elle:* Et quel âge a votre fille? 16. *Moi:* Elle a dix-sept ans. 17. *Elle:* Allons! bon! pas possible! A dix-huit ans on n'a pas une fille de dix-sept ans! 18. *Moi:* Chez nous on en a de bonne heure. 19. *Elle:* Evidemment! (Indiquant la photo.) Cette jeune fille est une amie, n'est-ce pas? 20. *Moi:* Certainement, c'est ma meilleure amie. 21. *Elle:* Alors, elle n'est pas votre fille! Votre sœur est la fille de votre père, et elle est sans doute une jeune fille charmante, comme d'ailleurs votre amie!

Répondez aux questions suivantes: 1. Pourquoi Mme Couzin me traitait-elle comme un fils? 2. Qu'est-ce qu'elle me faisait faire? 3. Qu'est-ce qui se passait pendant le petit déjeuner? 4. Combien de temps y a-t-il que je suis à Toulouse? 5. Que voit Mme Couzin d'intéressant dans ma chambre? 6. Quel âge a la jeune fille? 7. Qu'est-ce qui n'est pas possible? 8. Qui est la jeune fille? 9. De qui ma sœur est-elle la fille? 10. Faites un résumé de cette lecture.

II

ORAL AND WRITTEN EXERCISES

A. *Read in French.* 1. Quelle heure est-il? 2. Il est (8:10, 10:30, 11:40, 12 noon, 12:30 P.M., 12:45, 11:45 P.M., 1:00 A.M.). 3. 2 et 3 font 5. 4. 10 et 5 font 15. 5. 3 fois 6 font 18. 6. 10 fois 10 font 100. 7. 10 moins 4 égale 6. 8. 110 divisé par 2 égale 55. 9. ½ de 4 est 2. 10. ¾ de 12 est 9. 11. 1921. 12. 1933.

B. *Pronounce and translate.* 1. J'ai cinq pêches. J'en ai cinq. 2. le onze mai; le huit août 3. soixante et onze; quatre-vingt-un; quatre-vingt-onze 4. à trois heures; à dix heures précises; à sept heures moins dix 5. le cinquième; les deux tiers; les trois neuvièmes; le quart; trente et unième.

C. *Review of idioms. Translate.* 1. S'attendirent-ils à vous voir? 2. Se sera-t-il douté de quelque chose? 3. Vous allez nous manquer, mon ami. 4. A quoi bon se donner tant de peine? 5. Vous aurez beau protester, mon vieux; vous serez son gendre! 6. Qu'est-ce qui se passait? 7. Nous devons nous passer des articles de luxe. 8. Que vous avez l'air content!

D. *Review of verbs. If not given, supply the appropriate pronouns and put the infinitives in the tense and number indicated.* 1. (*1st Sing., Perf. Indic.*) battre, étendre, raconter, rencontrer, bâtir, descendre, monter. 2. (*3rd Sing., Past Def.*) répandre, rajeunir, écraser, être, avoir, gronder, emporter. 3. (*Pres. Subj.*) Il faut que vous (se dépêcher, l'ôter, répondre, obéir, réussir, s'en occuper). 4. (*3rd Plur. Fut.*) vendre, venir, oser, rougir, rendre, espérer, mener. 5. (*Perf. Subj.*) Je suis enchanté qu'elle (rester, s'en servir, parler, grandir, attendre).

E. *Translate.* 1. What time is it? 2. It is eight o'clock.* 3. It is nine ten A.M. 4. I will meet you at noon sharp. 5. They arrived at six-thirty. 6. They will be here in a half hour. 7. They shot him at a quarter past midnight. 8. How old is he? 9. He will be eight a week from today. 10. What day of the week is it today?

IRREGULAR VERBS

F. *Consult:* **ouvrir** (§157), **plaire** (§158), **Unit** 16.

(a) *Translate:* 1. Je souffre. 2. J'ai découvert. 3. Je lui plai-

* In France the official time of railroads and a few other public services is reckoned on a twenty-four hour basis. *One o'clock* A.M. is **une heure;** *noon* is **douze heures;** *one o'clock* P.M. is **treize heures;** *eight* P.M. is **vingt heures;** *midnight* is **vingt-quatre heures.**

sais. 4. Taisez-vous. 5. Il faut que je me taise. 6. Elle s'est tue. 7. Ça me plairait. 8. Il offrait. 9. Il offrirait. 10. Il souffrit.

(b) *Write:* 1. He opens it. 2. He has suffered. 3. You used to please me. 4. Let's be quiet. 5. They must be silent. 6. I stopped talking. 7. That will please her. 8. You were suffering. 9. We shall discover it. 10. They opened it (*P. Def.*).

III

OPTIONAL

G. *Translate. Consult:* **Idiomatic Expressions** (Chap. 16), and **Chapters** 6–12, **Lecture, Conversation** 16.

(a) 1. Today is Monday. 2. I prefer the second of the two novels. 3. The second soldier is not in step. 4. She gets up late in the morning; he gets up at six. 5. No! No! A thousand times no! You cannot buy my caresses. 6. She ate half of the apple and gave me a third of it. 7. Today is the twenty-first of March. 8. From the first of June on it is extremely hot in this country. 9. At the end of three months, one has had enough vacation. 10. Then one can work well until the next spring. 11. In our time one has to work the whole year. 12. A few years ago it was thought that, thanks to modern science, people were going to have much more leisure.

(b) *Review of idioms.* 1. It is a question of finishing this lesson. 2. You ought to send for the doctor. 3. Why doesn't she ever glance at you? 4. He cannot get along with anybody. 5. The students always listened attentively to that professor. 6. I bumped into a landmark in the dark. 7. The pilot had a narrow escape, but he didn't boast about his luck. 8. I wonder how he is going to get out of it. 9. I was expecting to find you at home. 10. Do you know what is going to happen to your friend?

IV

CONVERSATION 16

1. Quelle est la date? Quel jour (de la semaine) sommes-nous (est-ce) (est-on)? —Aujourd'hui c'est lundi, le premier (deux, etc.) septembre, etc., mil neuf cent cinquante-sept (soixante et un). —Quelle sera (était) la date demain (hier)?

2. Quelle heure est-il (à votre montre)? —Il est une heure (deux heures) dix (vingt-cinq, et quart, moins le quart, et demie, moins cinq, etc.) (à ma montre). Elle avance (retarde) de trois minutes. Attendez que je la remonte et que je la mette à l'heure.

3. A quelle heure est-ce que (Quelle heure était-il quand) vous avez commencé à étudier hier soir (fini d'étudier, quitté la maison, pris votre petit déjeuner)? . . . vous vous êtes couché (levé, rasé, mis à travailler)? . . . vous êtes parti pour l'école, arrivé à la classe, sorti hier soir, rentré)? —Il était huit heures du soir (du matin) quand j'ai commencé . . . je me suis couché . . . je suis parti . . . (à huit heures du soir, etc.)

4. En quelle année êtes-vous né? Savez-vous en quelle année est né votre père (votre grand-père, votre professeur, Napoléon (1769)). —Je suis né en (l'an) mil neuf cent. . . . Napoléon est né en 1769.

5. Combien de jours faut-il pour faire une semaine? Combien de semaines y a-t-il dans un mois? —Sept jours font une semaine. Il y a quatre semaines et deux ou trois jours dans un mois. Il y a soixante minutes dans une heure.

6. Quels sont les mois du printemps, de l'été, de l'automne, de l'hiver?

7. Quel temps fait-il au printemps? en été? en automne? en hiver? En quelle saison fait-il chaud? froid? pleut-il? En quel mois fait-il du vent? Neige-t-il au mois de juin?

8. Quel est le premier (dernier) jour de la semaine (mois de l'année) ?

9. Combien font dix et cinq? quinze et vingt? trente et quarante? cinquante et vingt-cinq? seize moins dix? quatorze moins sept? cent moins vingt? quatre-vingts moins cinq? vingt moins cinq? deux fois dix? trois fois vingt-cinq? huit fois dix? cent divisé par quatre? trente divisé par deux? cent cinquante divisé par soixante-quinze? —Dix et cinq font (égale) quinze, etc.

10. Combien de temps faut-il pour aller d'ici chez vous à pied (en auto, à bicyclette, en chemin de fer, en avion, en bateau)? —Il faut dix minutes pour y aller en auto, etc.

11. Combien de temps vous a-t-il fallu pour venir à l'école ce matin? Comment êtes-vous venu? —Je suis venu à pied et il m'a fallu une demi-heure pour venir.

Sujets de discussion et de conversation:

1. Est-ce que tout le monde devrait étudier une langue étrangère?

2. Pourrait-on dire que les Américains ne s'intéressent pas beaucoup aux langues étrangères?

3. Devrait-on commencer l'étude des langues étrangères dans les écoles primaires?

4. L'étude des langues étrangères contribue-t-elle à la connaissance de l'anglais?

5. Peut-on profiter au mieux d'un séjour à l'étranger sans savoir la langue du pays?

CHAPTER 17

INFINITIVES AND PREPOSITIONS

GRAMMAR

114. Infinitive as Complement of a Preceding Verb. Certain verbs are consistently followed by the infinitive without a preposition; some usually take the preposition **à**, others **de**. The lists below include the more important verbs in each of these categories. To some extent they are grouped according to their synonymic or antonymic meanings.

(1) Verbs that require no preposition before the complementary infinitive.

désirer	**voir**	**falloir**
souhaiter	**regarder**	**devoir**
vouloir	**apercevoir**	
	sentir	**savoir**
espérer	**entendre**	**pouvoir**
compter		
penser	**aller**	**faire**
croire	**venir**	**laisser**
	monter	
aimer *	**descendre**	**sembler**
aimer mieux	**envoyer**	**paraître**
préférer		
		oser

Il désire me voir.	He wishes to see me.
Elle sait lire.	She can read.
Je les vois venir.	I see them coming.

* Also occurs with **à**.

(2) Verbs that require the preposition **à**.

commencer *	**s'apprêter**	**obliger** †
se mettre	**se préparer**	**forcer** †
se prendre	**s'accoutumer**	**inviter**
continuer *	**s'habituer**	
		avoir
travailler	**apprendre**	
s'évertuer	**enseigner**	**aider**
chercher		
	réussir	
passer (le temps)	**arriver**	
rester		
tarder		
s'amuser		

Elle commence à comprendre.	She is beginning to understand.
Nous apprenons à parler français.	We are learning to speak French.

(3) Verbs that require the preposition **de**.

essayer	**oublier**	**éviter**
tâcher	**se souvenir**	**manquer**
tenter		**défendre**
	dire	**craindre**
finir	**demander**	**empêcher**
cesser	**commander**	**refuser**
achever	**ordonner**	
	prier	**regretter**
se dépêcher	**écrire**	**se contenter**
se hâter	**proposer**	**s'indigner**
s'empresser	**permettre**	**se fâcher**
		promettre
		jurer

Nous essayons d'apprendre à écrire.	We are trying to learn to write.
Elle m'a prié d'y aller.	She requested me to go there.

* These verbs are also followed by **de** except in conversation.
† These verbs require **de** when used passively.

(4) In French, the dependent infinitive is often used for translating the English present participle.

Je vous ai entendu chanter.	I heard you singing.
Ils finiront de fumer.	They will finish smoking.
Il continuait d'écrire.	He continued writing, or he was continuing to write.

115. The Perfect Infinitive. The perfect infinitive = **avoir** or **être** + a *past participle*. Rules for the agreement of the past participle are the same as those that apply when any compound tense is used.

avoir vu (e) (s)	to have seen
être sorti (e) (s)	to have gone out
s'être couché (e) (s)	to have gone to bed

OBSERVATION

Note that when a reflexive pronoun is used with the perfect infinitive, it must be in the same person as the subject pronoun.

Après nous être habillés, nous sommes sortis.	After dressing, we went out.

116. Other Prepositions with the Infinitive. Aside from the general treatment of prepositions with the infinitive given in §114, certain special cases must also be borne in mind. These are set out below.

(1) In French, several prepositions may be followed by the infinitive, *viz.*, **à, après, par, pour, sans, de** and expressions ending in **de.** Only **en** and **tout en** require the present participle. (Cf. §123, 3.)

Il est parti sans me voir.	He left without seeing me.

BUT

Il est parti sans que je l'aie vu.	He left without my seeing him.

OBSERVATION

Similarly, note that **pour** and **pour que, afin de** and **afin que, avant de** and **avant que, à moins de** and **à moins que** have the same preposition-conjunction relationship as **sans** and **sans que** in the sentences above.

(2) When used in a verbal construction, the preposition **après** must always be followed by the perfect infinitive.

Après avoir mangé il se coucha.	After eating, he went to bed.
Après s'être couché il s'endormit.	He went to sleep after going to bed.
BUT	
Après qu'il se fut couché je me couchai.	I went to bed after he had gone to bed.

OBSERVATION

Note that **après** + the *perfect infinitive* translates English *after* + the *present participle.* Also observe that **après que** does not take the subjunctive.

(3) The preposition **par** + the *infinitive* is used only after the verbs **commencer** and **finir.**

Il commença par me remercier.	He began by thanking me.
Il finit par se fâcher.	He finally got angry.
	OR
	He ended by getting angry.

OBSERVATION

In all other instances, such expressions as, *by doing something,* are expressed by means of **en** + the *present participle.* (Cf. §123, 3.)

Vous y arriverez en prenant la première rue à gauche.	You will get there by taking the first street to the left.

117. Preposition with Infinitive to Express Purpose. The preposition **pour** or **afin de** (*in order to*) must be used in French after a verb of motion in an expression that includes mention of place. In English, on the contrary, the preposition *to* alone suffices in such instances. These prepositions must also be used if either **assez** or **trop,** or their equivalents, forms a part of the expression.

Il y alla pour acheter un chapeau.	He went there (in order) to buy a hat.
Il est assez bête pour le croire.	He is stupid enough to believe it.
Elle a trop de bon sens pour épouser un homme pareil.	She is too wise to marry such a man.

OBSERVATIONS

(1) The use of **pour** stresses the purpose of an action but does not necessarily signify the completion of it. Thus, **Il est venu pour me voir** indicates his purpose but does not of necessity mean that he saw me. The sentence, **Il est venu me voir,** on the contrary, indicates that he actually did see me.

(2) When translating such sentences as those given above, do not ever translate **pour** by *for*.

118. *de* with Infinitives after Nouns and Adjectives. Most adjectives and nouns that take a complementary infinitive require **de** before the infinitive.

Il est temps de partir.	It is time to leave.
J'ai peur de tomber.	I am afraid of falling.
Avez-vous l'intention de rester?	Do you intend to remain?
Je suis content de vous voir.	I am glad to see you.
Il est facile de lire le français.	It is easy to read French.

OBSERVATION

From the above examples it is apparent that after adjectives and nouns **de** occurs before the complementary infinitive whenever the expression is impersonal, or idiomatic, or when the complementary infinitive has a direct object.

119. *à* with Infinitives after Nouns and Adjectives. Proper use of **à** before a complementary infinitive presents certain difficulties, as shown by the statements and examples set out below.

(1) After nouns and adjectives, the use of **à** before a complementary infinitive is relatively infrequent as compared with the use of **de.** The preposition **à** must be used, however, if the infinitive is passive in meaning, or if it denotes fitness or purpose. Learn the following examples thoroughly.

1. **J'ai quelque chose à faire.**	I have something to do. (*i.e.,* to be done)
2. **Voilà une maison à louer.**	There is a house to rent. (*i.e.,* to be rented)

3. **Il a une fille à marier.**	He has a daughter to be married. / He has a marriageable daughter.
4. **Cette pièce est intéressante à lire.**	This play is interesting to read. (*i.e.*, to be read)
5. **Le français est facile à lire.**	French is easy to read. (*i.e.*, to be read)
6. **C'est facile à faire.**	It (that) is easy to do. (*i.e.*, to be done)

BUT

7. **Il est facile de faire cela.**	It is easy to do that.

OBSERVATION

Note that in the first three examples above, the infinitive tells what is to be done to the noun. In sentences 4 and 5, the adjective expresses the peculiar fitness of the noun in relation to the action indicated by the infinitive. In sentence 6, the phrase **c'est** replaces **il est** to translate English *it* (*that*) *is* because the verb has a passive meaning. Carefully compare sentences 6 and 7.

(2) A few adjectives always require **à** before the infinitive. Among these are **prêt, prompt, premier, dernier,** and **seul.**

Je suis prête à vous suivre.	I am ready to follow you.
Vous êtes le seul à le croire.	You are the only one who believes it.

(3) Note carefully how the preposition **à** is used in each of the sentences set out below.

C'est-à-dire.	That is to say.
Tout est à refaire.	All is to be done again.
Elle chante à ravir.	She sings delightfully.
C'est une histoire à dormir debout.	That is a dull tale.

120. Word Order with the Infinitive. Careful study of the examples below should make clear what part the infinitive may have in altering the normal word order of a sentence.

(1) Whenever an infinitive is made negative, both parts of the negation, except **que** and **personne,** are usually placed together before it. The usual word order is *negation + pronouns + infinitive.*

Je suis content de ne pas y aller.	I am glad not to go there.
Il est difficile de ne pas le voir.	It is difficult not to see him.
Il m'a dit de ne plus y aller.	He told me not to go there any more.

BUT

Elle m'avait promis de ne voir personne.	She had promised me not to see anyone.
Il m'avait commandé de n'en prendre que deux.	He had ordered me to take only two of them.

(2) Both **tout** and **rien** precede the infinitive of which they are the object.

Il ne voulait rien croire.	He was unwilling to believe anything.
Il m'a promis de tout faire.	He promised me to do everything.
Il partit sans rien dire.	He left without saying anything.

(3) Pronouns precede the infinitive of which they are the object, except when the infinitive follows **faire.** In the latter case, all pronoun objects precede **faire.**

Je vous prie de lui dire de me le donner.	I beg you to tell him to give it to me.
Je le lui ai fait donner.	I had it given to him.
Je le lui ai fait faire.	I made him do it.

121. The Infinitive in French and in English. There is a striking difference between the English use and the French use of the infinitive. Some of the more important of these differences are set out below.

(1) In French, the infinitive must be used after verbs of perceiving. In English, the present participle is commonly used in this position. The English word order is *verb of perceiving + noun object + present participle.* The French word order is *verb of perceiving + infinitive + noun object.*

J'ai vu venir de loin un homme vêtu de noir.	I saw a man dressed in black coming from afar.
Il faut écouter parler vos cœurs.	You must listen to your hearts speak (*or* speaking).
Il entendit chanter un oiseau.	He heard a bird singing (*or* sing).

(2) After expressions of thinking and believing, the French infinitive must often be rendered into English by means of a whole clause.

Je crus voir un sourire sur ses lèvres.	I thought I saw a smile on his lips.
Il pensait arriver avant minuit.	He thought he would arrive before midnight.

(3) In French, a relative clause may replace the infinitive.

Il entend chanter un merle.	He hears a blackbird singing.
OR	
Il entend un merle qui chante.	
Elle le voyait courir vers nous.	She saw him running toward us.
OR	
Elle le voyait qui courait vers nous.	

122. How to Translate Certain English Prepositions. Certain English prepositions are variously translated into French, depending upon the particular sense the preposition is to convey. Some of the more common examples of these various translations are given below.

(1) The preposition *with,* which is usually translated by **avec,** is translated (*a*) by **à** when it expresses a distinguishing trait; (*b*) by the definite article when it expresses an accessory circumstance; (*c*) by **de** when it is equivalent to *by, from,* or *on account of.*

(*a*) **Cette femme au sourire de sphinx.**	That woman with the sphinx-like smile.
L'homme à la barbe noire.	The man with the black beard.

(*b*) **Je vous parle les larmes aux yeux.**	I speak to you with tears in my eyes.
(*c*) **La montagne était couverte de neige.**	The mountain was covered with snow.
Il pleura de chagrin.	He wept with chagrin.
Etes-vous content de moi?	Are you satisfied with me?

(2) English *from* is usually translated by **de.** To express the place from which a thing is taken, however, the French use **sur** or **dans.** In an expression that has to do with time, the French use **depuis, dès,** or **à partir de** for *from.*

Il prit le livre sur la table.	He took the book from the table.
Il prit le rasoir dans le tiroir.	He took the razor from (out of) the drawer.
Depuis (dès, à partir de) ce jour.	From that day on.

(3) When the preposition *about* means *concerning,* it is translated by **de,** except after the verbs **penser** and **songer.** With the latter, **à** is used. *E.g.,* **penser à, songer à.** When *about* means *approximately,* it is translated by **environ, près de, à peu près,** or **vers.**

De quoi parlez-vous?	What are you talking about?
A quoi pensez-vous?	What are you thinking about?
Environ (près de, à peu près) dix kilomètres.	About ten kilometers.
Vers dix heures. Vers 1800.	About ten o'clock. About 1800.

(4) Although the prepositions *as* and *like* are usually translated by **comme,** after certain verbs **en** or **de** may also be used. Note that the indefinite article is always omitted.

Il est mort en chrétien.	He died as a Christian.
Je vous parle en ami.	I speak to you as a friend.
Il me sert de secrétaire.	He serves me as a secretary.

IDIOMATIC EXPRESSIONS

à l'étranger	abroad	**au lieu de**	instead of
à moins de	unless	**avant de**	before
à outrance	to the limit	**en plein air**	in the open air
afin de	in order to	**en travers**	across, askew

I

LECTURE

Lisez à haute voix.

1. A moins d'avoir appris à fond une langue avant d'aller à l'étranger, le voyageur s'expose à de graves périls. 2. L'étranger doit lutter à outrance contre les trahisons de ces mots dits «faux amis» tels que **large** (*broad*), **ignorer** (*to be unaware of*), **lecture** (*reading*), etc. 3. En outre, il faut qu'il fasse attention à la prononciation de certains mots tels que **cheveux** et **chevaux, fou** et **feu, faim** et **femme.** 4. Egalement il ne faut pas que l'étranger se fasse des images, mutilées ou mal assimilées, de ces mots qui se ressemblent un peu par la forme extérieure: comme par exemple **matelot** et **matelas.** 5. Encore une fois, c'est madame Couzin qui me parle. 6. *Elle:* Vous rentrez de bonne heure cet après-midi. 7. *Moi:* Oui, madame, je suis fatigué et j'ai envie de faire un petit somme. 8. *Elle:* Quoi! un jeune homme comme vous se fatigue à se promener en plein air par un bel après-midi de printemps! 9. Au lieu de rentrer le pas traînant, le chapeau de travers, vous devriez rentrer la chanson aux lèvres. 10. Qu'est-ce que vous avez vu en ville? 11. *Moi:* J'ai vu des matelas. 12. *Elle:* Oh! vous avez vu des matelas! Et où étaient-ils vos matelas? 13. *Moi:* Ils étaient dans la rue, madame. 14. *Elle:* Des matelas dans la rue? Comme c'est drôle! Et qu'est-ce qu'ils faisaient dans la rue? 15. *Moi:* Ils s'y promenaient. 16. *Elle:* Par exemple! figurez-vous ça! Des matelas avec des pieds! Est-ce qu'ils se promenaient seuls? 17. *Moi:* Non, ils se promenaient avec des amies. 18. *Elle:* De plus en plus extraordinaire! Savez-vous ce que c'est qu'un matelas? 19. *Moi:* Un matelas c'est un homme qui voyage dans un bateau et qui regarde le monde par un hublot. 20. *Elle:* Oh! vous voulez dire un matelot! Comme vous confondez les mots!

Répondez aux questions suivantes: 1. Quand le voyageur s'expose-t-il à de graves périls? 2. Contre quoi doit-il lutter à outrance? 3. Faut-il se méfier des mots qui se ressemblent par la forme extérieure? 4. Pourquoi est-ce que je suis rentré de bonne heure? 5. Comment suis-je rentré? 6. Que faisaient les matelas que j'avais vus en ville? 7. Madame Couzin avait-elle raison de s'étonner? 8. D'après moi qu'est-ce que c'est qu'un matelas? 9. Quelle est la différence entre un matelas et un matelot? 10. Racontez cette histoire en vos propres termes.

II

ORAL AND WRITTEN EXERCISES

A. *When necessary, supply the correct preposition to complete the meaning.* 1. J'ai plusieurs lettres ____ écrire. 2. Elle est assez stupide ____ le faire. 3. Etaient-ils prêts ____ partir? 4. Qui était le dernier ____ vous voir? 5. Il est important ____ le lui rendre. 6. Ils s'amusaient ____ jouer aux quilles. 7. Nous désirons ____ faire nos adieux. 8. Pourquoi êtes-vous venu ____ me voir? 9. J'avais fini ____ le lire. 10. M. Dupin a une auto ____ vendre. 11. Il est difficile ____ acheter des pneus. 12. Demandez-lui ____ se dépêcher.

B. *Complete the sentences by translating the italicized English words.* 1. Je l'entends *singing.* 2. *Before beginning* son discours, il a bu un verre d'eau. 3. Ils avaient cessé *talking.* 4. *After speaking,* il s'assit. 5. *After dressing,* je suis descendu à la salle à manger. 6. Le commis-voyageur commença *by telling* une histoire scabreuse. 7. Il est difficile *not to admire* la bravoure. 8. Elle est sortie *without looking at us.* 9. Elle prit ses pantoufles *from* l'armoire. 10. *From that night on,* elle ne se fiait plus à ses promesses. 11. Il gagnait *about* deux cents dollars par mois. 12. Pourquoi me parlez-vous *as a friend*? 13. Il aime mieux boire *from* la bouteille. 14. Connaissez-vous cet homme *with the* nez fendu? 15. Méfiez-vous de ces hommes *with* yeux de souris!

C. ORAL. *Model:* **Après l'avoir vue je l'ai quittée.** 1. After leaving her I saw Raoul. 2. After talking to him I left him. 3. After leaving him I met Marie. 4. After meeting her I talked to her a moment. 5. After saying good morning to me she left me.

D. ORAL. *Model:* **Après être sorti je suis allé en ville.** 1. After going down town I returned home. 2. After arriving in Paris I stayed there two weeks. 3. After staying there two weeks I left for Italy. 4. After leaving for Italy I fell ill. 5. After falling ill I stopped **(descendre)** at a hotel.

E. ORAL. *Model:* **Après m'être levé je me suis lavé la figure.** 1. After washing my face I shaved. 2. After shaving I brushed my teeth. 3. After brushing my teeth I remembered that it was Saturday. 4. After remembering that it was Saturday I dressed. 5. After dressing I went down town to have a good time.

F. ORAL. *Model:* **J'ai quelque chose à faire.** 1. I have nothing to do. 2. He has a letter to write. 3. They **(on)** gave us a poem to learn. 4. Do you know where there is a house for rent? 5. Lend me a book to read.

G. ORAL. *Model:* **C'est facile à faire.** 1. That is easy to say. 2. That is amusing to see. 3. That man is hard to know. 4. Chinese is hard to read. 5. He will be the last to know it. 6. Your story is hard to believe.

H. ORAL. *Model:* **Il est dangereux de marcher dans la rue.** 1. It is dangerous to play with fire. 2. It is easy to lose one's **(son)** money. 3. It is hard to learn a foreign language. 4. It is time to leave. 5. Is it possible to dance without having learned to dance? 6. It is impossible to know the truth.

IRREGULAR VERBS

I. *Consult:* **acquérir** (§159), **conduire** (§160), **Unit** 17, **Conversation** 17.

(a) *Translate:* 1. Je l'acquiers. 2. Il faut que je l'acquière. 3. Je l'acquérais. 4. Je l'aurai acquis. 5. Il traduit. 6. Il traduisit. 7. Qui conduisait? 8. Qui conduirait? 9. Il faut que vous produisiez. 10. On a construit.

(b) *Write:* 1. He conquers. 2. He must conquer. 3. I would acquire it. 4. He had conquered. 5. I drive the car. 6. He produced (*P. Def.*). 7. We were translating. 8. They would construct. 9. I must translate. 10. I have conducted myself well.

III

OPTIONAL

J. *Translate.* 1. I am hungry enough to eat a horse. 2. I saw a woman with black eyes come into the room. 3. She was disguised as a Chinese woman. 4. I begged her to believe that she had nothing to fear. 5. Do you plan to spend the summer abroad? 6. We will be unable to win unless we do our best. 7. Our soldiers were struggling to the limit in order to defeat the enemy. 8. You ought to act instead of talking. 9. Daniel drank his coffee before going to look for the ladies. 10. After working in the open air during the summer, he had a good appetite. 11. That absent-minded professor always wears his vest askew. 12. I was thinking of that poor gentleman who has five daughters to marry off.

IV

CONVERSATION 17

1. Est-il facile (difficile) de parler français (d'écrire, de lire, de comprendre, de prononcer l'anglais, le chinois, etc.)? —(Moi je crois qu') il est facile de parler français, etc.

2. Est-ce que le français (russe, latin, etc.) est facile à parler? —Le français est difficile à parler mais facile à lire, etc.

3. Qu'est-ce que vous espérez (pensez, comptez, avez l'intention de) faire ce soir (demain, l'été prochain)? —J'espère (pense, compte, ai l'intention de) me faire couper les cheveux (aller en ville, faire un voyage, faire une promenade, faire des visites).

4. Comment passez-vous le temps quand vous n'avez rien à faire? —Je passe le temps à lire (écrire des sonnets, réfléchir, rêver, examiner ma conscience, penser à l'avenir, penser au passé, écouter la radio).

5. Comment allez-vous passer les vacances (de Noël, d'été)? —Je vais passer les vacances à travailler (voyager, m'amuser, ne rien faire, etc.).

6. Vous lavez-vous les mains avant de manger ou après avoir mangé? —Je me lave les mains. . . . Je me les lave. . . .

7. Vous peignez-vous avant de sortir ou après être rentré?

8. Allez-vous au cinéma avant d'étudier ou après avoir étudié?

9. Vous rasez-vous avant de vous coucher ou après vous être levé? — . . . avant de me coucher. . . . après m'être levé.

10. Est-ce que vous vous endormez tout de suite après vous être couché? —Je (ne) m'endors (pas). . . .

11. Etes-vous capable de (Est-il possible de . . . Pouvez-vous . . . Peut-on . . .) voir sans ouvrir les yeux (réussir sans faire un effort, apprendre sans étudier, comprendre sans bien écouter, faire une omelette sans casser des œufs)? —Je ne suis pas capable de, d' . . . Il n'est pas possible de, d' . . . Je ne peux pas . . . On ne peut pas. . . .

12. Etes-vous assez riche (trop pauvre) pour acheter un crayon (un livre, un paquet de cigarettes, une vieille auto, une auto neuve, une petite maison, un palais à Venise, un château en Espagne)? Avez-vous assez (trop peu) d'argent pour acheter un crayon, etc.? Etes-vous assez intelligent (naïf, ambitieux, patient) pour apprendre une langue étrangère (croire

tout ce qu'on vous dit, travailler douze heures par jour, compter toutes les étoiles du ciel) ? Avez-vous assez faim (sommeil) pour manger (dormir) un bonbon, un sandwich, un escargot, un cheval (vingt-quatre heures de suite) ?

13. Demandez à quelqu'un s'il est facile de parler français, si le latin est difficile à lire, ce qu'il espère faire ce soir, comment il passe le temps quand il n'a rien à faire, comment il va passer les vacances, s'il se lave les mains avant de manger, s'il se rase avant de se coucher, ou après s'être levé, s'il s'endort tout de suite après s'être couché, s'il est capable de parler sans ouvrir la bouche, s'il est assez riche pour acheter un château, s'il a assez faim pour manger un filet mignon.

Sujets de discussion et de conversation:

1. Peut-on être trop poli?
2. A-t-on jamais le droit de battre une femme?
3. Pourquoi discute-t-on rarement la politique en société?
4. Pour être heureux en ménage, faut-il que les époux partagent les mêmes opinions politiques et la même foi religieuse?
5. Etes-vous démocrate? républicain? socialiste? communiste? etc. Pourquoi l'êtes-vous?

CHAPTER 18

PRESENT PARTICIPLE : THE PASSIVE VOICE

GRAMMAR

123. The Present Participle. At the same time, a present participle functions as a verb and as an adjective. It is formed by dropping the first person plural present indicative ending **-ons,** and adding **-ant.** Aside from the so-called defective verbs, **avoir, être,** and **savoir** are the only exceptions to this rule, which applies to all regular and irregular verbs.

nous mangeons		**nous avons**	
mangeant	eating	**ayant**	having
nous choisissons		**nous sommes**	
choisissant	choosing	**étant**	being
nous vendons		**nous savons**	
vendant	selling	**sachant**	knowing

(1) When used as an adjective, the present participle agrees with the noun it modifies.

une femme charmante	a charming woman
une machine parlante	a talking machine
un film parlant	a talking film

(2) When the present participle retains its verbal force, it is invariable.

Elle vivait seule, parlant rarement aux voisins.	She lived alone, seldom speaking to the neighbors.
Je l'ai vu lisant une lettre.	I saw him reading a letter.

(3) The prepositions **en** or **tout en,** which are always followed by a present participle, are translated by *while, in, on,* or *by.* The **tout** stresses the simultaneous nature of the action.

En patinant, on apprend à patiner.	By skating, one learns to skate.
Il trouva son ami en rentrant chez lui.	He found his friend upon returning home.
Tout en me le donnant, il eut peur.	While giving it to me, he became afraid.

(4) In French, a subordinate clause is frequently employed in preference to the present participle. (Cf. §121.)

Je l'ai trouvé jouant au tennis.	I found him playing tennis.
OR	
Je l'ai trouvé qui jouait au tennis.	I found him playing tennis.
«L'Homme qui rit» est un roman de Victor Hugo.	"The Laughing Man" is a novel by Victor Hugo.
Le voilà qui chantait et buvait.	There he was, singing and drinking.

124. The Perfect Participle. The perfect participle = the *present participle* of **avoir** or **être** + a *past participle.* The agreement of the past participle is the same as in the compound tenses.

ayant fini	having finished
étant parti	having left
s'étant lavé	having washed
S'étant couchée, elle s'endormit.	Having gone to bed, she fell asleep.
OR	
Après s'être couchée, elle s'endormit.	Having gone to bed, she fell asleep.
L'ayant aperçue, je l'ai saluée.	Having seen her, I bowed.
OR	
Après l'avoir aperçue, je l'ai saluée.	Having seen her, I bowed.
Etant sorti de bonne heure, il est rentré à midi.	Having gone out early, he returned at noon.
OR	
Après être sorti de bonne heure, il est rentré à midi.	Having gone out early, he returned at noon.

OBSERVATION

There is no difference in meaning between the perfect participle and the perfect infinitive with **après.** (Cf. §116, 2.)

125. The Passive Voice. In the passive voice, the subject is represented as being acted upon. As in English, the passive voice is formed by placing the desired tense of **être** before the past participle of a transitive verb. The past participle agrees in gender and number with the subject.

FORMULA: The passive voice = the simple and compound tenses of **être** + *a past participle.*

Present	**je suis vu(e),** etc.	I am (am being) seen.
Imperfect	**j'étais vu(e),** etc.	I was (was being) seen.
Future	**je serai vu(e),** etc.	I shall (will) be seen.
Conditional	**je serais vu(e),** etc.	I should (would) be seen.
Past Def.	**je fus vu(e),** etc.	I was seen.
Pres. Subj.	**que je sois vu(e),** etc.	that I be (am, may be) seen.
Imp. Subj.	**que je fusse vu(e),** etc.	that I was (might be) seen.
Perfect	**j'ai été vu(e),** etc.	I was (have been) seen.
Pluperfect	**j'avais été vu(e),** etc.	I had been seen.
Fut. Perf.	**j'aurai été vu(e),** etc.	I shall (will) have been seen.
Cond. Perf.	**j'aurais été vu(e),** etc.	I should (would) have been seen.
Past Ant.	**j'eus été vu(e),** etc.	I had been seen.
Perf. Subj.	**que j'aie été vu(e),** etc.	that I was (have been) seen
Plup. Subj.	**que j'eusse été vu(e),** etc.	that I had been (might have been) seen

(1) An agent noun is preceded by the preposition **par** when the rôle of the agent is actively felt.

Il fut tué par un boulet.	He was killed by a cannon ball.
Ils ont été attaqués par un brigand.	They were assaulted by a brigand.
Le candidat est félicité par ses professeurs.	The candidate is congratulated by his professors.

(2) An agent noun is preceded by **de** after certain verbs that express emotion, and after such verbs as **couvrir, accompagner, assister,** and others that always govern **de.** If the idea expressed in the sentence implies that the action is habitual or customary, then **de** is used. On the whole, however, this use must be learned by observation.

Il est obéi de ses enfants.	He is obeyed by his children.
Elle est aimée de son père.	She is loved by her father.
La maison est entourée de beaux jardins.	The house is surrounded by beautiful gardens.
Elle est estimée de tous ses amis.	She is esteemed by all her friends.

(3) Imperfect and present tenses that denote a state or condition are false passives. They must not be confused with the real passive. The past participles of certain verbs cannot be translated literally.

Elle était blessée.	She was wounded.
La porte est ouverte.	The door is open.
Je serai levé à six heures.	I shall be up at six.
Je me fâche. Je suis fâché.	I am getting angry. I am angry.
Est-elle assise ou debout?	Is she sitting or standing?

126. Substitutes for the Passive Voice. The passive voice is not so frequently used in French as in English. It may be replaced (1) by using the verb in the active voice with **on** as subject; or (2), by using a reflexive verb.

(1) Depending upon the context of the sentence, the indefinite pronoun **on** is variously translated. *E.g., one, someone, we, they, people, you, I,* and so on. The pronoun **on** always takes a verb in the third person singular.

On parle dans le corridor.	People are talking in the hall.
Sera-t-on jaloux?	Are you perhaps jealous?
On n'étudie pas assez.	You (one, they, etc.) do not study enough.

Observe the following passive and active forms carefully, and note the characteristics of each.

Passive	*Active*
je suis vu	**on me voit**
j'étais vu	**on me voyait**
je serai vu	**on me verra**
je serais vu	**on me verrait**
je fus vu	**on me vit**
j'ai été vu	**on m'a vu**
j'avais été vu	**on m'avait vu**
j'aurai été vu	**on m'aura vu**
j'aurais été vu	**on m'aurait vu**
j'eus été vu	**on m'eut vu**

OBSERVATION

Although a construction with **on** is frequently substituted for the passive voice, nevertheless such constructions are not always translated as passives. This will become clear upon examining the sentences just above. *E.g.,* **On me voit** may mean either *I am seen* or *They (you, etc.) see me.* The sentence **On vole** means *They are flying.*

(*a*) The indefinite pronoun **on** is generally used instead of the passive to translate an English passive sentence in which the agent noun is not mentioned.

Ici on vend des fleurs.	Flowers are sold here.
On les punit.	They are punished.
On n'a pas envoyé de secours.	No aid was sent.
On a bâti cette maison l'année dernière.	This house was built last year.

(*b*) The use of **on** is obligatory when the subject of the passive sentence is acted on indirectly.

On me donne une pomme.	I am given an apple.
On m'a donné une pomme.	I was given an apple.
On lui a demandé de l'argent.	He was asked for some money.

OBSERVATION

The indefinite pronoun **on** may be written **l'on** for the sake of euphony after **si** (*if*), **que** (*that*), **et** (*and*), **où** (*where*), and **ou** (*or*).

(2) The reflexive verb replaces the passive voice if the subject is a thing, and if the action is considered to be habitual or normal.

Les fleurs se vendent en ville.	Flowers are sold downtown.
Les mots se divisent en syllabes.	Words are divided into syllables.
Une maison ne se bâtit pas d'un seul coup.	A home isn't built all at once.

IDIOMATIC EXPRESSIONS

à l'abri de	sheltered from	**en fait de**	with respect to
à portée de	within range of	**là-dedans**	inside, in it
à travers	across, through	**là-dessous**	under it, beneath
en dépit de	in spite of	**là-dessus**	thereupon

I

LECTURE

Lisez à haute voix.

Après la bataille

Mon père, ce héros au sourire si doux,
Suivi d'un seul housard qu'il aimait entre tous
Pour sa grande bravoure et pour sa haute taille,
Parcourait à cheval le soir d'une bataille
Le champ couvert de morts sur qui tombait la nuit.
Il lui sembla dans l'ombre entendre un faible bruit.
C'était un Espagnol de l'armée en déroute,
Qui se traînait sanglant sur le bord de la route,
Râlant, brisé, livide, et mort plus qu'à moitié,
Et qui disait : —A boire, à boire, par pitié!
Mon père, ému, tendit à son housard fidèle
Une gourde de rhum qui pendait à sa selle,
Et dit : —Tiens, donne à boire à ce pauvre blessé!
Tout à coup, au moment où le housard baissé
Se penchait vers lui, l'homme, une espèce de maure,
Saisit un pistolet qu'il étreignait encore,

Et vise au front mon père en criant: —Caramba!
Le coup passa si près que le chapeau tomba,
Et que le cheval fit un écart en arrière.
—Donne-lui tout de même à boire, dit mon père.

VICTOR HUGO (1802–1885)

Répondez aux questions suivantes: 1. Saviez-vous que le père de Victor Hugo était général? 2. Contre qui les Français s'étaient-ils battus? 3. Qui avait-été battu? 4. A peu près quelle heure était-il quand le général et son housard parcouraient le champ de bataille? 5. De quoi le champ était-il couvert? 6. Qu'est-ce qu'ils ont entendu dans l'ombre. 7. Décrivez l'Espagnol blessé. 8. Qu'est-ce qu'il disait? 9. Comment se fait-il que cet Espagnol parlait français? 10. Savez-vous comment on dit *eau* en espagnol? 11. Qu'est-ce que le général a tendu au housard? 12. Que voulait-il qu'il en fît? 13. Qu'est-ce que l'Espagnol a fait au moment où l'on lui offrait à boire? 14. Le coup a-t-il manqué de loin? 15. Lui auriez-vous donné tout de même à boire?

II

ORAL AND WRITTEN EXERCISES

A. *Substitute the passive voice for the active. E.g.,* **Le lion mangea notre pauvre ami. Notre pauvre ami fut mangé par le lion.** 1. Un gros mur entourait la ville. 2. L'ennemi entoura notre armée. 3. Ma mère a grondé son enfant. 4. Cette femme me déteste. 5. On n'oubliera jamais votre dévouement. 6. On n'a pas prouvé sa culpabilité. 7. Qui cueillera cette belle pomme? 8. L'écrivain voulait qu'on recueillît tous ses poèmes. 9. Il ne veut pas qu'on le reconnaisse. 10. Tout le monde avait admiré ce savant. 11. On n'a rien promis. 12. Les obus ont tué beaucoup de nos soldats. 13. Cette femme vous a trompé peut-être. 14. Elle vous trompera de nouveau.

B. *Substitute the active voice for the passive. E.g.,* **Le bandit a été saisi par les gendarmes. Les gendarmes ont saisi le bandit.** 1. L'Amérique fut découverte par Christophe Colomb. 2. Le criminel sera puni. 3. Par qui l'auto est-elle conduite? 4. Je ne suis pas connu de vous. 5. Rien n'a été promis par personne. 6. J'ai été trompé par vous. 7. Le vin avait été bu par quelqu'un. 8. Elle est aimée de tout le monde. 9. Je suis retenu par une affaire pressante. 10. Il veut être écouté. 11. De qui était-elle accompagnée? 12. Son nom n'est connu de personne ici.

C. *Translate the italicized English words.* 1. *Before dressing,* je me suis lavé la figure. 2. *After washing my face,* je me suis rasé. 3. *While dressing,* je pensais au petit déjeuner que j'allais prendre. 4. *Having finished dressing,* je suis descendu à la salle à manger. 5. *By talking,* on éclaircit les idées. 6. Quelle est cette jeune femme *looking at us*? 7. J'ai vu un chien *running toward us.* 8. *While strolling,* ils se regardaient tendrement. 9. Entendez-vous votre mère *calling you*? 10. *On seeing her,* il l'a saluée.

D. *Put the following verbs into the future, conditional, imperfect, and past definite.* 1. Il rencontre. 2. Il raconte. 3. Il vend. 4. Je viens. 5. Nous renvoyons. 6. Nous revoyons. 7. Il pleut. 8. Il pleure. 9. Ils montent. 10. Ils montrent. 11. Elle éteint. 12. Elle étend.

E. *Review of idioms, Lessons 12 to 18. Translate.* 1. Do you doubt what I have just said? 2. I suspected that. 3. I miss you a great deal. 4. We miss you also. 5. I almost saw you at the station. 6. What was happening? 7. What's the use of my doing without a car? 8. They came a week ago and will leave a week from today. 9. What day of the month is it? 10. Today is the tenth of April.

F. *Translate.* 1. Gray is worn in the spring. 2. That idiom isn't used in French. 3. They say that that isn't done in

France. 4. The jewels are shown to them. 5. The jewels were shown to them. 6. We were always scolded. 7. We are being made fun of. 8. French is spoken here. 9. His advice was asked. 10. I was given a bonbon and told to go home. 11. While we were strolling, we met our French teacher. 12. Having no money, I have been unable to continue my trip. 13. I was welcomed by my friend. 14. We were not in cannon range. 15. The house was destroyed by the bombs.

IRREGULAR VERBS

G. *Consult:* **cueillir** (§161), **suffire** (§162), **Unit** 18, **Conversation** 18.

(a) *Translate:* 1. Je cueille. 2. Je cueillerai. 3. Cueillons-en. 4. Ça suffit. 5. Ça suffira. 6. Il faut que vous l'accueilliez. 7. Il faut que ça suffise. 8. Ils cueillirent. 9. Ils cueilleront. 10. C'est suffisant.

(b) *Write:* 1. They gather. 2. We would gather. 3. Gather some. 4. That was enough. 5. That would be enough. 6. I must greet him. 7. He greeted me (*P. Def.*). 8. He will greet me. 9. That has sufficed me. 10. We would not have gathered them.

III

OPTIONAL

H. *Translate. Consult:* **Lecture, Conversation** 18. My father was riding across the field which was covered with dead. 2. He was followed by a single hussar. 3. Night was falling. 4. They seemed to hear a feeble sound. 5. It was a wounded Spaniard who was groaning on the edge of the road. 6. On seeing him my father was moved. 7. He told the hussar to give him a drink. 8. At the moment when he was holding out the flask of rum to the wounded man, the latter lifted the pistol which he was still grasping. 9. He aimed at my father's forehead but the shot missed. 10. My father said to give him a drink anyhow. 11. Is it better to wait or to make people wait for you?

12. Would you rather obey or have people obey you? 13. I was reared in Paris. 14. I would have been annoyed if the present president had not been elected. 15. If I were appointed in your place I would ask for a raise. 16. He speaks French well enough to make himself understood anywhere. 17. If he spoke French properly he would be elected president of the French Club. 18. I am going to propose you as a candidate, but I am afraid you will not be elected.

IV

CONVERSATION 18

1. Aimeriez-vous mieux (Préférez-vous . . . Vaut-il mieux . . .) aimer ou être aimé (tromper ou être trompé, battre ou être battu, tuer ou être tué, attendre ou vous faire attendre, donner ou qu'on vous donne, obéir ou qu'on vous obéisse, faire mal ou qu'on vous fasse mal, prêter ou emprunter, enseigner ou apprendre)? —J'aimerais mieux (Je préfère . . . Il vaut mieux . . .) être aimé, etc.

2. Où avez-vous été élevé? —J'ai été élevé à . . . (en . . . , au . . . , aux . . .).

3. Choisissez quelqu'un. Qui avez-vous choisi? Par qui avez-vous été choisi? —J'ai choisi. . . . J'ai été choisi par. . . .

4. Sauriez-vous me dire par qui l'Amérique (le Canada, la Baie d'Hudson, le Mississipi, le Pacifique) a été découvert(e)?

5. Qui a été élu à la dernière élection présidentielle? Qui sera (va être) élu à la prochaine élection?

6. Auriez-vous été fâché (surpris, étonné, désolé, ravi, enchanté, ennuyé) si le président actuel n'avait pas été élu? —J'aurais été . . . Je n'aurais pas été. . . .

7. Qu'est-ce que vous feriez si vous étiez nommé professeur de français à ma place? —Si j'étais nommé à votre place je donnerais plus de phrases à écrire (j'abolirais les examens, je serais moins indulgent, je ne me fâcherais jamais, je donnerais de bonnes notes à tout le monde, je ferais chanter des chansons

tous les jours, je parlerais souvent de ma jeunesse à Paris, je ne collerais personne, je ne collerais que . . . , je féliciterais les bons élèves, etc.).

8. Je propose M. Leblanc comme candidat à la présidence de cette classe (du Cercle Français). Qu'est-ce que vous ferez (feriez) si vous êtes (étiez) élu? —Si je suis (étais) élu, je ferai (ferais) de mon mieux pour seconder les efforts héroïques de notre (cher, distingué, pauvre, malheureux) professeur.

9. Si vous étiez élu membre de l'Académie Française aboliriez-vous le subjonctif? les accents? les verbes irréguliers? l'élision? la liaison? les verbes conjugués avec *être*? le partitif? —Si j'étais élu . . . j'abolirais. . . .

10. Parlez-vous français un peu mieux que l'année passée? assez couramment? comme un Français? assez bien pour vous faire comprendre? assez bien pour vous en tirer? comme une vache espagnole? comme il faut? aussi bien que le meilleur élève de la classe? mieux (moins bien) que n'importe qui? sans faute? sans accent? —Je (ne) le parle (pas). . . .

Sujets de discussion et de conversation:

1. La science suffit-elle au bonheur des hommes?

2. La science rendra-t-elle la guerre moderne si destructrice que les nations n'oseront plus se faire la guerre?

3. Les hommes sont-ils incapables de vivre en paix les uns avec les autres?

4. Faut-il désespérer des hommes et de l'humanité?

5. A-t-on raison de dire que les uniformes font une grande impression sur les femmes? Pourquoi les soldats portent-ils l'uniforme?

Part Two

IRREGULAR VERBS, IDIOMS, AND EXERCISES

IRREGULAR VERBS, IDIOMS, AND EXERCISES

UNIT 1: ALLER, ENVOYER

127. **Aller*** to go

The asterisk (*) indicates that all verbs so marked are conjugated with **être.**

		Present	*Pres. S.*	*Past Def.*
Fut.	**irai**	**vais**	**aille**	**allai**
Cond.	**irais**	**vas**	**ailles**	**allas**
Imp.	**allais**	**va**	**aille**	**alla**
Imp. S.	**allasse**	**allons**	**allions**	**allâmes**
Pres. P.	**allant**	**allez**	**alliez**	**allâtes**
Past P.	**allé**	**vont**	**aillent**	**allèrent**

The familiar imperative is irregular except when used with **y.**
Va-t-en. Go away. BUT **Vas-y.** Go there.

128. **Envoyer** to send

		Present	*Pres. S.*	*Past Def.*
Fut.	**enverrai**	**envoie**	**envoie**	**envoyai**
Cond.	**enverrais**	**envoies**	**envoies**	**envoyas**
Imp.	**envoyais**	**envoie**	**envoie**	**envoya**
Imp. S.	**envoyasse**	**envoyons**	**envoyions**	**envoyâmes**
Pres. P.	**envoyant**	**envoyez**	**envoyiez**	**envoyâtes**
Past P.	**envoyé**	**envoient**	**envoient**	**envoyèrent**

Like **envoyer: renvoyer** to send away, to dismiss

OBSERVATIONS

(1) For a list of the irregular verbs, and references to the sections in which they appear, cf. *Reference List of Irregular Verbs,* pages 221–223.

(2) Note the following abbreviations:

Fut.	= Future	*Pres. S.*	= Present Subjunctive
Cond.	= Conditional	*Past Def.*	= Past Definite
Imp.	= Imperfect	*Pres. P.*	= Present Participle
Imp. S.	= Imperfect subjunctive	*Past P.*	= Past Participle

IDIOMS

Il s'en va.	He is going away.
Je suis allé à sa (leur) rencontre.	I went to meet him (them).
Comment allez-vous? Ça va.	How are you? All right.
Allez chercher le médecin.	Go get the doctor.
Ce chapeau ne lui va pas.	That hat does not become her.
Il y va de sa vie.	His life is at stake.

EXERCISES ON IRREGULAR VERBS AND IDIOMS

A. *Pronounce and translate.* 1. S'en vont-ils? 2. Comment allez-vous? 3. Je vais très bien, merci. 4. Ça va? Oui, ça va très bien. 5. Il faut que j'aille chercher le médecin. 6. Cette robe ne vous va pas. 7. Vous dites toujours que mes robes ne me vont pas! Allez-vous-en! 8. Il y va de ma vie toutes les fois que je vous en parle. 9. Assez parlé! Allez chercher la vendeuse, s'il vous plaît. 10. Je vous les enverrai. 11. Envoyez chercher vos amis. 12. Ils s'en allèrent sans retourner la tête.

B. *Translate.* 1. I send. 2. Let us send. 3. They will go over there. 4. Are they leaving? 5. They are dismissing him. 6. Will they send it to John? 7. How are you today? 8. Are they going down town? 9. Would you go with me? 10. He went away. 11. Let's go away. 12. Go away. 13. This hat doesn't become me. 14. It becomes you perfectly **(à merveille).** 15. Your life is at stake if it doesn't become me!

C. *Conjugate:* 1. Je n'allais pas chez moi. 2. J'enverrai de mes nouvelles à tout le monde. 3. Si je m'en vais j'irai à Paris.

UNIT 2: DORMIR, TENIR

129. Dormir to sleep

		Present	*Pres. S.*	*Past Def.*
Fut.	**dormirai**	**dors**	**dorme**	**dormis**
Cond.	**dormirais**	**dors**	**dormes**	**dormis**
Imp.	**dormais**	**dort**	**dorme**	**dormit**
Imp. S.	**dormisse**	**dormons**	**dormions**	**dormîmes**
Pres. P.	**dormant**	**dormez**	**dormiez**	**dormîtes**
Past P.	**dormi**	**dorment**	**dorment**	**dormirent**

Like **dormir**: **endormir** to put to sleep; **s'endormir** to fall asleep; **mentir** to lie; **démentir** to contradict; **partir** * **(de)** to leave; **sortir** * **(de)** to go out; **bouillir** to boil; **servir (à, de)** to serve; **consentir (à)** to consent; **pressentir** to have a presentiment of, to foresee; **se repentir (de)** to repent; **sentir** to feel, to smell; and others.

OBSERVATION

The **-ill-** of **bouillir** is treated as a single letter. Hence it drops out where **-m-** drops out in the conjugation of **dormir**.

130. Tenir to hold

		Present	*Pres. S.*	*Past Def.*
Fut.	**tiendrai**	**tiens**	**tienne**	**tins**
Cond.	**tiendrais**	**tiens**	**tiennes**	**tins**
Imp.	**tenais**	**tient**	**tienne**	**tint**
Imp. S.	**tinsse**	**tenons**	**tenions**	**tînmes**
Pres. P.	**tenant**	**tenez**	**teniez**	**tîntes**
Past P.	**tenu**	**tiennent**	**tiennent**	**tinrent**

Like **tenir**: **appartenir** to belong; **contenir** to contain; **maintenir** to maintain; **obtenir** to obtain; **retenir** to retain; **soutenir** to sustain, defend; **venir** * to come; **devenir** * to become (of); **se souvenir (de)** to remember; **prévenir** to anticipate, to warn; **convenir** to agree, to suit; **revenir** * to return; and others.

IDIOMS

Il se servait de son crayon.	He was using his pencil.
Un crayon sert à écrire.	A pencil is used for writing.
Il m'a servi de guide.	He served me as a guide.
Il me tient au courant.	He keeps me informed (posted).
Je tiens à vous dire la vérité.	I insist on telling you the truth.
Je n'y tiens pas du tout.	I don't care at all for that.
Si je viens à le voir je le lui dirai.	If I happen to see him, I will tell him.
Ils en vinrent aux mains.	They resorted to fighting.
Nous convînmes du prix.	We agreed on the price.
Il vient de partir.	He has just left.
Il venait de partir.	He had just left.

EXERCISES ON IRREGULAR VERBS AND IDIOMS

A. *Pronounce and translate.* 1. Qui vous servait de secrétaire? 2. On se sert d'une fourchette pour manger. 3. Elle servait le repas. 4. Vous souvenez-vous de moi? 5. Allez-vous me tenir au courant? 6. Nous venions de le rencontrer. 7. Il tenait à assister à la conférence. 8. Qu'est-ce qu'il est devenu? 9. S'ils viennent à le voir, ils l'avertiront du danger. 10. Ils convinrent du prix et s'en allèrent. 11. Cette musique m'endort. 12. Il ne consentira pas à vous céder son bien. 13. Il soutiendra sa thèse demain. 14. Il se repentira de cette bêtise. 15. Je vous avais prévenu, mon ami!

B. *Translate.* 1. Do you sleep well? 2. My students are falling asleep. 3. I always put them to sleep. 4. We feel nothing. 5. They will leave. (*two ways*) 6. She is serving breakfast. 7. This raincoat belongs to me. 8. Will you keep me informed? 9. They were using my pen. 10. He was serving me as an interpreter. 11. Will they agree on the price? 12. They have just gone out.

C. *Conjugate:* 1. Je viens de finir mes devoirs. 2. Je me sers d'un crayon pour écrire. 3. Je tiendrai ma sœur au courant.

UNIT 3: METTRE, PRENDRE

131. Mettre to put, to put on

		Present	*Pres. S.*	*Past Def.*
Fut.	mettrai	mets	mette	mis
Cond.	mettrais	mets	mettes	mis
Imp.	mettais	met	mette	mit
Imp. S.	misse	mettons	mettions	mîmes
Pres. P.	mettant	mettez	mettiez	mîtes
Past P.	mis	mettent	mettent	mirent

Like **mettre: admettre** to admit; **commettre** to commit; **compromettre** to compromise; **omettre** to omit; **permettre** to permit; **promettre** to promise; **remettre** to put back, to hand to; **soumettre** to submit; **transmettre** to transmit; and others.

132. Prendre to take

Fut.	prendrai	prends	prenne	pris
Cond.	prendrais	prends	prennes	pris
Imp.	prenais	prend	prenne	prit
Imp. S.	prisse	prenons	prenions	prîmes
Pres. P.	prenant	prenez	preniez	prîtes
Past P.	pris	prennent	prennent	prirent

Like **prendre: reprendre** to take back, to resume, to continue; **apprendre** to learn; **comprendre** to understand; **entreprendre** to undertake; **se méprendre** to be mistaken; **surprendre** to surprise; and others.

IDIOMS

Il se met à chanter.	He begins to sing.
Il se mit en route.	He set out.
Il s'était remis de sa peur.	He had recovered from his fear.
Je vous mettrai au courant.	I will inform you.
Il va prendre la parole.	He is going to take the floor.

Il a pris son parti.	He has made up his mind.
Il prit un parti courageux.	He made a courageous decision.
Vous l'avez fait de parti pris.	You did it deliberately.
Prenez garde de tomber.	Be careful not to fall.
Prenez garde à fermer la porte.	Be careful to close the door.
Prenez garde!	Watch out!
Je l'ai pris en grippe.	I took a dislike to him.

EXERCISES ON IRREGULAR VERBS AND IDIOMS

A. *Translate.* 1. Où l'a-t-il mis? 2. Il ne vous promit rien. 3. Nous leur avions permis de partir. 4. Ils ne lui remettaient jamais leurs cahiers. 5. Il faut qu'elle mette son chapeau. 6. Quelle faute a-t-il commise? 7. Il se remit au travail. 8. Il se croit tout permis. 9. Nous nous sommes mis à rire. 10. Elle me promit de me mettre au courant. 11. Il tenait à se mettre en route. 12. Quand va-t-elle se remettre de sa maladie? 13. Le président prit la parole. 14. Ils avaient déjà pris leur parti. 15. Il faut prendre garde de vous faire mal.

B. *Conjugate the following present indicative verb forms in the imperfect, future, conditional, and past definite. E.g.,* **Il va. Il allait. Il ira. Il irait. Il alla.** 1. Il va. 2. Ils prennent. 3. Je prends. 4. Vous mettez. 5. Tu envoies. 6. Nous tenons. 7. Ils commettent. 8. Je viens. 9. Nous dormons. 10. Je sors.

C. *Translate.* 1. Take it. 2. They retake it. 3. They will undertake it. 4. Would you understand them? 5. Put on the hat. 6. Were you putting it on? 7. He handed it to him. 8. Do not compromise me. 9. They will go away. 10. The president was going to take the floor. 11. Will they recover from their illness? 12. Be careful to pronounce all the words. 13. Be careful not to promise too much. 14. Everyone must make up his mind.

D. *Conjugate:* 1. Si je comprenais la situation je prendrais mon parti. 2. Je mets mes gants avant de sortir. 3. Je viens de me souvenir de ma tante.

UNIT 4: NAÎTRE, VIVRE, MOURIR

133. Naître * to be born, to arise

		Present	*Pres. S.*	*Past Def.*
Fut.	**naîtrai**	**nais**	**naisse**	**naquis**
Cond.	**naîtrais**	**nais**	**naisses**	**naquis**
Imp.	**naissais**	**naît**	**naisse**	**naquit**
Imp. S.	**naquisse**	**naissons**	**naissions**	**naquîmes**
Pres. P.	**naissant**	**naissez**	**naissiez**	**naquîtes**
Past P.	**né**	**naissent**	**naissent**	**naquirent**

Like **Naître: renaître** (No Past Participle) to revive

134. Vivre to live

Fut.	**vivrai**	**vis**	**vive**	**vécus**
Cond.	**vivrais**	**vis**	**vives**	**vécus**
Imp.	**vivais**	**vit**	**vive**	**vécut**
Imp. S.	**vécusse**	**vivons**	**vivions**	**vécûmes**
Pres. P.	**vivant**	**vivez**	**viviez**	**vécûtes**
Past P.	**vécu**	**vivent**	**vivent**	**vécurent**

Like **vivre: survivre** to survive; **revivre** to revive

135. Mourir * to die

Fut.	**mourrai**	**meurs**	**meure**	**mourus**
Cond.	**mourrais**	**meurs**	**meures**	**mourus**
Imp.	**mourais**	**meurt**	**meure**	**mourut**
Imp. S.	**mourusse**	**mourons**	**mourions**	**mourûmes**
Pres. P.	**mourant**	**mourez**	**mouriez**	**mourûtes**
Past P.	**mort**	**meurent**	**meurent**	**moururent**

Like **mourir: se mourir** to be dying. Used only in the infinitive, the present and the imperfect.

EXERCISES ON IRREGULAR VERBS AND IDIOMS

A. *Translate.* 1. Je meurs de faim. 2. Il naquit pauvre. 3. On mourait jeune autrefois. 4. Ils vivront longtemps. 5. Elle était morte le lendemain. 6. Le soldat se mourait. 7. Elles vivaient heureuses. 8. En quelle année naquit Rousseau? 9. Ils survécurent à la bataille. 10. Elle est morte hier.

B. *Put the following sentences into (1) the perfect; (2) the pluperfect; (3) the future perfect; (4) the conditional perfect; (5) the perfect subjunctive. Prefix* **je regrette que (qu')** *to the perfect subjunctive.* 1. Il me sert de cuisinier. 2. Ils ne nous tiennent pas au courant. 3. Nous tenons à voir ce film. 4. Vous vous mettez à pleurer. 5. Tu vas à sa rencontre.

C. *Change the following simple tenses to their corresponding compound tenses. E.g.,* **Il nous l'envoie. Il nous l'a envoyée.** 1. Je vous les sers. 2. Je me sers de vos outils. 3. Il se souviendra de vous. 4. Qui prenait la parole? 5. Je suis content que vous en reteniez deux. 6. Tout le monde sortait. 7. Ce coquin vous compromettrait s'il le pouvait. 8. Vous n'entreprenez rien.

D. *Translate.* 1. We are dying. 2. We shall die. 3. He survived. 4. My grandfather is still living. 5. My aunt died last week. 6. I was born at Tarbes. 7. Had they died? 8. They used to keep me informed about everything. 9. Who has just taken the floor? 10. We set out early yesterday morning. 11. Had they recovered from their illness?

E. *Conjugate:* 1. Je suis né en 1929. 2. Si j'avais vécu au temps de Napoléon je serais mort il y a longtemps.

UNIT 5: POUVOIR, VOULOIR

136. Pouvoir to be able

		Present	*Pres. S.*	*Past Def.*
Fut.	**pourrai**	**peux or puis**	**puisse**	**pus**
Cond.	**pourrais**	**peux**	**puisses**	**pus**
Imp.	**pouvais**	**peut**	**puisse**	**put**
Imp. S.	**pusse**	**pouvons**	**puissions**	**pûmes**
Pres. P.	**pouvant**	**pouvez**	**puissiez**	**pûtes**
Past P.	**pu**	**peuvent**	**puissent**	**purent**

In the inverted interrogative, the **puis** form is generally used instead of **peux.**

137. Vouloir to want, to wish

		Present	*Pres. S.*	*Past Def.*
Fut.	**voudrai**	**veux**	**veuille**	**voulus**
Cond.	**voudrais**	**veux**	**veuilles**	**voulus**
Imp.	**voulais**	**veut**	**veuille**	**voulut**
Imp. S.	**voulusse**	**voulons**	**voulions**	**voulûmes**
Pres. P.	**voulant**	**voulez**	**vouliez**	**voulûtes**
Past P.	**voulu**	**veulent**	**veuillent**	**voulurent**

Imperative: The form **veuillez** = please, have the kindness, and similar expressions.

IDIOMS

Cela se peut.	That is possible.
Il se peut qu'il ait tort.	It is possible that he is (may be) wrong.
Je n'en peux plus.	I am exhausted. I'm all in.
Je n'y peux rien.	I can do nothing about it. I can't help it.
Que voulez-vous?	What can you expect?
Que voulez-vous que je fasse?	What do you expect (want) me to do?
Je veux bien vous aider.	I am (quite) willing to help you. OR I consent to help you.
Je l'ai prié de bien vouloir entrer.	I asked him please to come in.
J'en veux à tout le monde.	I have a grudge against everybody. OR I wish everyone harm.
Je lui en veux de l'avoir dit.	I am vexed at him for having said it.
Voulez-vous vous taire?	Will you be quiet?
Veuillez vous taire.	Please be quiet.
Cela ne veut rien dire.	That means nothing.

OBSERVATION

Note the following peculiarities of meaning of **pouvoir** and **vouloir**, depending upon tense or construction.

Je voudrais bien y aller.	I should certainly like to go there.
Il aurait voulu le faire.	He would have liked to do it.
S'il pouvait le faire, je pourrais le faire	If he could do it, I could do it. OR If he were able to do it, I should be able to do it.
Il aurait pu y aller.	He could have gone there. OR He would have been able to go there.

OBSERVATION

As illustrated below, note the differences in meaning between the imperfect and the perfect and past definite.

Imperfect	*Perfect* and *Past Definite*
Il voulait le faire.	**Il a voulu le faire.** **Il voulut le faire.**
He wanted to do it (*i.e.*, He had the desire or the mental attitude, but did not act.)	He insisted upon doing it. OR He tried to do it. (*i.e.*, He had the desire and acted upon it.)
Il ne voulait pas le faire.	**Il n'a pas voulu le faire.** **Il ne voulut pas le faire.**
He did not want to do it. (*i.e.*, He did not have the desire to do it, but we do not know what effect his unwillingness had upon his action.)	He would not do it. OR He refused to do it. (*i.e.*, His unwillingness was translated into action.)
Il pouvait le faire.	**Il a pu le faire.** **Il put le faire.**
He was able to do it. OR He could do it. (*i.e.*, He was capable of action, but he did not necessarily act.)	He succeeded in doing it. OR He managed to do it. (*i.e.*, His ability resulted in action.)

EXERCISES ON IRREGULAR VERBS AND IDIOMS

A. *Pronounce and translate.* 1. Qu'est-ce que vous voulez dire? 2. Veuillez vous asseoir, monsieur. 3. Pourquoi m'en voulez-vous? 4. Il a bien voulu me prêter son parapluie. 5. A qui en voulait-il? 6. Nous n'en pouvons plus. 7. Je voudrais bien la revoir. 8. Il aurait voulu y passer sa vie. 9. Il a voulu ouvrir la porte, mais elle était fermée à clef. 10. Après plusieurs heures de travail, il put trouver la solution. 11. Il se peut que vous ayez reçu une visite. 12. Maître Hauchecorne voulut protester. Toute la table se mit à rire. Il ne put achever son dîner et s'en alla, au milieu des moqueries.

B. *Translate.* 1. What is the matter? Are you exhausted? 2. What do you expect? I have been working since this morning. 3. Do you mean that you have worked all day? 4. Yes, now I should like to drink a lemonade. 5. Will you sit down? * 6. Couldn't you do anything about it? 7. We should like to go to Fond du Lac; we could have gone there last summer. 8. We tried to borrow some money, but we did not succeed in doing it. 9. Why do you have a grudge against me?

C. *Conjugate:* 1. Si je pouvais mourir je mourrais. 2. Si je voulais y aller je le ferais. 3. Si j'avais voulu rester chez moi j'aurais pu y rester.

UNIT 6: DEVOIR

138. Devoir to owe, etc.

		Present	*Pres. S.*	*Past Def.*
Fut.	**devrai**	**dois**	**doive**	**dus**
Cond.	**devrais**	**dois**	**doives**	**dus**
Imp.	**devais**	**doit**	**doive**	**dut**
Imp. S.	**dusse**	**devons**	**devions**	**dûmes**
Pres. P.	**devant**	**devez**	**deviez**	**dûtes**
Past P.	**dû**	**doivent**	**doivent**	**durent**

* Note that English *will*, used in this sense, expresses a polite form of request, and not the future. The French use **vouloir** + an *infinitive* to express this kind of request. *E.g.*, **Voulez-vous fermer la fenêtre?** *Will you close the window?*

Note the following English translations of the various tenses of devoir.

Il me doit dix francs.	He owes me ten francs.
Je dois vous dire la vérité.	I must tell you the truth.
Il doit être malade.	He must be ill. OR He is probably ill.
Le train doit arriver à huit heures.	The train is to arrive at eight o'clock.
Dois-je faire le thé?	Shall I (am I supposed to) make the tea?
Il me devait de l'argent.	He owed me some money.
Il devait dire la vérité.	He must have been telling the truth. OR He was obliged to tell the truth.
Il devait arriver bientôt.	He was to arrive soon.
Il a dû (*or* dut) le faire.	He had to do it. OR He must have done it.
Je devrais y aller.	I ought to (should) go there.
J'aurais dû y aller.	I ought to (should) have gone there.
Il devra partir.	He will have to leave.

OBSERVATION

The difficulty in translating **devoir** is due to the fact that in English the verb *ought* is defective; *i.e.*, it does not have a complete set of tenses. When in doubt, use the tenses of *to be supposed to* or of *to have to.* When **devoir** means *to owe,* it presents no such difficulties.

EXERCISES ON IRREGULAR VERBS AND IDIOMS

A. *Translate.* 1. «Ce pauvre M. Perrichon! il a dû passer une bien mauvaise nuit . . . heureusement ce duel n'aura pas lieu.» 2. Il devait être minuit quand la lune se leva. 3. Jean doit être dans le magasin. 4. Vous auriez dû me rendre ce livre plus tôt. 5. Elle doit se tromper. 6. Ils doivent arriver à huit heures. 7. Je croyais qu'ils devaient arriver à sept heures. 8. Combien vous dois-je? 9. Il devrait me payer tout ce qu'il me doit. 10. Ayant manqué l'autobus, ils durent prendre un taxi.

B. *Put the following sentences into (1) the imperfect, (2) the future, (3) the conditional, (4) the past definite, (5) the present subjunctive, and (6) the imperfect subjunctive. To the present subjunctive, prefix* **il doute que,** *and to the imperfect subjunctive,* **il doutait que.** 1. Il en veut à ses amis. 2. Ils prennent la parole. 3. Elle veut bien nous aider. 4. Il tient à vous voir.

C. *Translate.* 1. I have owed you that money for twenty years. 2. You should have paid me nineteen years ago **(il y a dix-neuf ans).** 3. I must have left my pocketbook at home. 4. You must have a checkbook? 5. Well, I ought to leave you presently if I am to take the seven o'clock train. 6. I was to leave sooner, but I had to visit my aunt. 7. She must suffer a great deal. 8. I ought to have done it. 9. She must have been here. 10. We had to go there (*two ways*).

D. *Conjugate:* 1. Je devrais lui rendre l'argent que je lui dois. 2. J'aurais dû leur rendre l'argent que je leur devais. 3. J'ai dû me lever de bonne heure ce matin. 4. C'est que je dois m'en aller.

UNIT 7: FAIRE

139. Faire to do, to make

		Present	*Pres. S.*	*Past Def.*
Fut.	**ferai**	**fais**	**fasse**	**fis**
Cond.	**ferais**	**fais**	**fasses**	**fis**
Imp.	**faisais**	**fait**	**fasse**	**fit**
Imp. S.	**fisse**	**faisons**	**fassions**	**fîmes**
Pres. P.	**faisant**	**faites**	**fassiez**	**fîtes**
Past P.	**fait**	**font**	**fassent**	**firent**

Like **faire: contrefaire** to imitate; **défaire** to undo, to unbutton; **refaire** to do again; **satisfaire** to satisfy; and others.

IDIOMS

Il fait semblant de dormir.	He pretends to sleep.
Il fait le sourd.	He plays deaf.
Vous lui faites mal.	You are hurting him.
Cela lui fait du bien.	That does him good.
Il leur fait peur.	He frightens them.
Cela me fait plaisir.	That gives me pleasure. OR That pleases me.
Ils se font à cette vie.	They are becoming accustomed (getting used) to this life.
Qu'est-ce que cela vous fait?	What is that to you?
Qu'est-ce que cela fait?	What does that matter?
Il fait froid; chaud; mauvais; beau; du vent; du soleil; glissant; jour; nuit; and so on.	It is cold; warm; bad weather; fair; windy; sunny; slippery; day; night; and so on.

CAUSAL USE OF FAIRE

The causal idea, usually expressed in English by a form of have + the *past participle* or the *infinitive,* is expressed in French by **faire** + an *infinitive.* Thus used, **faire** means *to have, to make, to get* + the meaning of the following infinitive. If the infinitive that follows **faire** has a direct object, then the object of **faire** is indirect. Both objects precede **faire** if they are pronouns.

Il a fait écrire les phrases aux élèves.	He had the students write the sentences.
Il leur a fait chanter une chanson.	He had them sing a song.
Il la leur a fait chanter.	He had them sing it.
Je lui ai fait bâtir une maison.	I had him build a house.
Je me suis fait bâtir une maison.	I had a house built for myself.
Il s'est fait couper les cheveux.	He had his hair cut.
Je me suis fait gronder	I got myself scolded.
Il me l'a fait voir.	He showed it to me.
Je l'ai fait entrer.	I admitted him. OR I showed him in.
Il le lui fit savoir.	He informed him of it.

EXERCISES ON IRREGULAR VERBS AND IDIOMS

A. *Translate.* 1. Qui vous a fait peur? 2. Ne faites pas le mort. 3. Qu'est-ce qui vous fait mal? 4. Il se fit mal au pied en tombant. 5. Vos paroles me font du bien. 6. Ils faisaient semblant de ne pas avoir peur. 7. Nous nous ferions vite à ce travail. 8. Cela ne me fait rien. 9. Vous êtes-vous fait faire une robe? 10. Il a fait boire du lait au chat.

B. *Translate.* 1. Il y alla. 2. Je les ai obtenus. 3. Il n'avait rien omis. 4. Les mettront-ils? 5. Tu t'endormais. 6. Vous l'appreniez. 7. Prenez garde! 8. Vous auriez dû le faire. 9. J'ai dû l'admettre. 10. Tenait-il à y entrer?

C. *Change the above sentences, whenever possible, to their corresponding compound or simple tenses. E.g.,* **Il y alla. Il y fut allé. Je les ai obtenus. Je les obtiens.**

D. *Translate.* 1. It is warm. 2. It will be windy. 3. You have hurt me. 4. Do not pretend to be sick. 5. Are you getting accustomed to his habits? 6. I shall have him do it. 7. He had them tell it. 8. Why did you frighten him? 9. What is that to him? 10. We were having a house built. 11. They informed him of it. 12. Will he have it sung to them?

E. *Conjugate:* 1. Je fais ce que je dois faire. 2. Si j'avais une auto je ferais un voyage. 3. Quand je serai riche je me ferai bâtir une maison.

UNIT 8: VALOIR, FALLOIR

140. Valoir to be worth, to win for

		Present	*Pres. S.*	*Past Def.*
Fut.	**vaudrai**	**vaux**	**vaille**	**valus**
Cond.	**vaudrais**	**vaux**	**vailles**	**valus**
Imp.	**valais**	**vaut**	**vaille**	**valut**
Imp. S.	**valusse**	**valons**	**valions**	**valûmes**
Pres. P.	**valant**	**valez**	**valiez**	**valûtes**
Past P.	**valu**	**valent**	**vaillent**	**valurent**

Like **valoir**: **équivaloir** to be equivalent; **prévaloir** to prevail, *Pres. S.* **prévale.**

141. Falloir to be necessary

Fut.	**faudra**			
Cond.	**faudrait**			
Imp.	**fallait**	**faut**	**faille**	**fallut**
Imp. S.	**fallût**			
Pres. P.				
Past P.	**fallu**			

IDIOMS

Il vaut mieux que vous vous taisiez.	It is better for you to be silent.
Cela ne vaut pas la peine.	That is not worth the trouble.
Ses efforts lui ont valu le succès.	His efforts won him success.
C'est une jeune fille comme il faut.	She is a nice (*or* proper) girl.
Il s'en faut de beaucoup qu'il ait raison.	He is far from being right.
Il est mort ou peu s'en faut.	He is dead, or almost so.
Il leur faut une auto.	They need (must have) a car.
Qu'est-ce qu'il vous faut?	What do you need?
Qu'est-ce qu'il vous faut!	What more do you want!
Il faut deux jours pour y aller.	It takes two days to go there.

The verb **falloir** also has the following meanings:

Il faut le faire.	It is necessary to do it.
Il ne faut pas le faire.	One must not do it.
Il me faut y aller.	I must (have to) go there.
Il faut que j'y aille.	I must (have to) go there.
Il ne faut pas que j'y aille.	I must not go there.
Il me faudra le faire.	I shall have to do it.

OBSERVATIONS

(1) The forms of the verb **falloir** can have no subject except the impersonal pronoun **il**.

(2) The subjunctive is required in the subordinate clause in order to avoid ambiguity, or to place emphasis upon the person who accomplishes the act.

Il faut y aller. It is necessary to go there.
Il faut que vous y alliez. You must go there.

(3) Distinguish carefully between **falloir,** when this verb expresses external compulsion or absolute necessity, and **devoir,** which expresses moral compulsion or an action prearranged or decided in advance.

Il faut que j'y aille. I have to (must) go there.
Je dois y aller. I must (am supposed to) go there.
Il doit chanter ce soir. He must (is to) sing this evening.

(4) Notice that the negative of the verb **falloir** is translated by *must not.* The phrase, *it is not necessary,* is translated by **il n'est pas nécessaire.**

EXERCISES ON IRREGULAR VERBS AND IDIOMS

A. *Translate.* 1. Qu'est-ce qui m'a valu votre sympathie? 2. Puisqu'il pleut à verse, il vaut mieux ne pas sortir. 3. Il ne vaut pas la peine de vous déranger. 4. Il faudra vous lever de bonne heure demain. 5. Ne faites pas attention à ce qui ne vous regarde pas. 6. Tenez-vous comme il faut. 7. Peu s'en est fallu qu'il ne tombât. 8. Je ne suis pas heureux — il s'en faut de beaucoup. 9. Il ne faut jamais battre une femme, même avec une fleur. 10. Combien d'argent vous faudrait-il pour vivre comme il faut?

B. *Translate, and then change to their corresponding simple tenses. E.g.,* **Il l'avait fait. Il le faisait.** 1. Il l'a mis. 2. Elle sera arrivée. 3. Nous l'avions pris. 4. Tu ne l'aurais jamais fait. 5. Elle est restée. 6. Je me suis endormi.

C. *Identify the following verb endings and give an example of each:* -ai, -iez, -aient, -ent, -sse, -^t, -a, -ont, -ais, -s, -ssent, -e, -es, -ez, -ons, -âmes, -âtes, -èrent, -is, -îmes, -it.

D. *Translate.* 1. It is necessary to do it. 2. I must do it (*three ways*). 3. I needed a car. 4. It would take you two days to go there. 5. We shall have to stay here. 6. What do they need? 7. One must eat to live. 8. It would be better to stay. 9. That isn't worth the trouble. 10. I need money. 11. He has fallen in love with you, or almost has.

E. *Conjugate:* 1. Je fais ce qu'il faut que je fasse. 2. J'ai tout ce qu'il me faut pour vivre heureux. 3. Il vaut mieux que je revienne demain.

UNIT 9: SAVOIR, CONNAÎTRE

142. Savoir to know (of facts); to know how

		Present	*Pres. S.*	*Past Def.*
Fut.	**saurai**	**sais**	**sache**	**sus**
Cond.	**saurais**	**sais**	**saches**	**sus**
Imp.	**savais**	**sait**	**sache**	**sut**
Imp. S.	**susse**	**savons**	**sachions**	**sûmes**
Pres. P.	**sachant**	**savez**	**sachiez**	**sûtes**
Past P.	**su**	**savent**	**sachent**	**surent**

OBSERVATION

The imperative forms of **savoir** are **sache, sachons, sachez.**

143. Connaître to know, to be acquainted with (persons or things)

Fut.	**connaîtrai**	**connais**	**connaisse**	**connus**
Cond.	**connaîtrais**	**connais**	**connaisses**	**connus**
Imp.	**connaissais**	**connaît**	**connaisse**	**connut**
Imp. S.	**connusse**	**connaissons**	**connaissions**	**connûmes**
Pres. P.	**connaissant**	**connaissez**	**connaissiez**	**connûtes**
Past P.	**connu**	**connaissent**	**connaissent**	**connurent**

Like **connaître: reconnaître** to recognize; **méconnaître** not to know; **paraître** to appear; **apparaître** to appear; **disparaître** to disappear; **paître** to graze; and others.

OBSERVATIONS

(1) To know a person is always **connaître,** never **savoir.**

(2) Note the following meanings of **savoir.**

Il sait lire.	He knows how to read. / He can read.
Je lui en sais gré.	I am grateful to him for it.
Il ne sait que faire.	He does not know what to do.
Je ne saurais vous le dire.	I cannot tell you.
Il sut enfin la vérité. / **Il a su enfin la vérité.**	He finally learned (discovered, found out) the truth.

IDIOMS

Il se connaît à la musique (en musique).	He is a good judge of music.
Je m'y connais.	I am a good judge of it.

OBSERVATION

The verb **savoir** means *to have the knowledge*; the verb **pouvoir** means *to have the ability, power,* or *permission* to do a thing.

EXERCISES ON IRREGULAR VERBS AND IDIOMS

A. *Translate.* 1. Il faut qu'elle sache la vérité. 2. On ne sut que plus tard la cause de sa mort. 3. Vous a-t-il reconnu? 4. Il se connaissait en chevaux. 5. Vous y connaissez-vous? 6. Ils vous savent gré de vos efforts. 7. Je ne le connais guère. 8. Il ne savait que faire. 9. Le livre a déjà paru. 10. Mme Loisel ne connaissait pas la misère, mais elle la connut.

B. *Fill in the italicized phrases and words with appropriate forms of* **savoir** and **connaître.** 1. *Do you know* mes amis? 2. Il *knew* toujours ses leçons. 3. *Are you acquainted with* cette ville? 4. Je *know* qu'ils ne vous aiment guère. 5. Je ne savais pas qu'il *knew how to swim.* 6. En voilà un qui *knows* ce dont il s'agit. 7. Ceux dont vous êtes en train de parler *do not know* *me.* 8. *I know that you know him.* 9. Je viens de vous dire tout ce que *I know about it.* 10. Vous dites qu'il ne vous reconnaît pas quoiqu'il *knows you* (*present subjunctive*)?

C. *Translate.* 1. I would recognize him anywhere. 2. He appeared happy. 3. She had disappeared. 4. I cannot tell you that. 5. I do not know what to do today. 6. They learned the truth (*two ways*). 7. We didn't know you were ill, but we found it out later. 8. We shall be grateful to you for that. 9. She was a good judge of literature, but her husband was a still better judge of it. 10. He knows how to fight, but he is unable to fight tonight.

D. *Conjugate:* 1. Je sais ce que je veux. 2. Je savais que je devais m'en aller. 3. Si je le connaissais je saurais son nom. 4. Si je l'avais reconnu j'aurais su ce qu'il voulait.

UNIT 10: ECRIRE, DIRE, LIRE

144. Ecrire to write

		Present	*Pres. S.*	*Past Def.*
Fut.	**écrirai**	**écris**	**écrive**	**écrivis**
Cond.	**écrirais**	**écris**	**écrives**	**écrivis**
Imp.	**écrivais**	**écrit**	**écrive**	**écrivit**
Imp. S.	**écrivisse**	**écrivons**	**écrivions**	**écrivîmes**
Pres. P.	**écrivant**	**écrivez**	**écriviez**	**écrivîtes**
Past P.	**écrit**	**écrivent**	**écrivent**	**écrivirent**

Like **écrire: décrire** to describe; **inscrire** to inscribe; **s'inscrire** to enroll; **récrire** to rewrite; and others.

145. Dire to say, to tell

Fut.	**dirai**	**dis**	**dise**	**dis**
Cond.	**dirais**	**dis**	**dises**	**dis**
Imp.	**disais**	**dit**	**dise**	**dit**
Imp. S.	**disse**	**disons**	**disions**	**dîmes**
Pres. P.	**disant**	**dites**	**disiez**	**dîtes**
Past P.	**dit**	**disent**	**disent**	**dirent**

Like **dire: redire** to say again.

Also like **dire,** except in the second person plural, *Pres. Ind.* and *Imperative:* **contredire** to contradict; **interdire** to forbid; **médire de** to slander; **prédire** to predict. These forms are **contredisez, interdisez, médisez,** and **prédisez.**

Also like **dire: maudire** to condemn, to accurse, in the infinitive, *Past P., Fut.,* and *Cond.* Otherwise like **finir.**

146. Lire to read

		Present	*Pres. S.*	*Past Def.*
Fut.	**lirai**	**lis**	**lise**	**lus**
Cond.	**lirais**	**lis**	**lises**	**lus**
Imp.	**lisais**	**lit**	**lise**	**lut**
Imp. S.	**lusse**	**lisons**	**lisions**	**lûmes**
Pres. P.	**lisant**	**lisez**	**lisiez**	**lûtes**
Past P.	**lu**	**lisent**	**lisent**	**lurent**

Like **lire: élire,** to elect; **relire,** to read again; and others.

IDIOMS

A vrai dire . . .	To tell the truth . . .
Pour ainsi dire . . .	So to speak . . .
C'est-à-dire . . .	That is to say . . .
Pour tout dire . . .	In a word . . .

EXERCISES ON IRREGULAR VERBS AND IDIOMS

A. *Pronounce and translate.* 1. Elle décrivit son voyage. 2. Nous l'avions décrite. 3. Il me lisait la lettre qu'il venait d'écrire. 4. Qui avait-on élu? 5. Elle s'était déjà inscrite à l'université de Grenoble. 6. La tolérance, c'est-à-dire, la manifestation suprême de la liberté, est quelque chose de très rare. 7. A vrai dire, je doute de sa sincérité. 8. Il faut lire et relire les bons livres. 9. C'était pour ainsi dire un chevalier sans peur et sans reproche. 10. Il a beau écrire des lettres conciliantes, elle ne les lira pas.

B. *Conjugate the following forms in the imperfect, future, conditional, past definite, and present subjunctive. Introduce the present subjunctive with* **il faut que.** *E.g.,* **Tu envoies. Tu envoyais. Tu enverras. Tu enverrais. Tu envoyas. Il faut que tu envoies.** 1. Je vais. 2. Ils savent. 3. Nous connaissons. 4. Elle écrit. 5. Il prend. 6. Vous mettez. 7. Vous dites. 8. Tu veux. 9. Elles viennent. 10. Je pars.

C. *Translate.* 1. Je suis sorti. 2. Je me suis couché. 3. Nous nous en souviendrons. 4. Ils devaient partir. 5. Je devrais l'ouvrir. 6. Il a dû vous voir. 7. Il me le fit voir. 8. Il a su la vérité.

D. *Translate.* 1. They are reading. 2. To tell the truth, he doesn't say anything. 3. She had written me. 4. He will describe it to you. 5. Do not say that. 6. I told them what you needed. 7. We should (ought to) read it. 8. You must tell it to us. 9. She does not love you, which means that she detests you, so to speak. 10. He will do without coffee, that is to say, henceforth he will drink only two cups a day. 11. Write us what you plan **(penser)** to do.

E. *Conjugate:* 1. Je dis ce qu'on veut que je dise. 2. Je lui ai lu l'histoire que j'avais écrite. 3. Si je lui écrivais elle ne lirait pas ma lettre.

UNIT 11: CRAINDRE, RIRE

147. Craindre to fear

		Present	*Pres. S.*	*Past Def.*
Fut.	**craindrai**	**crains**	**craigne**	**craignis**
Cond.	**craindrais**	**crains**	**craignes**	**craignis**
Imp.	**craignais**	**craint**	**craigne**	**craignit**
Imp. S.	**craignisse**	**craignons**	**craignions**	**craignîmes**
Pres. P.	**craignant**	**craignez**	**craigniez**	**craignîtes**
Past P.	**craint**	**craignent**	**craignent**	**craignirent**

Like **craindre: contraindre** to constrain; **plaindre** to pity; **atteindre** to attain; **dépeindre** to depict; **éteindre** to extinguish; **feindre** to feign; **geindre** to groan; **peindre** to paint; **joindre** to join; **rejoindre** to join, to meet; and others.

148. Rire to laugh

Fut.	**rirai**	**ris**	**rie**	**ris**
Cond.	**rirais**	**ris**	**ries**	**ris**
Imp.	**riais**	**rit**	**rie**	**rit**
Imp. S.	**risse**	**rions**	**riions**	**rîmes**
Pres. P.	**riant**	**riez**	**riiez**	**rîtes**
Past P.	**ri**	**rient**	**rient**	**rirent**

Like **rire: sourire** to smile.

IDIOMS

Il (se) riait de moi.	He was laughing at me.
Ils vous plaignent.	They pity you.
Ils se plaignent de vous.	They are complaining about you.

EXERCISES ON IRREGULAR VERBS AND IDIOMS

A. *Translate.* 1. Personne ne le craint. 2. Il avait bien dépeint cela. 3. Ne vous moquez pas de nous. 4. De quoi vous plaignez-vous? 5. Il ne nous atteindra jamais. 6. Nous rejoindront-ils au restaurant? 7. Rira bien qui rira le dernier. 8. Eteignez la lumière.

B. *Translate these idiomatic sentences.* 1. Tient-il à vous voir? 2. Y allait-il de leur vie? 3. Qui a pris la parole? 4. Pourquoi nous en voulait-elle? 5. Il leur fallait un bon bifteck. 6. Elle avait beau sourire, elle n'était pas heureuse. 7. Je voudrais lui dire un mot. 8. Nous en sauront-ils gré? 9. A quelle heure se mirent-ils en route? 10. Ils venaient de me mettre au courant de cela.

C. *Put the verb forms into the imperfect, the future, the present subjunctive, and the perfect subjunctive. Prefix* **je doute que (qu')** *to the subjunctive forms.* 1. Ils le font. 2. Ils les tiennent. 3. Vous le dites. 4. Nous le connaissons. 5. Elles le lisent.

D. *Translate.* 1. Will he laugh? 2. What do they fear? 3. Girls smile a great deal. 4. Do not pity us. 5. What picture will he paint? 6. You must **(il faut que)** meet us at the café. 7. Do students complain about their teachers? 8. Teachers never complain about their students!

E. *Conjugate:* 1. Je ris parce qu'il faut que je rie. 2. Je crains ce qu'il faut que je craigne. 3. Si je ne le craignais pas je ne me plaindrais pas de lui.

UNIT 12: BOIRE, VOIR

149. Boire to drink

		Present	*Pres. S.*	*Past Def.*
Fut.	**boirai**	**bois**	**boive**	**bus**
Cond.	**boirais**	**bois**	**boives**	**bus**
Imp.	**buvais**	**boit**	**boive**	**but**
Imp. S.	**busse**	**buvons**	**buvions**	**bûmes**
Pres. P.	**buvant**	**buvez**	**buviez**	**bûtes**
Past P.	**bu**	**boivent**	**boivent**	**burent**

OBSERVATION

The verb **boire** is generally used to translate the word *to drink*. When speaking of prepared beverages, the French normally use the verb **prendre.**

150. Voir to see

Fut.	**verrai**	**vois**	**voie**	**vis**
Cond.	**verrais**	**vois**	**voies**	**vis**
Imp.	**voyais**	**voit**	**voie**	**vit**
Imp. S.	**visse**	**voyons**	**voyions**	**vîmes**
Pres. P.	**voyant**	**voyez**	**voyiez**	**vîtes**
Past P.	**vu**	**voient**	**voient**	**virent**

Like **voir: entrevoir** to catch sight of; **revoir** to see again; **pourvoir†** to provide; **dépourvoir†** to strip, to leave destitute; **prévoir‡** to foresee.

† Unlike **voir,** the past definite of these verbs is **pourvus, dépourvus,** and so on.

‡ The future is regular: **prévoirai.**

EXERCISES ON IRREGULAR VERBS AND IDIOMS

A. *Translate.* 1. Il ne buvait jamais de vin. Il prenait une tasse de café au lait tous les matins. 2. Ils ne nous avaient vus que le lendemain. 3. Nous ne l'avions pas vu partir. 4. Il voulait qu'elle le vît. 5. Quand vous nous les enverrez, nous les verrons. 6. Ils ne se sont jamais revus. 7. Elle était dépourvue de tout. 8. Elles ne prévoyaient jamais que les difficultés. 9. J'avais bu trop d'eau. 10. L'armée est bien pourvue de munitions. 11. Il faut qu'elle le voie. 12. Il n'osait plus rien boire.

B. *Review of idiomatic sentences.* 1. Ils ne s'en rendront jamais compte. 2. On vous prend en grippe, mon ami. 3. Tout à l'heure le caissier va vous remettre vos gages. 4. Personne ne lui savait gré de ses services. 5. Pourquoi tenez-vous toujours à me donner tort? 6. Elle aura beau essayer, elle ne pourra pas se faire à votre façon de vivre. 7. C'est un homme qui en veut à tout le monde. 8. Il se remit à nous expliquer son dilemme. 9. Je ne saurais me passer de cigares. 10. Il venait de prendre la parole.

C. *Put the following verb forms into the perfect, the future, the imperfect, the pluperfect, the present subjunctive, and the perfect subjunctive. Prefix* **je suis fâché que** *to the subjunctive forms.* 1. Tu vas. 2. Ils viennent. 3. Nous revenons. 4. Il meurt. 5. Ils s'en vont. 6. Vous sortez. 7. Elles partent.

D. *Translate.* 1. He did not drink it. 2. We shall see you later. 3. He had never foreseen that possibility. 4. He sees only his own interests. 5. I can't do without that. 6. John just drank some poison. 7. Never have a grudge against your teacher. 8. They insisted on leaving. 9. They will see you presently. 10. He had not realized that.

E. *Conjugate:* 1. Je bois tout ce que je vois. 2. Si j'avais soif je le boirais. 3. Si je le buvais je ne verrais plus rien.

UNIT 13: ASSEOIR, COURIR

151. Asseoir [1] to seat

		Present	*Pres. S.*	*Past Def.*
Fut.	**asseyerai**	**assieds**	**asseye**	**assis**
Cond.	**asseyerais**	**assieds**	**asseyes**	**assis**
Imp.	**asseyais**	**assied**	**asseye**	**assit**
Imp. S.	**assisse**	**asseyons**	**asseyions**	**assîmes**
Pres. P.	**asseyant**	**asseyez**	**asseyiez**	**assîtes**
Past P.	**assis**	**asseyent**	**asseyent**	**assirent**

Like **asseoir**: **s'asseoir** to sit down; **rasseoir** to reseat; **se rasseoir** to sit down again; and others.

152. Courir to run

Fut.	**courrai**	**cours**	**coure**	**courus**
Cond.	**courrais**	**cours**	**coures**	**courus**
Imp.	**courais**	**court**	**coure**	**courut**
Imp. S.	**courusse**	**courons**	**coarions**	**courûmes**
Pres. P.	**courant**	**courez**	**couriez**	**courûtes**
Past P.	**couru**	**courent**	**courent**	**coururent**

Like **courir**: **accourir** to run up; **parcourir** to run over, to go through.

EXERCISES ON IRREGULAR VERBS AND IDIOMS

A. *Translate.* 1. Je m'assieds. 2. Je le fais asseoir. 3. Je suis assis. 4. Il s'assit sans bruit. 5. Asseyons-nous. 6. Rasseyez-vous. 7. Ils s'étaient assis. 8. Allaient-elles s'asseoir? 9. Il parcourait le champ. 10. Les badauds accoururent.

B. *Review of idiomatic sentences.* 1. Que ce chapeau lui va bien! 2. Il y allait de son prestige. 3. Il devrait se servir de tout. 4. Qui vous a mis au courant de ce qui se passait? 5. Nous

[1] This verb has other forms: *Fut.* **assiérai** or **assoirai**; *Cond.* **assiérais** or **assoirais**; *Imp.* **assoyais**; *Pres.* **assois**; *Pres. S.* **assoie**; *Pres. P.* **assoyant.**

n'y tiendrons nullement. 6. En viendront-ils aux coups? 7. Gaston se connaît en vins. 8. Ont-ils déjà pris un parti?

C. *Translate.* 1. Sit down, please. 2. Where is she sitting? 3. Had you already sat down? 4. Have they sat down again? 5. You must run fast. 6. They will run through the fields. 7. My prestige was at stake. 8. He can run fast. 9. You will have to run. 10. I was going to run over the exercises. 11. Are you going to run fast? 12. Will John run to school?

D. *Conjugate:* 1. Je m'étais assis près de la fenêtre. 2. Si je peux courir je courrai. 3. Si je pouvais courir je courrais.

UNIT 14: PLEUVOIR, SUIVRE

153. Pleuvoir to rain

		Present	*Pres. S.*	*Past Def.*
Fut.	**pleuvra**			
Cond.	**pleuvrait**			
Imp.	**pleuvait**	**pleut**	**pleuve**	**plut**
Imp. S.	**plût**			
Pres. P.	**pleuvant**			
Past P.	**plu**			

154. Suivre to follow

Fut.	**suivrai**	**suis**	**suive**	**suivis**
Cond.	**suivrais**	**suis**	**suives**	**suivis**
Imp.	**suivais**	**suit**	**suive**	**suivit**
Imp. S.	**suivisse**	**suivons**	**suivions**	**suivîmes**
Pres. P.	**suivant**	**suivez**	**suiviez**	**suivîtes**
Past P.	**suivi**	**suivent**	**suivent**	**suivirent**

Like **suivre: poursuivre** to pursue, to prosecute; **s'ensuivre** to follow, to result (*always impersonal*); *e.g.,* **il s'ensuit (que, qu')** it follows, the result is.

IDIOMS

Il pleut à verse.	It is pouring down rain.

EXERCISES ON IRREGULAR VERBS AND IDIOMS

A. *Translate.* 1. Puisqu'il pleut à verse il vaut mieux ne pas sortir. 2. S'il avait plu je ne serais pas sorti. 3. Pleuvra-t-il demain? 4. Il poursuivit le voleur. 5. Je regrette qu'il pleuve tous les jours. 6. Les hommes les suivirent-ils? 7. Il s'ensuivait que. . . . 8. Il fut content qu'elle l'eût poursuivi. 9. Avait-il plu? 10. Je les suis.

B. *Review of idioms.* 1. Cela se peut. 2. Il n'en pouvait plus. 3. Il veut bien vous aider. 4. Elle en voulait même à ses amies. 5. Voulez-vous fermer la porte? 6. Veuillez vous asseoir. 7. Ne nous faites pas peur. 8. Elle se fera à cette manière de vivre. 9. Attendez. Je vous le ferai voir. 10. Il fera beau demain. 11. Cette nouvelle nous ferait du bien.

C. *Identify person, number, and tense.* 1. aimai 2. fut 3. fût 4. allèrent 5. montrai 6. montrerai 7. s'en alla 8. enverra 9. renverront 10. reverront.

D. *Exercise on* **aller** *and* **s'en aller.** 1. We are going to school. 2. We are going to leave tomorrow. 3. He was going to speak to you about it. 4. They will go away soon. 5. At what hour is he going away? 6. Did they go to see your friends? 7. When will you go to Paris? 8. When are you going to go away? 9. He went away in the direction of the river. 10. They are going to take a dislike to you.

E. *Translate.* 1. Is it raining? 2. Did it rain last night? 3. It was pouring down rain. 4. I am not taking his course. 5. He had followed them. 6. They pursued the goat. 7. It does not follow from that that they will be happy. 8. He would not follow you. 9. Follow us and say nothing. 10. Are you going to inform him?

F. *Conjugate:* 1. Je pense, donc je suis. 2. Je suis un cours de français. 3. Je ne veux pas qu'il pleuve.

UNIT 15: RECEVOIR, CROIRE

155. Recevoir to receive

		Present	*Pres. S.*	*Past Def.*
Fut.	**recevrai**	**reçois**	**reçoive**	**reçus**
Cond.	**recevrais**	**reçois**	**reçoives**	**reçus**
Imp.	**recevais**	**reçoit**	**reçoive**	**reçut**
Imp. S.	**reçusse**	**recevons**	**recevions**	**reçûmes**
Pres. P.	**recevant**	**recevez**	**receviez**	**reçûtes**
Past P.	**reçu**	**reçoivent**	**reçoivent**	**reçurent**

Like **recevoir: apercevoir** to perceive, to notice; **concevoir** to conceive; **décevoir** to deceive, to disappoint; and others.

156. Croire to believe

Fut.	**croirai**	**crois**	**croie**	**crus**
Cond.	**croirais**	**crois**	**croies**	**crus**
Imp.	**croyais**	**croit**	**croie**	**crut**
Imp. S.	**crusse**	**croyons**	**croyions**	**crûmes**
Pres. P.	**croyant**	**croyez**	**croyiez**	**crûtes**
Past P.	**cru**	**croient**	**croient**	**crurent**

IDIOMS

Il ne s'est aperçu de rien.	He perceived (noticed, saw) nothing.
A l'en croire, tout est perdu.	If he is to be believed, all is lost.
Je crois que oui (non).	I believe so (not).
Il se croit tout permis.	He thinks he may do anything.

EXERCISES ON IRREGULAR VERBS AND IDIOMS

A. *Translate.* 1. Qu'est-ce qu'il croirait? 2. Elles nous auraient crus. 3. Je veux qu'ils me croient. 4. On ne croit pas les menteurs. 5. Vous m'avez déçu. 6. Vous êtes-vous aperçu de quelque chose? 7. Il ne s'en était pas aperçu. 8. Elle reçoit les jeudis. 9. Il est difficile de concevoir une telle bêtise. 10. Il avait reçu votre lettre.

B. *Review of idioms.* 1. Ils vont arriver tout à l'heure. 2. Jean vient d'entrer dans le hangar. 3. J'ai appris cette nouvelle il y a une heure. 4. Il y a un mois qu'il me tient au courant de cette affaire. 5. Combien de temps y a-t-il que vous vous en occupez? 6. Voici deux mois que je m'en tire tant bien que mal. 7. Ils venaient de s'en apercevoir. 8. Elle travaillait dans le jardin depuis le matin. 9. Je ne ferais pas autrement s'il y allait de ma vie. 10. Depuis quand tenez-vous à des bêtises pareilles?

C. *Conjugate the following verb forms in the tense in which they are given. E.g.,* **Je pars: je pars, tu pars, il part, nous partons, vous partez, ils partent.** 1. Je sors. 2. Je partais. 3. Je suis venu. 4. Je deviendrai. 5. Je reçois. 6. J'étais descendu. 7. Je courrai. 8. Il faut que j'apprenne. 9. Elle doute que je l'aie vue. 10. Je m'en suis souvenu. 11. Je reviendrais.

D. *Translate.* 1. He received my letter. 2. Will he receive mine? 3. I wrote on the envelope, "Please Forward." **(prière de faire suivre)** 4. The bandit followed us. 5. What course will you take **(suivre)**? 6. The police pursued the thief. 7. Are they going to prosecute that criminal? 8. Do you believe that? 9. I would never have believed it if I hadn't seen it. 10. I knew he noticed it.

E. *Conjugate:* 1. Je ne me suis aperçu de rien. 2. Il faut que je reçoive mon ami. 3. Je croyais pouvoir me passer de tabac. 4. Je crois ce qu'on veut que je croie.

UNIT 16: OUVRIR, PLAIRE

157. Ouvrir to open

		Present	*Pres. S.*	*Past Def.*
Fut.	**ouvrirai**	**ouvre**	**ouvre**	**ouvris**
Cond.	**ouvrirais**	**ouvres**	**ouvres**	**ouvris**
Imp.	**ouvrais**	**ouvre**	**ouvre**	**ouvrit**
Imp. S.	**ouvrisse**	**ouvrons**	**ouvrions**	**ouvrîmes**
Pres. P.	**ouvrant**	**ouvrez**	**ouvriez**	**ouvrîtes**
Past P.	**ouvert**	**ouvrent**	**ouvrent**	**ouvrirent**

Like **ouvrir: couvrir** to cover; **découvrir** to discover, to uncover; **offrir** to offer; **souffrir** to suffer; and others.

158. Plaire to please

Fut.	**plairai**	**plais**	**plaise**	**plus**
Cond.	**plairais**	**plais**	**plaises**	**plus**
Imp.	**plaisais**	**plaît**	**plaise**	**plut**
Imp. S.	**plusse**	**plaisons**	**plaisions**	**plûmes**
Pres. P.	**plaisant**	**plaisez**	**plaisiez**	**plûtes**
Past P.	**plu**	**plaisent**	**plaisent**	**plurent**

Like **plaire: déplaire** to displease; **taire** to say nothing about, conceal; and others. Unlike **plaire,** the verb **taire** takes no circumflex accent in the third person singular, *Pres. Ind. E.g.,* **il tait.**

IDIOMS

Il se plaît à vous taquiner.	He takes pleasure in teasing you.
Il se tait.	He keeps quiet. OR He ceases to speak.

EXERCISES ON IRREGULAR VERBS AND IDIOMS

A. *Translate.* 1. Ouvrez la porte, s'il vous plaît. 2. Je me plais à me taire. 3. S'il découvre la vérité, il ne la taira pas. 4. L'auriez-vous tue si vous l'aviez sue? 5. Que tout le monde se taise! 6. Permettez que je vous offre quelque chose à boire. 7. Nous avons tant souffert lors de sa mort. 8. Il cherchait une femme qui sût se taire. 9. Les montagnes étaient couvertes de neige. 10. Jacques Cartier découvrit le Canada. 11. Si je ne savais pas la réponse, je me tairais. 12. Toutes ces tracasseries me déplaisent. 13. Plût à Dieu. . . . 14. A Dieu ne plaise.

B. *Review of Idioms. Translate.* 1. Prends garde de tomber. 2. Ils prirent un parti courageux. 3. Tâchez de vous conduire en homme de bien. 4. Elle ne se riait jamais de personne. 5. Ils vous en sauront gré. 6. Il pleuvait à verse. 7. Ces deux messieurs se valent. 8. Ils ont dû se tromper. 9. Vous devriez faire attention.

C. *Review of Verbs. Supply the correct pronouns, and put the infinitives in the person and tense indicated.* 1. (*3rd Plur., Pres. Ind.*) retenir, revenir, vouloir, pouvoir. 2. (*1st Sing., Fut.*) faire, devenir, vouloir, pouvoir. 3. (*3rd Sing., Imp.*) craindre, courir, éteindre, lire. 4. (*1st Plur., Cond.*) savoir, obtenir, devoir, envoyer. 5. (*3rd Sing., Past Def.*) plaindre, voir, lire, faire.

D. *Review of* **devoir.** *Translate.* 1. He is to join us at the café. 2. You ought to accompany him. 3. At what time are they to arrive? 4. They were to arrive on the seven o'clock train. 5. They must have missed it. 6. Little John had to go (*two ways*) to the grocer's before going to school. 7. You should have told me that. 8. She must be in the kitchen. 9. Husbands must obey their wives. 10. You should not say what you have just said.

E. *Translate.* 1. Christopher Columbus discovered America in 1492. 2. Keep quiet, please. 3. If you discover the truth, keep it quiet. 4. He took pleasure in making others suffer. 5. That will please me a great deal.

F. *Conjugate:* 1. Je me plais à me taire. 2. J'ouvrirai la porte s'il le faut. 3. Je la faisais souffrir. 4. Je n'ai rien découvert d'intéressant.

UNIT 17: ACQUÉRIR, CONDUIRE

159. Acquérir to acquire

		Present	*Pres. S.*	*Past Def.*
Fut.	**acquerrai**	**acquiers**	**acquière**	**acquis**
Cond.	**acquerrais**	**acquiers**	**acquières**	**acquis**
Imp.	**acquérais**	**acquiert**	**acquière**	**acquit**
Imp. S.	**acquisse**	**acquérons**	**acquérions**	**acquîmes**
Pres. P.	**acquérant**	**acquérez**	**acquériez**	**acquîtes**
Past P.	**acquis**	**acquièrent**	**acquièrent**	**acquirent**

Like **acquérir: conquérir** to conquer; **s'enquérir** to inquire; and others.

160. Conduire to conduct, to drive, to take

		Present	*Pres. S.*	*Past Def.*
Fut.	**conduirai**	**conduis**	**conduise**	**conduisis**
Cond.	**conduirais**	**conduis**	**conduises**	**conduisis**
Imp.	**conduisais**	**conduit**	**conduise**	**conduisit**
Imp. S.	**conduisisse**	**conduisons**	**conduisions**	**conduisîmes**
Pres. P.	**conduisant**	**conduisez**	**conduisiez**	**conduisîtes**
Past P.	**conduit**	**conduisent**	**conduisent**	**conduisirent**

Like **conduire: éconduire** to show out (rudely); **reconduire** to show out (politely); **introduire** to introduce, to bring in; **produire** to produce; **réduire** to reduce; **reproduire** to reproduce; **séduire** to seduce; **traduire** to translate; **construire** to construct; and others.

EXERCISES ON IRREGULAR VERBS AND IDIOMS

A. *Translate.* 1. Comment traduit-on le mot «esprit»? 2. Le champ ne produisit rien cette année-là. 3. On n'éconduit jamais une femme au sourire séduisant. 4. La ferme que vous avez acquise ne produira jamais rien. 5. Pourvu que nous acquérions des bases nous vaincrons facilement l'ennemi. 6. La culture de la pomme de terre fut introduite en France au dix-septième siècle. 7. En se conduisant bien, on acquiert une bonne réputation. 8. Vous partez? Permettez que je vous reconduise. 9. Ils me réduisirent au désespoir en m'éconduisant. 10. Elle s'était mal conduite à mon égard.

B. *Conjugate the following verbs in the tense in which they occur.* 1. Il faut que je le mette. 2. Je crains. 3. Je m'en suis servi. 4. Je voudrais le faire. 5. Je m'en souviendrai. 6. Il regrette que je sois venu. 7. J'ouvre. 8. Je lui en enverrai. 9. Il est content que je l'aie vue. 10. J'écrivis. 11. J'avais craint.

C. *Review of idiomatic peculiarities of* **vouloir, pouvoir,** *and* **savoir.** 1. The tenant would not move. 2. Did you know that the Dupins are going to Lyons? 3. I learned only yesterday that they intended to go there. 4. We didn't succeed in convincing him of it. 5. He cannot tell you that. 6. We should like to see them. 7. I tried to rescue him but I couldn't. 8. Could you do it if you had time? 9. Could you see them when they came to your house? 10. Madame Loisel learned that the necklace was an imitation **(fausse)**.

D. *Translate.* 1. Translate the sentence, please. 2. You would reduce it to nothing. 3. He had conducted himself well. 4. He constructed a house. 5. He produced it (*P. Def.*). 6. You must translate more exactly.

E. *Conjugate:* 1. Si je le traduis je le traduirai bien. 2. Je conduisais l'auto que j'avais acquise. 3. Je vais me faire construire une maison.

UNIT 18: CUEILLIR, SUFFIRE

161. Cueillir to gather

		Present	*Pres. S.*	*Past Def.*
Fut.	**cueillerai**	**cueille**	**cueille**	**cueillis**
Cond.	**cueillerais**	**cueilles**	**cueilles**	**cueillis**
Imp.	**cueillais**	**cueille**	**cueille**	**cueillit**
Imp. S.	**cueillisse**	**cueillons**	**cueillions**	**cueillîmes**
Pres. P.	**cueillant**	**cueillez**	**cueilliez**	**cueillîtes**
Past P.	**cueilli**	**cueillent**	**cueillent**	**cueillirent**

Like **cueillir: accueillir** to welcome, to greet; **recueillir** to gather, to gather up, to collect; and others.

162. suffire to suffice, to be enough

Fut.	**suffirai**	**suffis**	**suffise**	**suffis**
Cond.	**suffirais**	**suffis**	**suffises**	**suffis**
Imp.	**suffisais**	**suffit**	**suffise**	**suffit**
Imp. S.	**suffisse**	**suffisons**	**suffisions**	**suffîmes**
Pres. P.	**suffisant**	**suffisez**	**suffisiez**	**suffîtes**
Past P.	**suffi**	**suffisent**	**suffisent**	**suffirent**

EXERCISES ON IRREGULAR VERBS AND IDIOMS

A. *Translate.* 1. Il suffit de bien chercher pour le trouver. 2. Les paroles douceâtres ne suffisaient plus. 3. «Cueillez dès aujourd'hui les roses de la vie.» (Ronsard) 4. Qui vous a accueilli quand vous avez frappé à ma porte? 5. Je veux que tu cueilles une poignée de fleurs. 6. Je recueille des documents. 7. La bonne volonté est très bien, mais ne suffit pas. 8. Elle est allée dans le verger pour cueillir un panier de pommes. 9. La politesse exige qu'on acueille les invités le sourire aux lèvres. 10. Il ne suffit plus de vouloir la défaite de l'ennemi, il faut l'obtenir à force d'efforts assidus et ardents.

B. *Idiomatic contrasts. Translate.* 1. Je m'assieds. Je suis assis. 2. Il me fait taire, et puis il se tait. 3. Il ne se plaint pas de moi, parce qu'il me plaint. 4. Il me sert de secrétaire. Il se sert de moi pour avancer ses petits intérêts. 5. On sert le dîner. Le dîner est servi. 6. Il connaît les musées. Il se connaît en peinture. 7. Y a-t-il des étudiants assez bêtes pour croire ce dicton? «Celui qui connaît bien ses professeurs ne doit pas savoir ses leçons.» 8. Prenez garde à aller tout droit, mais prenez garde de tomber. 9. Riez, mais ne vous riez pas de nous. 10. Il vint à les voir. Ils venaient de sortir.

C. *Review of* **faire.** 1. Was it warm yesterday? 2. No, it was cold. 3. Why do you pretend to sleep? 4. I shall have him do it. 5. Will you get a haircut tomorrow? 6. What is hurting you? 7. I hurt my finger. 8. I can't get used to this climate. 9. What is that to us? 10. Don't frighten me in that manner.

D. *Translate.* 1. That is no longer enough. 2. They welcomed us on the threshold. 3. He must not gather those cherries. 4. Roger is collecting documents for his thesis. 5. A half pound of sugar a week will suffice for you. 6. While strolling, we shall gather some raspberries. 7. We found them gathering strawberries in the field. 8. If a dollar were enough for you, I would give it to you. 9. He is feared by everybody. 10. We were shown some beautiful buildings. 11. Dinner is served at eight.

E. *Conjugate:* 1. Il veut que je cueille une poignée de fleurs. 2. Je recueille des documents pour ma thèse. 3. Il suffit que je fasse un effort. 4. J'ai l'honneur de conjuguer la dernière phrase de ce livre.

REFERENCE LIST OF IRREGULAR VERBS

The number after the verb refers to the section where the verb is presented. For orthographic changes cf. §11.

	Section		Section
sortir	129	taire	158
souffrir	157	tenir	130
soumettre	131	traduire	160
sourire	148	transmettre	131
soutenir	130		
se souvenir de	130	valoir	140
suffire	162	venir	130
suivre	154	vivre	134
surprendre	132	voir	150
survivre	134	vouloir	137

THE CONJUGATION OF REGULAR VERBS IN SIMPLE AND COMPOUND TENSES

Infinitive (*l'infinitif*)

donner *to give*	**finir** to finish	**vendre** *to sell*

Present Participle (*le participe présent*)

donnant *giving*	**finissant** *finishing*	**vendant** *selling*

Past Participle (*le participe passé*)

donné *given*	**fini** *finished*	**vendu** *sold*

Present Indicative (*le présent*)

I give, am giving, do give, etc.	*I finish, am finishing, do finish, etc.*	*I sell, am selling, do sell, etc.*
je donne	je finis	je vends
tu donnes	tu finis	tu vends
il donne	il finit	il vend
nous donnons	nous finissons	nous vendons
vous donnez	vous finissez	vous vendez
ils donnent	ils finissent	ils vendent

Imperfect (Past Descriptive, *l'imparfait*)

I was giving, used to give, gave, etc.	*I was finishing, used to finish, finished, etc.*	*I was selling, used to sell, sold, etc.*
je donnais	je finissais	je vendais
tu donnais	tu finissais	tu vendais
il donnait	il finissait	il vendait
nous donnions	nous finissions	nous vendions
vous donniez	vous finissiez	vous vendiez
ils donnaient	ils finissaient	ils vendaient

Future (*le futur*)

I shall (will) give, etc.	*I shall (will) finish, etc.*	*I shall (will) sell, etc.*
je donnerai	je finirai	je vendrai
tu donneras	tu finiras	tu vendras
il donnera	il finira	il vendra
nous donnerons	nous finirons	nous vendrons
vous donnerez	vous finirez	vous vendrez
ils donneront	ils finiront	ils vendront

Conditional (Past Future, *le conditionnel*)

I would give, etc.	*I would finish, etc.*	*I would sell, etc.*
je donnerais	je finirais	je vendrais
tu donnerais	tu finirais	tu vendrais
il donnerait	il finirait	il vendrait
nous donnerions	nous finirions	nous vendrions
vous donneriez	vous finiriez	vous vendriez
ils donneraient	ils finiraient	ils vendraient

Past Definite (Past Absolute, *le passé simple*)

I gave, etc.	*I finished, etc.*	*I sold, etc.*
je donnai	je finis	je vendis
tu donnas	tu finis	tu vendis
il donna	il finit	il vendit
nous donnâmes	nous finîmes	nous vendîmes
vous donnâtes	vous finîtes	vous vendîtes
ils donnèrent	ils finirent	ils vendirent

Present Subjunctive (*le présent du subjonctif*)

(*that*) *I* (*may*) *give, etc.*	(*that*) *I* (*may*) *finish, etc.*	(*that*) *I* (*may*) *sell, etc.*
(que) je donne	(que) je finisse	(que) je vende
(que) tu donnes	(que) tu finisses	(que) tu vendes
(qu')il donne	(qu')il finisse	(qu')il vende
(que) nous donnions	(que) nous finissions	(que) nous vendions
(que) vous donniez	(que) vous finissiez	(que) vous vendiez
(qu')ils donnent	(qu')ils finissent	(qu')ils vendent

Imperfect Subjunctive (*l'imparfait du subjonctif*)

(*that*) *I* (*might*) *give, etc.*	(*that*) *I* (*might*) *finish, etc.*	(*that*) *I* (*might*) *sell, etc.*
(que) je donnasse	(que) je finisse	(que) je vendisse
(que) tu donnasses	(que) tu finisses	(que) tu vendisses
(qu')il donnât	(qu')il finît	(qu')il vendît
(que) nous donnassions	(que) nous finissions	(que) nous vendissions
(que) vous donnassiez	(que) vous finissiez	(que) vous vendissiez
(qu')ils donnassent	(qu')ils finissent	(qu')ils vendissent

Imperative (*l'impératif*)

donne	*give*	finis	*finish*	vends	*sell*
donnons	*let us give*	finissons	*let us finish*	vendons	*let us sell*
donnez	*give*	finissez	*finish*	vendez	*sell*

AUXILIARY VERBS **avoir** AND **être**

(See Chapter IV §§ 31–37)

		Present participle (le participe présent)		*Past participle* (le participe passé)	
avoir	to have	**ayant**	having	**eu**	had
être	to be	**étant**	being	**été**	been

Present

avoir *I have*		**être** *I am*	
j'ai	nous avons	je suis	nous sommes
tu as	vous avez	tu es	vous êtes
il a	ils ont	il est	ils sont

Imperfect

I had		*I was*	
j'avais	nous avions	j'étais	nous étions
tu avais	vous aviez	tu étais	vous étiez
il avait	ils avaient	il était	ils étaient

Past definite

I had		*I was*	
j'eus	nous eûmes	je fus	nous fûmes
tu eus	vous eûtes	tu fus	vous fûtes
il eut	ils eurent	il fut	ils furent

Future

I shall have		*I shall be*	
j'aurai	nous aurons	je serai	nous serons
tu auras	vous aurez	tu seras	vous serez
il aura	ils auront	il sera	ils seront

Conditional

I would have		*I would be*	
j'aurais	nous aurions	je serais	nous serions
tu aurais	vous auriez	tu serais	vous seriez
il aurait	ils auraient	il serait	ils seraient

SUBJUNCTIVE MOOD

Present

(that) I (may) have		*(that) I (may) be*	
que j'aie	que nous ayons	que je sois	que nous soyons
que tu aies	que vous ayez	que tu sois	que vous soyez
qu'il ait	qu'ils aient	qu'il soit	qu'ils soient

Imperfect

(that) I (might) have		*(that) I (might) be*	
que j'eusse	que nous eussions	que je fusse	que nous fussions
que tu eusses	que vous eussiez	que tu fusses	que vous fussiez
qu'il eût	qu'ils eussent	qu'il fût	qu'ils fussent

IMPERATIVE MOOD

(see §36, obs. 2)

have			be		
aie	ayons	ayez	sois	soyons	soyez

COMPOUND TENSES

I. Verbs conjugated with *avoir,* i.e., all verbs except those in II and III. II. Verbs conjugated with *être* (see § 38, 2, for the list of such verbs). III. Reflexive verbs. Any verb which can take a direct or indirect object can be made reflexive.

I	II	III
	Perfect (Past Indefinite, *le passé composé*)	
I gave, have given, etc.	*I went, have gone, etc.*	*I got up, have got up, etc.*
j'ai donné	je suis allé(e)	je me suis levé(e)
tu as donné	tu es allé(e)	tu t'es levé(e)
il a donné	il est allé	il s'est levé
nous avons donné	nous sommes allé(e)s	nous nous sommes levé(e)s
vous avez donné	vous êtes allé(e)(s)	vous vous êtes levé(e)(s)
ils ont donné	ils sont allés	ils se sont levés
	Pluperfect (Past Perfect, *le plus-que-parfait*)	
I had sold, etc.	*I had come, etc.*	*I had said to myself, etc.*
j'avais vendu	j'étais venu(e)	je m'étais dit
tu avais vendu	tu étais venu(e)	tu t'étais dit
il avait vendu	il était venu	il s'était dit
nous avions vendu	nous étions venu(e)s	nous nous étions dit
vous aviez vendu	vous étiez venu(e)(s)	vous vous étiez dit
ils avaient vendu	ils étaient venus	ils s'étaient dit
	Future Perfect (*le futur antérieur*)	
I shall (will) have finished, etc.	*I shall (will) have died, etc.*	*I shall (will) have kept silent, etc.*
j'aurai fini	je serai mort(e)	je me serai tu(e)
tu auras fini	tu seras mort(e)	tu te seras tu(e)
il aura fini	il sera mort	il se sera tu
nous aurons fini	nous serons mort(e)s	nous nous serons tu(e)s
vous aurez fini	vous serez mort(e)(s)	vous vous serez tu(e)(s)
ils auront fini	ils seront morts	ils se seront tus

Conditional Perfect (Past Conditional, *le conditionnel passé*)

I would have been, etc.	*I would have gone out, etc.*	*I would have seen myself, etc.*
j'aurais été	je serais sorti(e)	je me serais vu(e)
tu aurais été	tu serais sorti(e)	tu te serais vu(e)
il aurait été	il serait sorti	il se serait vu
nous aurions été	nous serions sorti(e)s	nous nous serions vu(e)s
vous auriez été	vous seriez sorti(e)(s)	vous vous seriez vu(e)(s)
ils auraient été	ils seraient sortis	ils se seraient vus

Past Anterior (*le passé antérieur*)

I had had, etc.	*I had fallen, etc.*	*I had washed (myself), etc.*
j'eus eu	je fus tombé(e)	je me fus lavé(e)
tu eus eu	tu fus tombé(e)	tu te fus lavé(e)
il eut eu	il fut tombé	il se fut lavé
nous eûmes eu	nous fûmes tombé(e)s	nous nous fûmes lavé(e)s
vous eûtes eu	vous fûtes tombé(e)(s)	vous vous fûtes lavé(e)(s)
ils eurent eu	ils furent tombés	ils se furent lavés

Perfect Subjunctive (*le subjonctif passé*)

(*that*) *I gave,* (*may*) *have given, etc.*	(*that*) *I stayed,* (*may*) *have stayed, etc.*	(*that*) *I escaped,* (*may*) *have escaped, etc.*
(que) j'aie donné	(que) je sois resté(e)	(que) je me sois sauvé(e)
(que) tu aies donné	(que) tu sois resté(e)	(que) tu te sois sauvé(e)
(qu') il ait donné	(qu') il soit resté	(qu') il se soit sauvé
(que) nous ayons donné	(que) nous soyons resté(e)s	(que) nous nous soyons sauvé(e)s
(que) vous ayez donné	(que) vous soyez resté(e)(s)	(que) vous vous soyez sauvé(e)(s)
(qu') ils aient donné	(qu') ils soient restés	(qu') ils se soient sauvés

Pluperfect Subjunctive (*le plus-que-parfait du subjonctif*)

(*that*) *I had taken, might have taken, etc.*	(*that*) *I had been born, might have been born, etc.*	(*that*) *I had complained, might have complained, etc.*
(que) j'eusse pris	(que) je fusse né(e)	(que) je me fusse plaint(e)
(que) tu eusses pris	(que) tu fusses né(e)	(que) tu te fusses plaint(e)
(qu') il eût pris	(qu') il fût né	(qu') il se fût plaint
(que) nous eussions pris	(que) nous fussions né(e)s	(que) nous nous fussions plaint(e)s
(que) vous eussiez pris	(que) vous fussiez né(e)(s)	(que) vous vous fussiez plaint(e)(s)
(qu') ils eussent pris	(qu') ils fussent nés	(qu') ils se fussent plaints

FRENCH-ENGLISH VOCABULARY

Most words whose meaning and form may be related to their grammatical function or determined by it have been included in the Index rather than in the vocabulary. Thus, pronouns and adjectives, except descriptive adjectives, have been put in the Index. Entered in the Vocabulary are nouns, verbs, adverbs, prepositions, conjunctions, interjections, and descriptive adjectives.

A

à to, at, in, for, with
abandonner to desert, to abandon, to leave (*behind*)
abbé *m.* priest (A title generally given to French priests of low rank.)
abolir to abolish
abord: d'abord in the first place, at first; **tout d'abord** the very first thing
aboyer to bark
abri *m.* shelter; **à l'— de** safe from, sheltered by
absence *f.* absence
absent absent
absolument absolutely, positively
accent *m.* accent, tone
accepter to accept, to take; **— de** + *Inf.* to agree to
accomodé (à) adapted (*to*)
accompagner to accompany, to go with; **accompagné de** accompanied (*attended*) by
accomplir to accomplish, to perform
accord *m.* agreement; **être d'—** to agree
accourir to run up, to come running up, to hasten to the spot
s'accoutumer (à) to accustom (*one's self*)
accueil *m.* welcome
accueillir to receive, to (*make*) welcome
accusation *f.* accusation, charge
acheter to buy, to purchase
achever to finish, to complete, to perfect; **— de s'habiller** to finish dressing
acquérir to acquire, to get
acquitter to pay, to acquit
activité *f.* activity, stir, bustle
actuel -lle present-day, current
adieu *m.* good-by, leave-taking; **faire ses adieux (à)** to take one's leave, to say good-by (*to*); (**Adieu** is sometimes used as a greeting in certain parts of France.)
admettre to admit, to allow (*of*), to receive
admirer to admire, to wonder at
adorer to adore
adresse *f.* address
adresser to address, to direct, to call; **s'— à** to turn to, to go to, to call upon, to speak to
adroitement adroitly, skillfully
affaire *f.* affair, matter, dealing, thing; **affaire de cœur** love affair
affecter to affect, to pretend, to feign
affirmer to affirm, to vouch for

affreux -euse frightful
afin de + *Inf.* in order to; **afin que** + *Subj.* in order that, so that
Afrique *f.* Africa
âge *m.* age; **quel — avez-vous?** How old are you?
âgé aged, elderly, old
agir to act; **s'— de** to be a question of. **Il s'agit de le faire.** It is a question (*matter*) of doing it. **Il ne s'agit pas de cela.** That is not the point (*at issue*).
agricole *adj.* agricultural, farm
agneau *m.* lamb
aigre sour, tart, sharp, bitter
aigu pointed, acute, sharp
ailleurs elsewhere; **d'—** besides, moreover
aimable lovable, agreeable, likable, pleasant, kind
aimer to love, to like; **— beaucoup** to be fond of; **— mieux** to prefer; **j'aimerais mieux** + *Inf.* I'd rather; **— (à)** + *Inf.* to like to
aîné eldest, elder
ainsi thus, in this way, so, so then; **—soit-il!** So may it be! **ainsi que** as well as, as
air *m.* air, look; **en plein —** in the open air; **avoir l'air pauvre** to look poor
aise *f.* ease, convenience, gladness, comfort; **mal à son —** uncomfortable, ill at ease
aise *adj.* glad
ajouter to add
allemand German
Allemagne *f.* Germany
aller to go, to be going to, to be about to, to walk, to fit; **s'en —** to go away; **— à la rencontre de** to go to meet (*someone*); **— à sa (leur, votre,** *etc.*) **rencontre** to go to meet him, her (them, you, *etc.*), **Comment allez-vous?** How are you? **Ça va!** All right! **ça va beaucoup mieux** things are much better; **— chercher** to go (*and*) get. **Ce chapeau ne lui va pas.** That hat does not become her. **y — de** to be at stake; **— à pied** to walk
allons: — ! Bon! Come now! that's silly! **— donc!** Nonsense! Well!
allumer to light (*up*), to kindle, to brighten
allumette *f.* match
alors then (*at that time*), so, in that case, thereupon
âme *f.* soul
amener to bring, to lead
américain American
Amérique *f.* America
ami *m.*, **amie** *f.* friend
amitié *f.* friendship
amour *m.* love
amoureux *m.* lover, sweetheart; **tomber — de** to fall in love with
amuser to amuse, to entertain; **s'— (à)** to have a good time (*in*)
an *m.* year (*unit of time*); **avoir dix-huit ans** to be eighteen years old
ancien ancient, former
âne *m.* ass
ange *m.* angel
Angleterre *f.* England
anglais (Anglais) English (Englishman)
animal *m.* animal; **— favori** pet; **foi d'—** upon my word of honor
année *f.* year (*duration of time*)
anniversaire *m.* birthday, anniversary
anthropophage *m.* anthropophagite, cannibal

anthropophagie *f.* anthropophagy, cannibalism
août *m.* August
apercevoir to perceive (*with the eyes*), to discern, to catch sight of; **s'— de** to become aware of, to notice
apéritif *m.* appetizer
apparaître to appear suddenly
appartement *m.* an apartment, a flat, rooms (*for lodging*)
appartenir (à) to belong (*to*)
appeler to call; **s'—** to be named. **Comment vous appelez-vous?** What is your name?
applaudir to applaud
appliquer to apply
apporter to bring (*along*), to carry, to fetch
apprendre (à) to learn (*to*); **— par cœur** to memorize
s'apprêter (à) to get ready (*to*)
s'approcher (de) to approach, to come (*get*) near, to bring (*draw, move*) near
approuver to approve (*of*)
appuyer to support, to lean, to prop, to rest
après *prep.* after; *adv.* afterwards; **d'—** according to, adapted from; **— que** *conj.* after
après-demain *adv.* the day after tomorrow
après-midi *m.* or *f.* afternoon; **l'—** in the afternoon
arbre *m.* tree
ardent fiery, ardent
argent *m.* money, silver; **—comptant** cash
armée *f.* army
armoire *f.* wardrobe, closet
arracher (à) to tear out, to snatch (*from*), to pull away
arranger to suit
arrêter to arrest, to stop; **s'—** to stop (*one's self*)
arrière: en — backward
arrivée *f.* arrival
arriver to arrive (*at, in*); **— à** + *Inf.* to succeed in; **— à quelqu'un** to happen, to occur (*to one*). **Qu'est-ce qui arrive?** What is happening?
art *m.* art
article *m.* article, thing; **— de luxe** luxury item
artillerie *f.* artillery
artisan *m.* handicraftsman, artisan
as *m.* ace
aspirateur *m.* vacuum cleaner
aspiration *f.* aspiration, ambition
aspirer (à) to desire, to aspire (*to*)
assassin *m.* assassin, murderer
asseoir to seat: **s'—** to sit down
assez (de) enough, sufficiently, rather
assidu assiduous, diligent
assiette *f.* plate; **— à pâtée** a dish for dog food
assimiler to assimilate
assis seated
assister to help, to assist; **— à** to be present at, to attend
assurer to assure; **s'—** to make sure
athlète *m.* athlete
attaquer to attack
atteindre (à) to hit, to reach, to attain
attendant: en — meanwhile; **en — que** till, until
attendre to wait for, to await, to expect; **s'— à** to expect, to look forward to; **— que** + *Subj.* to wait until
attention *f.* care, attention; **faire**

— **à** to pay heed to, to notice; **presque sans y faire** — in a casual manner
attrape! take that!
attraper to overtake, to catch
aucun (*with* **ne** *before the verb*) no, none, not any
augmenter to increase, to grow
aujourd'hui today, now
auparavant previously, before, earlier
auprès (de) near, close to, with, alongside
aussi too, also; therefore (*when introducing a clause*)
aussitôt immediately, forthwith; — **que** as soon as
Australie *f.* Australia
autant (de) as much, so much, as many; **d'— plus que** all the more because, so much the more that
auteur *m.* author
auto *f.* auto; **en** — by car
autobus *m.* bus
automne *m.* autumn; **en** — in autumn
autour (de) about, around
autre other, different; **l'un l'—** each other; **l'un et l'—** both; **l'un à l'—** to each other; — **chose** something else; **d'— part** on the other hand
autrefois formerly, once upon a time
autrement otherwise
autrui *m. n.* or *pron.* others, another
avance *f.* advance; **en (d')—** early, ahead of time; **être en** — to be early
avancer to advance, to hasten; to be fast (*watch*)
avant *prep.* before; — **de** + *Inf.* before; — **que** + *Subj.* before; **en** — forward!
avant-hier *adv.* the day before yesterday
avare miserly, stingy, avaricious
avec with
avenir *m.* future; **à l'—** in the future
aventure *f.* adventure, experience; **à l'—** at random
avertir to warn, to notify
aveugle blind
avion *m.* airplane; **en** — by airplane; **par** — by air (mail)
avis *m.* opinion, sentiment, advice, impression
avocat *m.* lawyer
avoir to have; — **l'air (de)** to seem; — **beau** + *Inf.* to (*do*) in vain. **Elle a beau protester.** It is useless for her to protest. — **besoin (de)** to need. **Qu'avez-vous?** What is the matter? — **chaud** to be warm; — **envie (de)** to feel like; — **faim** to be hungry; — **froid** to be cold; — **honte (de)** to be ashamed (*of*); — **lieu** to take place; — **mal à la tête** to have a headache; — **peur (de)** to be afraid (*of*); — **raison** to be right; — **soif** to be thirsty; — **sommeil** to be sleepy; — **tort** to be wrong. **Qu'est-ce qu'il y a?** What's the matter? **Il y a que j'ai faim.** (The matter is) I'm hungry. **Qu'y a-t-il pour votre service, messieurs?** What can I do for you, gentlemen? **Combien y a-t-il d'ici au Louvre?** How far is it from here to the Louvre?
avouer to confess, to acknowledge, to admit
avril *m.* April

B

badaud *m.* loafer, booby, idler

bagage *m.* baggage, luggage
bague *f.* (*finger*) ring
baiser to kiss (*the lips, hand, etc.*); **embrasser** to embrace (and kiss) a person
baiser *m.* kiss
baisser to lower
bal *m.* ball, dance
balancement *m.* swaying (*motion*), balancing
balayer to sweep (*away*)
balle *f.* ball, bullet, shot
banquier *m.* banker
barbe *f.* beard
barboter to splash about
bas, basse low; **à** — down with; **en** — downstairs; **de — en haut** from head to foot; **à voix basse** in a whisper, in a low voice
bas *m.* stocking
base *f.* basis, foundation, base
basilique *f.* basilica
bataille *f.* battle
bateau *m.* boat; **en** — by boat
bâtiment *m.* building
bâtir to build
battre to beat; **se** — to combat, to fight
beau, bel *m.*, **belle** *f.* beautiful, handsome, fair; **avoir** — + *Inf.* to be useless (in vain)
beaucoup (de) much, a great deal (*of*), many
beau-fils *m.* son-in-law
beau-frère *m.* brother-in-law
beau-père *m.* father-in-law
beauté *f.* beauty
Belge *m., f.* and *adj.* Belgian
Belgique *f.* Belgium
belle-fille *f.* daughter-in-law
belle-mère *f.* mother-in-law
belle-sœur *f.* sister-in-law
bénir to bless
berger *m.* shepherd
besoin *m.* need; **avoir — de** to (*be in*) need (*of*), to need (*to*)
bête *f.* animal, beast
bête *adj.* stupid, foolish
bêtise *f.* stupidity, nonsense, folly
beurre *m.* butter
bibliothèque *f.* library
bicyclette *f.* bicycle; **à** — by bicycle
bien well, good, all right, very, very much, indeed; — **que** although; **ou** — or else; — **entendu** of course; **tant — que mal** rather poorly, somehow. **Eh — !** Well!
bien *m.* property, possession, piece of property, goods; **homme de** — gentleman
bientôt soon; **à** — good-by for the present, see you later
bière *f.* beer
bifteck *m.* beefsteak
bijou *m.* jewel
bille *f.* marble
billet *m.* ticket, note
bise *f.* north wind
blanc *m.*, **blanche** *f.* white
blasé jaded
blesser to wound, to hurt, to shock
blessure *f.* wound
bleu blue
blouse *f.* blouse, smock (The loose overgarment usually worn by French peasants or workingmen.)
bœuf *m.* ox, beef; **œil de** — a round window
boire to drink
bois *m.* wood(s)
boîte *f.* box
bol *m.* bowl, basin
bombe *f.* bomb
bon, bonne well, good. **Bon!** Fine! **Allons! bon!** Come now! That's silly! **A quoi** — ? What's the use? — **marché** cheap

bonheur *m.* happiness, good fortune, luck
bonjour *m.* good morning, good day, *etc.*
bonne *f.* housemaid, servant
bonsoir *m.* good evening, good night
bouche *f.* mouth
bonté *f.* kindness, goodness
boudoir *m.* boudoir
boue *f.* mud
bouillir to boil
boulanger *m.* baker
boulet *m.* cannon ball
bouleversement *m.* overthrow, ruin, upsetting
bouleverser to upset, to disturb
bourrelier *m.* harness maker
bourse *f.* purse, scholarship
bousculer to jostle, to toss (*about*)
bout *m.* end, tip; **au — de** (*of time*) after
bouteille *f.* bottle
boutique *f.* shop; **fonds de —** remnants
boxe *f.* boxing
bras *m.* arm
brave good, fine, worthy, brave
bravoure *f.* bravery, daring
bref in short, in brief
Brésil *m.* Brazil
brésilien Brazilian
briller to shine, to glisten
briser to break
brosse *f.* brush; **— à dents** toothbrush
brosser to brush
bruit *m.* noise, sound
brun brown, dusky
brusquement bluntly, gruffly, hastily, abruptly
bûcher *fig.* to drudge, to cram, to burn the midnight oil
budget *m.* budget
bureau *m.* desk, office

C

ça *colloquial abbrev. of* **cela; C'est ça!** That's right!
çà *adv.* here, thither; **ah! çà!** now (*then*).
cabaret *m.* tavern
cache-cache *m.* hide-and-seek
cacher to hide
cadeau *m.* gift, present
café *m.* coffee, a café, a restaurant, a coffeehouse
cahier *m.* notebook
caillou *m.* pebble, stone
caissier *m.* treasurer, cashier
camarade *m.* or *f.* comrade, chum
camion *m.* truck
campagne *f.* country; **à la —** in the country
candidat *m.* candidate
canif *m.* pocket knife
canon *m.* cannon, gun, artillery
cantatrice *f.* singer
caoutchouc *m.* caoutchouc, rubber; *pl.* rubbers (*footwear*)
capable capable, able
capitaine *m.* captain
capitale *f.* capital (*city*)
captif *m.* captive, prisoner
car *conj.* for
caractère *m.* character; **avoir bon —** to be good natured
carré square
carrément squarely, firmly
carrière *f.* career
carte *f.* card, map
cas *m.* case
casque *m.* helmet
casser to break (*off*), to shatter
catégorique proper, absolutely, explicit, categorical
catholique Catholic
cause *f.* cause, reason, trial; **à — de** on account of
causer to chat, to cause
céder to yield, to give up

célèbre famous, celebrated
célébrer to celebrate
célibataire *m.* bachelor, single man
cendre *f.* ashes
cent hundred
centaine: une — about a hundred
centime *m.* centime (The hundredth part of a franc.)
cercle *m.* circle, club
cerise *f.* cherry
cesser (de) to stop, to cease
chacal *m.* jackal
chacun *pron.* each, each one, everyone
chagrin *m.* sorrow, grief
chaise *f.* chair
chaleur *f.* heat
chameau *m.* camel
chambre *f.* room, bedroom
champ *m.* field; **sur-le-champ** at once, immediately
chance *f.* luck; **avoir de la** — to be lucky; **bonne** — good luck
changer (de) to change
chanson *f.* song
chanter to sing
chapeau *m.* hat
chaque *adj.* each, every
charmant charming, delightful
charmé charmed, delighted
charpentier *m.* carpenter
charrue *f.* plow
chasse *f.* hunt, hunting
chat *m.* cat
château *m.* castle
chaud *adj.* warm, hot; *n. m.* heat, warmth; **avoir** — to be warm (*of living things*); **faire** — to be warm (*of the weather*)
chaussette *f.* sock
chef *m.* chief, head; — **d'équipe** foreman
chemin *m.* way, road; — **de fer** railroad; **en** — **de fer** by train; — **faisant** on the way; **faire son** — to get along, to advance
chemise *f.* shirt
chêne *m.* oak
chèque *m.* check; **carnet de —s** checkbook
cher, chère dear, expensive
chercher to look for; — **à** to strive to, to try to; **envoyer** — to send for; **aller** — go and get
chéri dear, beloved, darling
cheval *m.* horse; **à** — on horseback
chevalier *m.* knight
cheveux *m. pl.* hair
chèvre *f.* she-goat, nanny goat
chez to, in, at, the house (room, quarters, shop, *etc.*) of
chic *m.* style; *adj.* stylish, smart
chien *m.* dog
chimique chemical
chimiste *m.* chemist
Chine *f.* China
chinois Chinese
chocolat *m.* chocolate
choisir to choose
choix *m.* choice
chose *f.* thing; **autre** — something else; **pas grand'chose** not much
chou *m.* cabbage
chrétien Christian
chrysanthème *m.* chrysanthemum
chute *f.* fall
ciel *m.* (*pl.* **cieux**) sky, heaven
cigale *f.* cicada, grasshopper, locust
cigare *m.* cigar
cinéma *m.* moving picture
cinquante fifty
cinquième fifth part
citoyen *m.* citizen
civil *m.* civilian
civilisation *f.* civilization, culture
classe *f.* class
clé (clef) *f.* key; **fermer à** — to lock

climat *m.* climate
cœur *m.* heart; **de bon —** gladly
coiffeur -euse *m.* and *f.* hairdresser, barber
coiffure *f.* hair-do
coin *m.* corner
colère *f.* anger, rage; **se mettre en —** to get angry; **être en —** to be angry
collège *m.* college
coller to paste, to glue; *fig.* (*of a student*) to fail, to flunk
colonie *f.* colony
combien (de) how many, how much, how; **— de temps?** how long
commander to order
comme as, like, how, just as; **— ci — ça** so so
commencer (à, de) to begin (*to*)
comment how
commerçant *m.* tradesman, merchant
commettre to commit
commis voyageur *m.* traveling salesman
communiste *m., f.; adj.* communist
compagnon *m.* companion
complet, complète complete, full; **être au —** to be full
complet *m.* suit of clothes
compléter to complete
composé *adj.* composed; *n. m.* compound
comprendre to understand, to comprise, to comprehend
compromettre to compromise, to commit
comptant *adj.* ready money; (*of money*) **argent —** cash
compte: en fin de — in the end, in the long run
compter to count, to number, to comprise, to intend, to believe (*firmly*)
concevoir to conceive
conciliant conciliating
condamner to condemn, to sentence
conduire to lead, to conduct, to drive, to take, to bring; **se —** to behave
conférence *f.* lecture
conférencier *m.* lecturer
confondre to confound, to confuse
conjuguer to conjugate
connaissance *f.* knowledge, acquaintance; **faire la — de** to meet (*someone*)
connaître to know, to be acquainted with; **se — à** (*or* **en**) to be a judge (*connoisseur*) of
conquérir to conquer, to win, to acquire
conseil *m.* advice, counsel, council
conseiller to advise
consentir (à) to consent
conséquent: par — consequently, so, therefore
considérable considerable, rather large, great
consister (de) to be composed (*of*), to consist (*of*)
conspirateur *m.* conspirator
constater to verify, to ascertain, to establish, to declare, to note, to state
constitution *f.* constitution
construire to construct, to build
consulter to consult
consumer to consume; **se —** to decay
contenir to contain, to hold
se contenir to contain one's self, to keep within bounds
content (de) glad, happy (*over, at*)
se contenter (de) to be satisfied, to be content (*with*)

continuer (à, de) to continue (*to*), to go on (*with*)
contraindre (de) to constrain, to compel, to force (*to*)
contraire: au — on the contrary, indeed
contrarier to vex, to contradict, to annoy, to provoke, to interfere with
contre against, contrary to
contrebande *f.* smuggled goods
contredire to contradict, to disprove, to gainsay
contrefaire to imitate, to deform, to counterfeit
contribuer to contribute
contrition *f.* contrition, penitence, remorse
convaincre to convince
convenir to agree, to suit, to become, to be proper
conversation *f.* conversation
coquin *m.* rascal
corde *f.* cord, rope, string
correction *f.* correction, lesson in behavior
corridor *m.* lobby, corridor
corriger to correct; **se** — to reform
corse *adj.* Corsican; *n.* **(Corse)** Corsican
côte *f.* coast;
côte d'Azur the French Riviera
côté *m.* side, direction; **à — de** beside, alongside of; **de ce** — in this (*or* that) direction; **de mon** — for my own part; **de tous —s** on all sides; **du — de** in the direction of (*toward*); **d'un** — on the one hand; **de l'autre — (de)** on the other side (*of*)
cou *m.* neck
se coucher to go to bed, to lie down
couleur *f.* color
coup *m.* blow, shot, stroke; **à — sûr** certainly; **du même** — at the same time; **jeter un — d'œil** to glance; — **sur** — in succession; — **d'état** the overthrow of a government; — **de fusil** gunshot; — **de grâce** the finishing stroke *or* blow; — **de main** helping hand; — **de maître** master stroke; — **de pied** a kick; — **de théâtre** an unexpected event
coupe *f.* cup, drinking bowl
couper to cut (*off* or *out*)
courage *m.* courage, pluck
courageux, courageuse courageous; **peu** — cowardly
couramment fluently
courant *m.* current, stream; **être au** — to be informed *or* posted on; **tenir au** — to keep informed *or* posted; **mettre au — de** to inform
courber to bend, to curve; **se** — to stoop, to bend over
courir to run (*about*), to hurry
courrier *m.* mail
cours *m.* course; **suivre un** — to take a course
court short
cousin *m.* cousin
couteau *m.* knife
coûter to cost
couturier -ère *m.* and *f.* dressmaker
couverture *f.* blanket
couvrir (de) to cover (*with*)
craie *f.* chalk
craindre to fear (*to*)
crainte *f.* fear, dread; **de — de** for fear of, for fear that
cravate *f.* necktie
crayon *m.* pencil
crème *f.* cream
creux *m.* hollow, cavity; — **de l'estomac** pit of the stomach

cri *m.* a shout; **pousser un —** to utter a cry, to scream
crier to shout, to cry out, to yell
crime *m.* crime
criminel *m.* criminal
croire to believe, to believe to be; **— à, en** to believe in. **Je crois bien!** I should say so!
crotte *f.* mud, mire
cueillir to gather
cuisine *f.* kitchen, cookery
cuisinier *m.* **-ère** *f.* cook
culotte *f.* knee breeches
culpabilité *f.* guilt, culpability
cultivateur *m.* farmer
cultiver to cultivate, to till
culture *f.* culture, cultivation, education
curiosité *f.* curiosity

D

dactylo(graphe) *m.* or *f.* typist
dame *f.* lady
dandiner to sway, to twist
Danemark *m.* Denmark
danger *m.* danger, peril
danois Danish
dans in, into, to
danser to dance
danseur *m.* **danseuse** *f.* dancer
date *f.* date
davantage *adv.* more, any more, any further, any longer
de of, about, concerning, from, out of
dé *m.* a die, *i.e.,* one of a pair of dice
débarrasser to rid, to clear away; **se — de** to rid one's self of, to get rid of
déboire *m.* vexation, mortification
debout standing; **être** (*or* **se tenir**) — to stand
décembre *m.* December
décevoir to disappoint, to deceive
déchirer to tear (*up, open*), to rend
décider (de + *Inf.*) to decide (*to*); **se — à** to decide (if decision is difficult to make)
déclarer to declare
déconcerter to disconcert, to upset
découverte *f.* discovery
découvrir to uncover, to discover
décrire to describe
défaire to defeat, to undo; **se — de** to get rid of
défaite *f.* defeat
défaut *m.* defect, fault, flaw
défendre (à quelqu'un de) to defend, to forbid (*someone to*)
défiance *f.* distrust
dégoût *m.* disgust, mortification
dégoûter to disgust
déguiser to disguise
déjà already
déjeuner *m.* lunch; **le petit —** breakfast
délicat delicate, dainty
délices *f. pl.* delight, pleasure, raptures; **avec —** blissfully
demain tomorrow; **à —** good-by until tomorrow
demander to ask, to ask for; **se —** to wonder; **— pardon à** to beg someone's pardon
démarrer to unmoor, to get under way, to start
déménagement *m.* the moving of household goods, change of residence
démentir to deny, to contradict, to belie
demeure *f.* residence, dwelling, abode
demeurer (à) to live, to reside, to stay (*at*), to remain
demi (*or* **demi-**) half
démission *f.* resignation; **donner la —** to resign

démocrate *m. or f.* democrat
demoiselle *f.* young lady, young girl
dent *f.* tooth
dépêche *f.* dispatch, telegram
dépêcher to hurry, to dispatch; **se — (de)** to make haste, to hurry (to)
dépeindre to depict, to portray
dépit *m.* spite; **en — de** in spite of
dépenser to spend
déplacement *m.* displacement, change of place, a wandering about
déplaire (à) to displease, to offend, to dislike; **ne vous déplaise** if you don't mind
déployer to unfold, to deploy; **rire à gorge déployée** to split one's sides laughing
dépourvoir to leave unprovided for, to leave destitute
depuis since, from, ever since; **— que** (*ever*) since
déranger to disturb, to trouble
dernier last, latter; **ces mois —s** in recent months
dernièrement recently
dérobée: à la — on the sly, by stealth
déroute *f.* rout, defeat
derrière *prep.* behind
derrière *m.* rear, haunches
dès from, since, by, *i.e.,* not later than; **— que** as soon as, since
désagréable disagreeable, unpleasant
désaltérer to quench the thirst of, to refresh
désastre *m.* disaster
descendre to descend, to go down, to stop at a hotel; (*trans.*) to get down, to go down *or* to come down a staircase, to set down, to land
désert *m.* desert, wilderness
désespérer to despair, to give up all hope
désespoir *m.* despair, grief
déshabiller to undress; **se —** to undress (one's self)
désir *m.* desire
désirer to desire, to wish
désolé disconsolate
désormais henceforth
dessiner to draw
dessous *m.* underside; **au-dessous (de)** below, under; **là-dessous** under there
dessus *m.* top; **au-dessus (de)** above; **là-dessus** on it, thereupon; **tenir le —** to hold the upper hand
destructeur, destructrice destructive
détester to detest, to dislike
détruire to destroy
deux two; **courbé en —** bent double
devant in front of
dévasté devastated
devenir to become (*of*), to grow, to get
deviner to divine, to guess, to foretell
devoir to owe, ought, must, to be supposed to (*Cf.* §*138 for idiomatic uses.*)
devoir *m.* duty; *pl.* lessons
dévouement *m.* devotion, zeal
diable *m.* devil, (*the*) deuce
dictionnaire *m.* dictionary
dicton *m.* saying, proverb
dieu *m.* god *or* God
différence *f.* difference
différent different
difficile difficult, hard
difficulté *f.* difficulty
dilemme *m.* dilemma
dimanche *m.* Sunday
dîner *m.* dinner
dîner to dine, to eat

dire to say, to tell; **à vrai —** to tell the truth; **pour ainsi —** so to speak; **c'est-à —** that is to say; **entendre —** to hear; **dire son fait à quelqu'un** to tell someone what you think of him
se diriger (à *or* **vers)** to go toward
discours *m.* speech; **prononcer (faire) un —** to make a speech
discussion *f.* discussion
discuter to discuss
disparaître to vanish, to disappear
dispendieux *m.*, **dispendieuse** *f.* spendthrift; *adj.* expensive
se disposer (à) to be disposed, to be about to
disposition *f.* disposal, service
disque *m.* disc, record
distinguer to distinguish, to see
distraction *f.* inattention, absent-mindedness, recreation, diversion
distrait absent-minded
divers various, different
diviser to divide
dix ten
dix-huit eighteen
dix-neuf nineteen
dix-sept seventeen
dizaine *f.* about ten
document *m.* document
dodo: faire — to sleep (*baby talk*)
doigt *m.* finger
dollar *m.* dollar
domestique *adj.* domestic
domestique *m.* or *f.* servant
dommage *m.* damage, loss. **C'est — !** It's a pity!
dompter to conquer, to subdue, to overcome
donner to give; **— raison à** to side with; **— sur** to face, to open upon; **— tort à** to side against
dormir to sleep
douanier *m.* customhouse officer
douceâtre sweetish
doucement softly, gently; **tout —** gradually, nicely, bit by bit, gently
douleur *f.* grief, pain
doute *m.* doubt; **sans —** no doubt, unquestionably
douter (de) to doubt; **se — de** to suspect
douteux *m.*, **douteuse** *f.* doubtful
doux *m.*, **douce** *f.* sweet, mild, gentle
douzaine: une — de a dozen, twelve
doyen *m.* dean
dramaturge *m.* dramatist
drap *m.* cloth, bed sheet
droit *m.* right, custom, duty; **tout —** straight ahead
droite *adj. f.* upright, erect; **toute —** fully erect
droite *f.* right-hand side; **à —** on the right *or* to the right
drôle droll, comical, odd
duel *m.* duel
dur hard, tough
durant during

E

eau *f.* water
éblouir to dazzle
éblouissant dazzling
ébrécher to indent, to notch, to make a dent in
écart *m.* a stepping aside, a digression; **à l'—** aside, to one side
échapper to escape; **l'— belle** to have a narrow escape
échouer to fail, to flunk an examination
éclair *m.* lightning, a flash of lightning

éclaircir to clarify, to explain, to brighten
éclairer to light (*up*), (*fig.*) to enlighten
éclater to burst (*forth*), to explode, to crash
école *f.* school; **à l'—** to (at) school; **— primaire** elementary school
éconduire to show out rudely
économe thrifty, economical
économiser to economize, to save
écouter to listen to
écraser to crush, to smash, to run over
s'écrier to exclaim, to cry out
écrire to write
écrivain *m.* writer
effacer to erase
effarouché startled, frightened, alarmed
effet *m.* effect, result; **en —** in reality, indeed, in fact
effort *m.* effort, endeavor
égal equal; **cela m'est —** that's all the same to me, I don't care
également equally, alike, likewise
égaler to equal
égard *m.* regard, consideration; **à cet —** in this (*that*) respect
église *f.* church
élégant elegant, graceful, refined
élève *m.* or *f.* student, pupil
élever to raise, rear, to elevate; **s'—** to rise, to increase, to go up
éleveur *m.* rancher
élire to elect
élision *f.* elision (*dropping a final vowel*)
éloquent eloquent
emballer to pack (*up*), to put in jail, (*fig.*) to carry away
embarras *m.* embarrassment, perplexity
embarrassant embarrassing, humiliating
embrasser to kiss, to embrace, to clasp
émotion *f.* emotion, stir, agitation
s'emparer (de) to seize, to take possession of
empêcher (de) to prevent, to hinder, to keep (*from*)
emplir (de) to fill (*up*) (*with*)
employé *m.* employee, clerk; **— de bureau** office worker
employer to employ, use, make use of
empoigner to grasp, to lay hold of, to grab
emporter to take away, to carry off
s'empresser (de) to hasten, to be eager (*to*), to lose no time (*in*)
emprunter (à) to borrow (*from*)
emprunteuse *f.* borrower
ému moved
enchanté (de) delighted (*to*), very glad (*to*)
enchanter to delight, to enchant
encore again, still, yet, also; **— une fois** once again; **non seulement . . . mais encore** not only . . . but also
encourager to encourage
encre *f.* ink
endormir to put to sleep; **s'—** to go to sleep, to fall asleep
endroit *m.* place, spot
enfant *m.* or *f.* child, boy, lad, girl, infant
enfin finally, in short, after all
engager to engage, to hire
engraisser to grow fat
enlever to take off, to remove, to carry off, to kidnap
ennemi *m.* enemy, foe
ennui *m.* boredom, vexation
ennuyer to bore, to tire, to annoy; **s'—** to be (become) weary or bored
s'enquérir (de) to inquire (*about*)

enragé rabid, mad
enrhumer to give a cold to someone; **s'—** to catch cold; **être enrhumé** to have a cold
enseigner (à) to teach (*to*)
ensemble together, at the same time
ensuite then, afterward, next
s'ensuivre to follow, to result
entendre to hear, to understand; **— dire** to hear (something) said; **— parler de** to hear of; **bien entendu** of course; **c'est entendu** agreed, it is understood; **s'— avec** to get along with
entente *f.* understanding, agreement
enthousiaste enthusiastic
entourer (de) to surround (*with, by*)
entre between, among
entrer (dans) to enter, to go in
entreprendre to undertake
entrevoir to have (*or* to catch) sight of, to catch a glimpse of
enveloppe *f.* envelope
envie *f.* desire, envy; **avoir — (de)** to feel like. **J'en meurs d'—!** I'm just dying to!
environ about, nearly
envoyer to send; **— chercher** to send for
épais *m.* **épaisse** *f.* thick, dense
épargner to spare
épicier *m.* grocer
époque *f.* epoch, time; **à cette —-là** at that time
épouser to marry, to wed
époux *m.* husband; *pl.* husband and wife
épris (de) in love (*with*)
équipe *f.* team, crew, gang; **chef d'—** foreman
équivaloir to be equivalent *or* tantamount to
errer to wander, to err, to rove, to stray
érudit *m.* scholar, learned man
escargot *m.* snail
Espagne *f.* Spain
espagnol Spanish
espèce *f.* species
espérance *f.* hope, expectation
espérer to hope (*for*), to expect
espoir *m.* hope, expectation
esprit *m.* spirit, mind, wit, intellect
essayer (de) to try (*to*), to try on
essuyer to wipe (*away*), to dry
estimer to esteem, to respect
et and; **et . . . et** both . . . and
établir to establish
état *m.* state, condition
Etats-Unis *m. pl.* United States
été *m.* summer; **en —** in the summer
éteindre to extinguish, to put out
étendre to stretch (*out*), to extend, to spread (*out*)
étoile *f.* star; **à la belle —** in the open air, under the open sky
étonner to astonish, to amaze; **s'— (de)** to wonder (*at*)
étrange strange, foreign
étranger *m.* foreigner; **à l'—** abroad
être to be; **— d'accord** to agree; **— au courant de** to be informed; **— en avance** to be early; **— en retard** to be late; **n'y — pour rien** to have nothing to do with, *i.e.*, not to be involved in; **— en train (de)** to be in the act of. **C'est ça!** That's right! **C'est qu'il est malade.** The fact is, he is sick. **N'est-ce pas?** Isn't it? *or* That's true, isn't it? **C'en est fait de moi!** I'm done for! **Y êtes-vous?** Do you understand it?

étreindre to grasp, to clasp (*conjugated like* **craindre** §147)
étroit narrow
étude *f.* study
étudiant *m.* student
étudier to study
s'évanouir to faint, to vanish
événement *m.* event
s'évertuer (à) to strive, to exert one's self (*to*)
évidemment evidently, obviously
éviter to avoid, to shun, to keep from
examen *m.* examination
examiner to examine
exemplaire *m.* model, copy (*of a book*)
exemple *m.* example; **par** — for example, for instance. Well of all things! Imagine that!
exercer to exercise
exercice *m.* an exercise
exiger to require, to exact, to demand
exister to exist
expérience *f.* experience, experiment
expliquer to explain
exposer to expose, to state
extérieur *m.* exterior, outside
exterminer to exterminate, to wipe out, to kill
extraordinaire extraordinary, unusual

F

fable *f.* fable, story
face *f.* front, forepart of a building, aspect, face; **en — (de)** opposite, facing
fâcher to vex, to make angry; **se** — to become angry; **être fâché** to be angry (sorry)
facile easy
façon *f.* way, manner, fashion; **de cette** — in this way (manner); **à la — de** after the manner of
façonner to fashion, to make, to work
facteur *m.* postman
faible weak, feeble, faint
faiblesse *f.* weakness, frailty
faillir + *Inf.* to miss, to fail; to be on the verge (point) of, to come near, almost
faim *f.* hunger; **avoir** — to be hungry
faire to do, to make; — **attention** to pay attention; **se — à** to become accustomed to, to adjust one's self to; — **son chemin** to advance, to thrive; — **beau** to be nice (*weather*); — **du bien** to help; — **chaud** to be warm (*weather*); — **froid** to be cold (*weather*); — **glissant** to be slippery; — **jour** to be daylight; **se — mal à** to hurt one's self; — **mal à** to hurt (someone); — **mauvais** to be bad (*weather*); — **de son mieux** to do one's best; — **peur à** to frighten; — **plaisir à** to please; — **tout son possible** to do one's best; — **des progrès** to make progress; **se — du mauvais sang** to fret, to worry; — **savoir** to inform; — **semblant de** to seem, to pretend (*to*); — **du soleil** to be sunny; — **un somme** to take a nap; — **le sourd** to pretend to be deaf; — **le tour de** to walk around, to take a stroll through; — **des mauvais tours à** to play bad tricks on; — **du vent** to be windy; — **voir** to show. **Qu'est-ce que cela nous fait?** What is that to us? **Qu'est-ce que cela fait?** What does that matter?

fait *past p.* **en être — de** to be the end of, to be over with
fait *m.* fact; **en — de** with respect to; **dire son — à quelqu'un** to tell someone what you think of him; **surprendre sur le —** to catch in the act
falloir to be necessary, to be needed; **comme il faut** properly. **Peu s'en faut qu'il ne meure.** He is within an inch of dying. **Il s'en faut de beaucoup** very far from it. **Il me faut un tire-bouchon.** I need a corkscrew.
fameux *m.*, **fameuse** *f.* famous, notorious
famille *f.* family
famine *f.* famine, dearth
fardeau *m.* burden, load
farouche wild, sullen, grim, mean-looking
fatigué tired, weary
fatiguer to tire
faute *f.* fault, mistake; **— de** for (through) lack of, for want of
fauteuil *m.* armchair
faux *m.*, **fausse** *f.* false, insincere, mistaken
favori *m.*, **favorite** *f.* favorite; **animal —** *m.* pet
feindre to feign, to make a pretense, to pretend, to sham
féliciter to congratulate
femme *f.* woman, wife
fendu split, cracked
fenêtre *f.* window
ferme firm, steady, fast, resolute
ferme *f.* farm
fermer to close; **— à clé** to lock (*up*)
fermier *m.* farmer
féroce ferocious
fertilisé fertilized
fête *f.* holiday, party, birthday
feu *m.* fire; **mettre le — à** to set fire to
février *m.* February
ficelle *f.* string, twine
ficher to drive in; (*slang*) **se — de** to make fun of. (*slang*) **Fichez-moi (Fiche-moi) la paix!** Beat it! Leave me alone!
fidèle faithful
fier to entrust; **se — à** to trust, to rely upon
fier *adj.* proud, haughty
figure *f.* face, shape
figurer to figure, to represent; **se —** to imagine, to fancy
fille *f.* girl, daughter; **jeune —** girl, young lady
fillette *f.* little girl, lassie
film *m.* film, picture; **— parlant** a sound motion picture
fils *m.* son; **petit-fils** grandson
fin *f.* end; **à la —** finally, in the long run, at last; **en — de compte** in the end
finances *f. pl.* finances
financier *m.* financier
finir (de) to finish; **— par** + *Inf.* (to) finally; **à n'en plus —** interminably; **en — avec** to be done (through, finished) with
flamme *f.* flame, passion
flatter to flatter
fleur *f.* flower
fleuve *m.* river
foi *f.* faith, belief; **— d'animal** upon my word of honor
fois *f.* time, *i.e.*, a particular occasion; **à la —** at the same time, at once; **toutes les — que** whenever, as often as; **une —** once
folâtre sportive, playful, frolicsome
fonction *f.* function
fonctionnaire *m.* functionary, official, office worker
fond *m.* bottom, depth, back-

ground, most remote part; **à —** thoroughly, fully; **au —** in the main, at (the) bottom, in reality
fondre to melt
fonds de boutique *m. pl.* remnants
force *f.* strength; **à — de** by, through, by dint of
forcer (à, de) to force, to compel, to oblige (*to*)
forme *f.* shape, frame
fort strong, very, exceedingly, clever
forteresse *f.* fortress; **— roulante** tank
fou, fol *m.* **folle** *f.* crazy, mad, insane, wild
fouiller to search (*a person*), to pry into, to go through
foule *f.* crowd, throng
fouler to trample on, to tread (*upon*)
fourchette *f.* a table fork
fourmi *f.* ant
fournir to furnish, to supply, to provide
frais *m.*, **fraîche** *f.* fresh
franc *m.* franc (A French silver coin; until 1919 worth about twenty cents.)
franc *m.*, **franche** *f.*, frank, sincere
français *adj.* French; **Français, Française** Frenchman, Frenchwoman
France *f.* France
franchement frankly, really
franchir to cross, to leap over, to clear
frapper to strike, to hit
frein *m.* bridle, brake; **mettre un — à** to curb, to halt, to check
frère *m.* brother
frisson *m.* chill, shudder, thrill
frivole frivolous
froid *m.* cold; **faire —** to be cold (*weather*); **avoir —** to be cold
fromage *m.* cheese
front *m.* forehead, front
fuite *f.* flight, escape, evasion; **prendre la —** to run away
fumer to smoke
fumer to fertilize, to manure
fur: au fur et à mesure in proportion, gradually as
fusil *m.* gun

G

gabelou *m.* tax collector (An abusive name given to custom-house tax collectors. The word dates from the time of Louis XIV.)
gages *m. pl.* wages, pay
gagner to earn, to win, to gain, to reach a place
gai gay, merry, gleeful
gaiement gaily, merrily
galant courteous, gallant
galère *f.* galley; **vogue la —** happen what may *or* come what may
galon *m.* lace, braid, stripe
gamin *m.* lad, urchin, little scamp
gant *m.* glove
garçon *m.* boy, lad, young man; waiter; bachelor
garde *f.* watch, guard; **prendre — (à)** to watch out (*for*), to be careful (*of*); **prendre — de** + *Inf.* to take care not to
garder to keep, to guard, to watch over; **— le souvenir** to remember
gaspiller to waste, to squander
gâteau *m.* cake
gauche left, awkward
gauche *f.* left hand, left side, left; **à —** on (*to*) the left
gazouillement *m.* chirping, warbling

geindre to groan
geler to freeze
gémir to groan, to sigh, to lament
gendarme *m.* policeman, gendarme
gendre *m.* son-in-law
gêne *f.* uneasiness, annoyance, embarrassment, pecuniary difficulty
général *adj.* general, all-round
général *m.* general
généreux *m.,* **généreuse** *f.* generous
génie *m.* genius
genou *m.* knee
genre *m.* species, kind, sort, style
gens *m.* people, persons
gentil *m.,* **gentille** *f.* nice. **Comme c'est gentil de sa part!** How nice of him!
gentiment prettily, nicely (*ironically*); **tout —** very nicely, quite simply
géologue *m.* geologist
geste *m.* gesture, action, motion
glacer to freeze (*up*), to ice, to chill
glissant slippery
golf *m.* golf
gorge *f.* throat; **rire à — déployée** to split one's sides laughing
gosse *m.* brat, urchin, youngster
gourde *f.* flask
goutte *f.* drop, small amount; gout; **se ressembler comme deux gouttes d'eau** to be as like as two peas in a pod
grâce *f.* grace, mercy, charm
grain *m.* grain, bead
grammaire *f.* grammar
grand tall, large, great, big
grandir to grow (*up*), to increase
grand'mère *f.* grandmother
grand-père *m.* grandfather
gras *m.,* **grasse** *f.* fat
gratter to scratch
grave serious, grave
gré *m.* will, inclination; **à son —** to his liking; **en savoir — à** to be grateful to someone for (something)
grenade *f.* grenade
grimper to climb
grippe *f.* dislike; **prendre (quelqu'un) en —** to take a dislike to (someone)
gris gray
gronder to scold
gros *m.,* **grosse** *f.* big, large, stout
grossir to make bigger, to augment, to enlarge
groupe *m.* group
guère: ne . . . guère hardly, scarcely
guérir to cure, to get well, to heal
guerre *f.* war; **faire la —** to wage war
guide *m.* or *f.* guide

H

* *The* **h** *is to be aspirated in words preceded by an asterisk.*

habiller to dress; **s'—** to dress (one's self)
habitant *m.* inhabitant, occupant
habituer to accustom; **s'— (à)** to become accustomed (*to*), to get used (*to*)
habitude *f.* habit, custom; **d'—** usually, generally
***hache** *f.* axe
***haïr** to hate
Haïti *f.* Haiti
hallucination *f.* hallucination
***hangar** *m.* shed
***happer** to nab, to snap up
***hardi** *m.,* **hardie** *f.* bold, daring, impudent
***hardiment** boldly, impudently

***haricot** *m.* bean; — **vert** string bean
***hâter** to hasten, to hurry up; **se — (de)** to hurry (*to*)
***haut** high, tall; **en** — upstairs; **de — en bas** from top to bottom; **à haute voix** aloud
***hauteur** *f.* height
hélas! alas
herbe *f.* grass
hériter to inherit
***héros** *m.* hero
heure *f.* hour; **à l'—** on time. **A la bonne — !** Well and good! Fine! **de bonne —** early; **tout à l'—** presently, in a little while; a little while ago, just now (*with a past tense*). **A tout à l'— !** I'll be seeing you! So long!
heureusement happily, fortunately
heureux *m.,* **heureuse** *f.* happy
***heurter** to bump, to run against, to knock; **se — contre** to bump into
***hibou** *m.* owl
hier yesterday; **avant- —** day before yesterday; **— soir** last night, last evening
histoire *f.* story, history
hiver *m.* winter
homme *m.* man; **— de bien** gentleman
honnête honest
honneur *m.* honor
***honni** dishonored, disgraced. **Honni** (*or* **Honi**) **soit qui mal y pense.** Evil be to him who evil thinks.
honorer to honor
***honte** *f.* shame; **avoir — (de)** to be ashamed (*of*)
hôtel *m.* hotel
***housard** *m.* hussar
***hublot** *m.* small porthole
***huit** eight; **— jours** a week
***huitaine** *f.* about eight, eight days
humain human
humaniste humanistic
humanité *f.* humanity, mankind; **cours d'Humanités** Humanities Course
hypocrisie *f.* hypocrisy

I

ici here
idée *f.* idea, notion
ignorer not to know, to be unaware of
ignorance *f.* ignorance
ignorant ignorant
il *impers.* there; **— y a** there is, there are. **Qu'y a-t-il pour votre service?** What will you have?
île *f.* island; **— des tropiques** tropical island
illettré illiterate
image *f.* image, picture
immense immense, huge, mighty
impatienter to make impatient; **s'—** to lose one's patience, to fret
important important
importer to concern, to matter, to import; **N'importe!** No matter! It doesn't matter! **n'importe où** anywhere; **n'importe qui** anyone; **n'importe quoi** anything; **n'importe quel livre** any book
impression *f.* impression
impuissant powerless, impotent
inaperçu unperceived
incapable incapable
incendie *m.* fire
incendier to burn down, to set fire to
incident *m.* incident, event, occurrence

inconnu unknown, strange
inconnu *m.*, **inconnue** *f.* stranger, unknown person
inconvénient *m.* inconvenience, disadvantage
indéfini indefinite
indépendant independent
index *m.* forefinger, index (*of a book*)
indifférent indifferent, unconcerned
indigner to anger, to make angry; **s'—** to be indignant, to become angry
indiquer to indicate, to point out, to show
individu *m.* individual
industriel *m.* manufacturer
infiniment infinitely, endlessly
infirmière *f.* nurse
influence *f.* influence
ingénieur *m.* engineer
injurieux *m.*, **injurieuse** *f.* abusive, insulting, swearing
innocence *f.* innocence
inouï unheard of, extraordinary
inscrire to inscribe, to register; **s'—** to enroll, to register, to enter one's name
instant *m.* instant; **à l'—** instantly, immediately
instinct *m.* instinct
instinctif instinctive
instituteur -trice *m.* and *f.* teacher
insu: à l'— (de) unknown to; **à mon —** unknown to me
insulter to insult, to abuse
intelligent intelligent, shrewd, sharp
intention *f.* intention, purpose; **avoir l'— de** to intend to
interdire to prohibit
intéressant interesting
intéresser to interest; **s'— à** to be interested in, to take an interest in
intérêt *m.* interest, concern
interroger to question closely, to examine, to interrogate
introduire to show in, to bring in
invitation *f.* invitation
inviter (à) to invite (*to*), to ask (*to*)
invité *m.*, **invitée** *f.* guest
ironique ironical
irriter to irritate, to anger
Italie *f.* Italy
italien *m.*, **italienne** *f.* Italian
ivrogne *m.* drunkard
ivrogne *adj.* tipsy

J

jaloux *m.*, **jalouse** *f.* jealous
jamais ever, never; **ne . . . jamais** never
jambe *f.* leg
janvier *m.* January
Japon *m.* Japan
japonais Japanese
jaune yellow
jardin *m.* garden
jeter to throw; **— un coup d'œil (sur, à)** to glance (*at*)
jeudi *m.* Thursday
jeune young
jeunesse *f.* youth
joindre to join
joli pretty
jouer to play; **— à** to play a game; **— de** to play an instrument
jouir de to enjoy
joujou *m.* toy
jour *m.* a day as a unit of time; **de nos —s** at present, nowadays; **ce jour-là** on that day; **huit —s** a week
journal *m.* newspaper
journée *f.* a day as a unit of accomplishment; *e.g.*, a day's work
joyau *m.* jewel

joyeux *m.*, **joyeuse** *f.* joyful, merry
juillet *m.* July
juin *m.* June
jupe *f.* skirt
jurer to swear
jusque till, until; **jusqu'à** up to, until; **jusqu'à ce que** until
juste just, equitable; **au —** exactly, precisely
justement precisely, exactly, in fact. **Voilà — !** That's just it!
justice *f.* justice, probity, courts of justice

K

kilogramme, kilo *m.* kilogram (*about 2 1/5 pounds*)
kilomètre *m.* kilometer (*about 3/5 of a mile*)

L

la the, her, it
là there, yonder
là-bas over there
là-dedans within, in there, in it (them), inside
là-dessous under there
là-dessus thereupon, on that, above
labourer to plow, to till
laboureur *m.* farmer
laisser to leave, to let, to allow, to permit, to leave behind
lait *m.* milk
laitier *m.* milkman
lancer to throw
langue *f.* tongue, language
large broad, wide, ample; **bien — comme la main** no wider than one's hand
larme *f.* tear
lavandière *f.* laundress, washerwoman
laver to wash; **se —** to wash one's self
le the, him, it
leçon *f.* lesson
lecture *f.* reading
léger *m.*, **légère** *f.* light, giddy
légume *m.* vegetable
lendemain *m.* the following day
lenteur *f.* slowness, tardiness
les the, them
lestement briskly, freely
lettre *f.* letter
lever to raise; **se —** to get up
lèvre *f.* lip
liaison *f.* linking (*of a final consonant*)
libération *f.* liberation
liberté *f.* liberty
libre free; **d'un pas —** with a light step
licol *or* **licou** *m.* halter
lieu *m.* place, spot; **avoir —** to take place; **au — de** in the place of, instead of, in lieu of
lieutenant *m.* lieutenant
lièvre *m.* hare
linguistique linguistic
lion *m.* lion
lire to read
lit *m.* bed
litre *m.* liter (*1.057 quart*)
littérature *f.* literature
livide livid
livre *m.* book
livre *f.* pound
locomotive *f.* locomotive, a railroad engine
locution *f.* phrase, expression
loin far; **au —** far away, in the distance; **de —** from a distance
long *m.*, **longue** *f.* long; **à la longue** in the long run
longtemps a long while, a long time; **plus —** longer
lors de at the time of
lorsque when (*Not used for asking a question.*)
louer to praise; to rent, to hire

Louisiane *f.* Louisiana
loup *m.* wolf
loyal loyal
lumière *f.* light
lundi *m.* Monday
lune *f.* moon; — **de miel** honeymoon
lunettes *f. pl.* spectacles
lutter to struggle, to wrestle
luxe *m.* luxury; **articles de —** luxury items

M

machine *f.* machine; **taper à la —** to type
maçon *m.* mason
mademoiselle *f.* miss
magasin *m.* a store, a shop, a warehouse
magnifique magnificent, splendid, fine
mai *m.* May
maigrir to grow thin, to become lean
main *f.* hand; **à la —** in my (your, his, *etc.*) hand; **en venir aux —s** to resort to fighting
maintenant now
maintenir to maintain
mais but
maïs *m.* corn
maison *f.* house
maître *m.* master, teacher
mal *adv.* badly, wrongly
mal *m.* (*pl.* **maux**) evil, ill; **avoir — à la tête** to have a headache; **se faire —** to hurt one's self; **pas —** not badly; **— à son aise** uncomfortable, ill at ease; **tant bien que —** rather poorly, somehow
malade ill, sick
maladie *f.* illness, disease
malgré in spite of; **— que** in spite of
malheur *m.* misfortune
malheureusement unfortunately
malheureux *m.*, **malheureuse** *f.* unhappy
malle *f.* trunk; **faire sa —** to pack one's trunk
manger to eat
manie *f.* mania, folly
manière *f.* manner, fashion, way
manifestation *f.* manifestation
manquer to fail, to be lacking, to miss (*Cf. idioms*, page 161.)
manteau *m.* cloak, cape
manufacturer to manufacture
manuscrit *m.* manuscript
se maquiller to apply one's "make-up"
marché *m.* market; **bon (meilleur) —** cheap (cheaper)
marche: se mettre en — to start
marcher to walk, to march. **Ça marche bien.** Everything is progressing nicely.
mardi *m.* Tuesday
marguerite *f.* daisy
mari *m.* husband
mariage *m.* marriage
marier to marry off, to give in marriage; **se — (avec)** to marry, to get married
mars *m.* March; **Mars** Mars
match *m.* match (game)
matelas *m.* mattress
matelot *m.* sailor
maternel maternal, motherly
matin *m.* morning
maudire to curse
maure *m.* Moor
maussade sulky, sullen, bad-tempered
mauvais bad
mécanicien *m.* mechanic
méchant mean, naughty, wicked
méconnaître to be unable to recognize, to overlook

mécontent dissatisfied, displeased
médecin *m.* a doctor, a physician
médiocre mediocre, ordinary
médire (de) to slander
méditer to meditate, to plan
méfiant distrustful, suspicious
méfier: se — de to mistrust, to distrust
meilleur better; **le —, la —e** the best
mêler to mingle, to mix; **se — (de)** to meddle (*with*), to become involved (*in*)
même same, even, very; **quand —** just the same (even though); **tout de —** just the same
menacer to threaten
ménage housekeeping; **en —** in married life
ménagère *f.* housewife, housekeeper
mener to lead, to conduct, to take (*to*)
menteur *m.* liar
mentir to lie, to tell a lie; **— comme quatre** to lie like a thief
menton *m.* chin
méprendre: se — (à) to be mistaken, to make a mistake (*about*)
mépris *m.* contempt, scorn
merci *m.* thanks, (I) thank you
mercredi *m.* Wednesday
mère *f.* mother
mériter to merit
merle *m.* blackbird
merveille *f.* wonder, marvel; **à —** wonderfully, marvelously (well)
messieurs *m. pl.* gentlemen, *Messrs. s.,* monsieur
mesure *f.* a measure, a step (procedure), a standard; **à — que** in proportion as, as, accordingly as; **au fur et à — que** in proportion as, gradually as
métier *m.* trade, occupation, calling
mètre *m.* meter (*39.37 inches*)
mettre to put, to put on; **— au courant** to inform; **— le feu à** to set fire to; **se — à** + *Inf.* to begin to; **se — en route** to set out; **se — à table** to sit down at the table; **— un frein à** to curb, to check, to halt; **se — en marche** to start; **— à l'heure** to set (*a watch*)
meunier *m.* miller
mexicain *m.* Mexican
Mexique *m.* Mexico
midi *m.* noon; south
miel *m.* honey; **la lune de —** the honeymoon
mieux *adv.* better; **tant —** so much the better; **valoir —** to be better; **profiter au —** to profit fully
mignon *m.,* **mignonne** *f.* delicate, pretty, neat, dainty
milieu *m.,* middle, environment; **au — de** in the midst of
militaire *m.* soldier
mille *m.* mile **(1.6 kilomètres)**
mille thousand (spelled **mil** when used with dates.)
milliard *m.* billion
million *m.* million
mince thin, slender
mine *f.* appearance; **avoir bonne —** to look well
ministre *m.* minister, cabinet minister, secretary
minuit *m.* midnight
minute *f.* minute
mise: bien — well dressed, in style
misère *f.* misery, distress, poverty, wretchedness
mission *f.* mission
mobilier *m.* furniture

mode *f.* mode, way, fashion; **être à la —** to be in fashion
moderne modern
modeste modest, unassuming, unpretentious
modiste *m.* or *f.* milliner
moindre *adj.* less; **le —** least
moins *adj.* less; **à — que** + *Subj.* unless; **à — de** + *Inf.* unless; **au —** at least (*quantity*); **du —** at least (*concession*)
mois *m.* month; **ces — derniers** in recent months
moitié *f.* half
moment *m.* moment, instant
monde *m.* world; **tout le —** everybody
mondial world-wide
monsieur *m.*, gentleman, sir, *Mr.*; *pl.* **messieurs** gentlemen
monstre *m.* monster
montagnard *m.* a mountaineer, a hillbilly
montagne *f.* mountain
monter to climb, to go up, to get in, to carry up; **— en voiture** to get in (aboard) a carriage or train
montre *f.* watch
montrer to show; **se —** to appear
moquer: se — (de) to mock, to make fun of, to make a fool of
moquerie *f.* mockery, scoffing; *pl.* jeers
moral moral
morale *f.* ethics, morality
morceau *m.* piece, bit, morsel
mordre to bite
mort *f.* death; **la — dans l'âme** in despair, disconsolate; *m.* the dead man
mot *m.* word
mou, mol, *m.*, **molle** *f.* soft
mouche *f.* a fly, a beauty patch, a beauty spot
mourir to die. **J'en meurs d'envie!** I'm just dying to! **se —** to be dying
moutardier *m.* a mustard-maker, a mustard pot
mouton *m.* sheep
mouvement *m.* motion, movement, impulse
mouvoir to move
moyen *m.* means, medium
muet *m.*, **muette** *f.* dumb, mute, silent
mule *f.* a she-mule, a slipper
mur *m.* wall
murmure *m.* whisper
musée *m.* museum
musicien *m.* musician
musique *f.* music
mutiler to mutilate
mutuellement mutually
mystère *m.* mystery

N

nager to swim
naguère lately, not long ago (*or* since)
naïf *m.*, **naïve** *f.* simple, unsophisticated
naître to be born
narrateur *m.* narrator, speaker
nation *f.* nation
nature *f.* nature
naturellement naturally
navrer to distress, to break the heart of
ne: for the uses of **ne** cf. §8, §19, §39, §87, and §88. **ne . . . ni . . . ni** neither . . . nor
nécessaire necessary
nécessité *f.* necessity, need
neige *f.* snow
neiger to snow
nettoyer to clean, to wipe clean
neuf *m.*, **neuve** *f.* new, brand new. **Quoi de neuf?** What's new? What do you know?
neuf nine

neveu *m.* nephew
nez *m.* nose
ni neither, nor; **ne . . . ni . . . ni** neither . . . nor; **ni moi non plus** nor I either
nièce *f.* niece
nier to deny
Noël *m.* or *f.* Christmas
noir black
Noiraud Blacky
nom *m.* name
nombreux *m.*, **nombreuse** *f.* numerous
nommer to name, to appoint
non no
nord *m.* north
normand *m.* Norman
note *f.* note, grade, mark
nourriture *f.* nourishment, food
nouveau, nouvel, *m.*, **nouvelle** *f.* new; **de nouveau** again. **Qu'y a-t-il de nouveau?** What's new? What do you know?
nouvelle *f.* a piece of news, tidings, a short story
novembre *m.* November
nuage *m.* cloud
nuit *f.* night; **cette —** tonight
nul no, no one; **nulle part** nowhere
nullement not at all, by no means
nu-pieds barefoot

O

obéir (à) to obey
objet *m.* object, thing, article
obliger (à, de) to oblige, to compel, to force
s'obscurcir to become dark
obtenir to obtain
observation *f.* observation, comment
obus *m.* shell
occasion *f.* opportunity, occasion
occuper to occupy
s'occuper (de) to look after, to busy (concern) one's self with, to attend to
octobre *m.* October
œil (*pl.* **yeux**) *m.* eye; **jeter un coup d'— (sur, à)** to glance (at)
œil-de-bœuf *m.* a round window
œuf *m.* egg
offre *f.* offer, proposal
offrir to offer, to buy, to present
oignon *m.* onion
oiseau *m.* bird
ombre *f.* shadow
omelette *f.* omelet
omettre to omit
oncle *m.* uncle
onde *f.* wave; *fig.* stream, pool of water
onze eleven
opinion *f.* opinion
opposer to oppose; **— un refus catégorique** to refuse absolutely (the request)
or *conj.* now, well
or *m.* gold
orateur *m.* orator, speaker; **— ambulant** itinerant orator
ordinaire ordinary, customary, usual; **d'—** usually
ordonner (de) to order, to command (to)
oreille *f.* ear
original original, eccentric
orphelin *m.* orphan
oser to dare, to venture
ôter to take off, to remove
ou or; **ou . . . ou** either . . . or; **ou bien** or else
où where
oublier (de) to forget (to)
oui yes; **mais —** yes indeed
outil *m.* tool, implement
outrage *m.* outrage, gross insult
outrager to outrage, to offend
outrance *f.* extreme, excess; **à —** to the death

outre: en — in addition, besides
ouvert opened
ouvrir to open

P

page *f.* page; **à la — cinq** on page five
paille *f.* straw
pain *m.* bread
paisible peaceful, quiet
paître to graze, to feed
paix *f.* peace
palais *m.* palace
panier *m.* basket
panne *f.* engine trouble; **avoir une —** to have engine trouble *or* a breakdown
pantoufle *f.* slipper
papa *m.* papa, daddy
pape *m.* Pope
papier *m.* paper
paquebot *m.* steamer
paquet *m.* package
par by, through, per
paraître to appear
parapluie *m.* umbrella
parce que because
parcourir to travel over, to go through, to run through, to glance through
pardessus *m.* overcoat
pardonner (à) to pardon, to forgive
pareil like, similar, such
parent *m.* kinsman, relative; *pl.* relatives, parents
paresseux -euse lazy
parfait perfect, complete, great
parfait *m.* (*gram.*) perfect tense
parler to speak; **entendre — (de)** to hear (of)
parole *f.* word, promise, speech; **en vos propres —s** in your own words
part *f.* share, part, side; **à —** aside; **d'autre —** on the other hand; **de la — de** in behalf of. **Je viens de la — de M. Amiel.** I (represent) have come in behalf of M. Amiel. **d'une —** on the one hand; **nulle —** nowhere; **quelque —** somewhere
partager to share
parti *m.* party, side; **prendre son —** to make up one's mind
particulier special, private
partir (de) to leave, to depart, to set out
partout everywhere
parvenir to attain, to reach
pas no, not; **ne . . . pas** not, no. **N'est-ce — ?** Isn't it? Shall we not? *etc.* **— du tout** not at all
pas *m.* step, footstep; **d'un — libre** with a lively step
passage *m.* passage, path; **s'ouvrir un —** to make or cut one's way through
passager -ère temporary
passant *m.* passer-by, pedestrian
passé défini *m.* past definite
passer (à) to pass or spend time; **se —** to happen; **se — de** to do without; **— à l'étranger** to go abroad; to betray
passion *f.* passion
pasteur *m.* pastor; shepherd
pâtée *f.* dog food, paste for fattening poultry; **assiette à —** a dish for dog food
patiner to skate
patrie *f.* native country, fatherland
patron *m.* boss
pauvre poor
pauvreté *f.* poverty, destitution
payer to pay (*for*)
pays *m.* country, region, district
paysage *m.* landscape
pêche *f.* a peach; fishing, angling; **aller à la —** to go fishing

peigner to comb; **se —** to comb one's hair
peindre to paint
peine *f.* pain, grief; **à —** hardly, scarcely. **Ce n'est pas la — !** Don't mention it! It isn't worth while!
peintre *m.* painter
peinture *f.* painting
pencher to lean, to bend, to incline
pendant during, for; **— que** while
pendre to hang
pénétrant penetrating
pénétrer to penetrate, to go through
pénible painful, hard, troublesome
péniblement painfully
pensée *f.* thought, opinion; pansy
penser to think; to intend, to plan; **— de** to have an opinion of; **— à** to think of *or* about, *i.e.,* to turn one's thoughts toward
pension *f.* boarding house
perdre to lose, to ruin; **— de vue** to lose sight of
père *m.* father
perfectionner to perfect, to improve
perfide perfidious, treacherous
péril *m.* danger, peril
périr to perish
perlé *adj.* pearled; **rire —** musical or tinkling laughter
permettre (de) to permit (to)
personne *m. pron., used with or without* **ne,** anybody, nobody; **ne . . . personne** not anyone, no one, nobody
personne *f.* person; *pl.* people
persuader to persuade, to convince
perte *f.* loss; **à — de vue** as far as the eye can reach
pessimiste *m.* pessimist
petit small
petit-fils *m.* grandson
peu little, few, not very; **— à —** little by little; **— de** little, not much; **— élégant** inelegant, not very refined; **(le) un —** a little, the few; **à — près** almost, about, nearly so, so-so
peur *f.* fear; **de — de** for fear of; **de — que** for fear that, lest; **avoir —** to be afraid
peut-être perhaps, maybe
pharmacie *f.* drug store
philosophie *f.* philosophy
photo *f.* photo
photographe *m.* photographer
phrase *f.* sentence
pièce *f.* play; room; piece; coin; each; apiece
pied *m.* foot; **à —** afoot; **au petit —** on a small scale, small fry; **aller à —** to walk
piéton *m.* pedestrian
pieusement piously
pipe *f.* pipe, a tobacco pipe; **fumer la —** to smoke a pipe
pire *adj.* worse
pis *adv.* worse; **tant —** so much the worse
pistolet *m.* pistol
pitié *f.* pity
place *f.* square, seat, position, job
placer to place, to get a job for
plafond *m.* ceiling
plaindre to pity; **se — (de)** to complain about
plaire (à) to please; **s'il vous plaît** please. **A Dieu ne plaise!** God forbid! **Plût à Dieu!** Would to God (Heaven)!
plaisir: Au —! It's been a pleasure! Good-by!
plancher *m.* floor
plein full; **en — air** in the open air

pleurer to weep
pleuvoir to rain; — **à verse** to rain in torrents (to rain cats and dogs)
plombier *m.* plumber
pluie *f.* rain
plume *f.* feather, pen
plupart: la — de most
plus more; **de — en —** more and more; **ni moi non —** nor I either; **— tôt** sooner; **d'autant — que** all the more as, because
plusieurs several; **à — reprises** on several occasions, repeatedly
plutôt rather
pneu (*pl.* **-s**) *m.* tire
poche *f.* pocket
poème *m.* poem
poète *m.* poet
poignée *f.* handful
point no, not, not at all; **ne . . . point (de)** not any, no
point *m.* point, period; **au — de vue** from the standpoint of
pois *m.* pea; **petits —** green peas
poisson *m.* fish
poitrine *f.* chest, breast
poli polite
police *f.* police
policier *m.* policeman
politesse *f.* politeness
politique political
politique *m.* politician
politique *f.* policy, politics
Polonais *m.* Polish
pomme *f.* apple; **— de terre** potato
pompier *f.* fireman
porc *m.* pork
pont *m.* bridge
port *m.* port; **— d'entrée** port of entry
porte *f.* door; **— d'entrée** entrance door
portée *f.* reach, import; **à — de** within reach (range) of
portefeuille *m.* pocketbook, portfolio
porter to carry, to wear; **se —** to be (when speaking of one's health)
porteur *m.* porter
Portugal *m.* Portugal
portugais Portuguese
poser to place; to ask (*a question*)
posséder to possess, to own
possession *f.* possession
possible possible. **Pas — !** That's impossible!
poste *m.* position, employment; **— de T.S.F.** radio set, wireless
poste *f.* post office; **— restante** general delivery
potentiel potential
pou *m.* flea
poudre *f.* powder, dust
poule *f.* hen
poupée *f.* doll
pour for; + *Inf.* in order to; **— que** in order that, so that
pourquoi why
poursuivre to pursue, to prosecute
pourtant however
pourvoir to provide, to supply with, to see to, to attend to
pourvu que provided that
pousser to push, to grow; **— un cri** to utter a cry
pouvoir to be able, can; **cela se peut** that is possible; **il se peut que . . .** it is possible (likely) that . . . **Il n'en peut plus.** He's all in (exhausted). **Nous n'y pouvons rien.** We can do nothing about it.
pouvoir *m.* power
pratique practical
pratique *f.* practice, dealing
pratiquer to practice; **— le sport** to engage in sports
précédent preceding, former

précéder to precede, to go before
précis precise, exact; **neuf heures —es** exactly nine o'clock
prédire to predict, to foretell
préférer to prefer, to like better
préjudiciable prejudicial, detrimental
premier first
prendre to take; **— garde (à)** to be careful to (of); **— garde (de)** + *Inf.* to watch out (for), to be careful not to; **— en grippe** to take a dislike to; **— la parole** to take the floor; **— un parti** to come to a decision; **de parti pris** deliberately; **s'en — (à)** to blame; **se — (à)** to begin (to); **— la fuite** to run away. **Il s'y prend avec soin.** He goes about it carefully.
préoccuper to engage, to preoccupy the mind
préparer to prepare
près near; **— de** near, close to; **à peu —** about, nearly so, so-so; **de —** closely
présence *f.* presence
présent present; **à —** at present, now
présenter (à) to introduce, to present; **se —** to present one's self, to appear
presque almost, nearly
pressant pressing, urging
pressentir to have a presentiment of, to anticipate
presser to press, to squeeze, to hurry; **être pressé** to be in a hurry
prestige *m.* prestige
prêt (à) ready, willing (*to*)
prétendre to claim (*to*), to assert, to intend
prêter to lend; **— l'oreille** to listen attentively
prêteur *m.* lender
prêtre *m.* priest
prévaloir to prevail
prévenir to anticipate, to warn, to inform, to forestall
prévoir to foresee, to anticipate
prier (de) to beg, to request (*to*)
prière *f.* prayer, request; **— de faire suivre** please forward
principal principal
printemps *m.* spring; **au —** in the spring
prisonnier *m.* prisoner
prix *m.* price, prize; **à tout —** at any cost; **à vil —** dirt cheap
problème *m.* problem
prochain next
produire to produce
professeur *m.* professor, teacher
profiter to profit; **— au mieux** to profit fully
profond deep, profound
profondément deeply, profoundly
progrès *m.* progress; **faire des —** to improve, to make progress
projet *m.* project, plan
projeter to plan
promenade *f.* walk, stroll; **faire une — en auto** to take an automobile ride
promener to take out for a walk; **se —** to stroll, to go for (take) a walk (ride, *etc.*)
promesse *f.* promise
promettre (de) to promise (*to*)
prompt prompt
prononcer to pronounce, to declare, to say; **— un discours** to make a speech
prononciation *f.* pronunciation
prophète *m.* prophet
propos *m.* remark; **à —** by the way, opportunely; **à — de** concerning, about
proposer to propose, to offer, to suggest
propre own, clean

propriétaire *m.* or *f.* owner
propriété *f.* property
protester to protest
prouver to prove, to show
proverbe *m.* proverb
provision *f.* store, stock, supply, food; *pl.* provisions
prudemment prudently, cautiously, warily
prudent prudent
public *m.* public; **grand —** general public
puis then, afterward (*indicates what happens next*)
punir to punish
pur pure

Q

qualité *f.* quality; **—s requises** qualifications
quand when; **— même** just the same (even if)
quant à as to, as for, with regard to
quarante forty
quart *m.* quarter
quartier *m.* section, a district of a town
quatorze fourteen
quatre four
quatre-vingts eighty
quatre-vingt-dix ninety
que *conj.* and *adv.* that, which, whom, so that, when, than (*often not translated*); **ne . . . que** only, but, except
quelconque (just) any, any whatsoever
quelque some; *pl.* a few
quelque however, whatever
quelque chose *m.* something
quelquefois sometimes
quelque part somewhere
quelqu'un(e) somebody, someone
question *f.* question; **poser (faire) une —** to ask a question
quille *f.* a ninepin, a skittle
quintuplettes *f.* quintuplets
quinze fifteen
quitter to leave, to quit
quoi what; **avoir de — vivre** to have something (the means) to live on. **A — bon?** What's the use? **Il n'y a pas de — .** You are welcome. **— de neuf?** What's new? **de —** (sufficient) means
quoique although, though

R

rabais *m.* reduction, discount, rebate
raconter to tell, to relate
raisin *m.* grape; **des —s secs** raisins
raison *f.* reason; **avoir —** to be right
rajeunir to make (to grow) young
râler to groan (as when dying)
ramasser to pick up
rancunier rancorous, spiteful, vindictive
rangé steady, reliable
ranger to arrange, to set in order, to draw up (around); **se —** to take one's stand, to draw up
rappeler to recall; **se —** to remember; **— au bon souvenir de** to remember (someone) to (somebody)
rapporter to bring (carry) back, to bring in, to report; **s'en — à** to leave it up to (anyone)
rare rare, uncommon, scarce, unusual
rarement rarely, seldom
raser to shave, to skim over, to touch lightly
rasoir *m.* razor
rasseoir to seat again; **se —** to sit down again

râteau *m.* rake
ravine *f.* ravine, gully
ravir to delight, to carry off; **à —** wonderfully, admirably
récemment recently
réception *f.* reception, party
recevoir to receive; to see (people); to invite
recherche *f.* search, quest; **à la — de** in search (quest) of; **à sa —** in search (quest) of him (her, it)
récolte *f.* harvest
reconduire to show out again
réconfortant comforting, strengthening
reconnaissant grateful
reconnaître to recognize
récrire to rewrite
recueil *m.* collection, volume
recueillir to gather, to collect
reculer to draw (go, fall) back, to retreat, to postpone; **à reculons** backward
redire to repeat, to say again
réduire to reduce, to oblige
refaire to do again, to recommence, to go over again
réfléchir to reflect
réfugié *m.* refugee
refus *m.* refusal, denial
refuser (de) to refuse, to deny (*to*)
regarder to look, to look at, to regard (concern); **— de près** to look at closely; **— par** to look out (through). **Cela ne nous regarde pas.** That doesn't concern us.
règle *f.* rule, ruler
regretter (de) to regret, to be sorry, to miss
reine *f.* queen
rejeter to throw back, to reject, to put out
rejoindre to rejoin, to meet again, to catch up with
religieux *m.*, **religieuse** *f.* religious
relire to reread
remarquer to note, to observe, to notice
se rembrunir to get *or* grow dark, to become sad
remède *m.* remedy
remercier to thank
remettre to put back, to postpone, to hand in; **se — (de)** to recover (*from*)
remonter to go up again, to wind a watch, to go (travel) up
remplaçant *m.* substitute
remplacer to replace, to serve as a substitute
remplir (de) to fill (*with*)
renaître to be born again, to revive
rencontre *f.* meeting; **aller** *or* **venir à la — de quelqu'un** to go *or* come to meet someone. **Je vais à sa (leur) — .** I go to meet him, her (them).
rencontrer to meet by accident
rendre to give back, to return; to make, to render; **— compte de** to account for; **se —** to surrender; **se — à** to go to; **se — compte de** to realize
renouveler to renew, to replenish
rentier *m.* person of property
rentrer to return home; **— en possession** to regain possession
renverser to upset, to overthrow
renvoyer to send again, to send away, to dismiss
répandre to spread, to scatter, to spill
reparler (de) to speak again (*of*)
repas *m.* meal
repasser to iron
se repentir (de) to repent (*of*)
répéter to repeat

répondre (à) to answer; **— de** to answer for
réponse *f.* answer
repos *m.* rest, tranquillity
repousser to repel, to push back, to grow again
reprendre to resume, to take back, to go on (*with*), to begin again; **se —** to correct one's self
reprise *f.* resumption, revival; **à plusieurs —s** on several occasions
reproche *m.* reproach
reproduire to reproduce
républicain(e) *n.* and *adj.* republican
république *f.* republic
réputation *f.* reputation, name, fame
ressembler (à) to resemble, to look like
restaurant *m.* restaurant
reste *m.* remainder, remnant, rest; **au —** besides, moreover; **du —** besides, moreover
rester (à) to stay, to remain, to be left (*to*)
résumé *m.* summary
retard *m.* delay; **être en —** to be late
retarder to delay; to be slow (*watch*)
retenir to retain, to keep, to hold on to
retour *m.* return; **être de —** to be back, to have returned
retourner to return; **se —** to turn round
réunir to join again, to unite, to meet
réussir (à) to succeed (*in*), to accomplish, to carry through, to pass an examination
révéler to reveal, to disclose
revenir to return, to come back
rêve *m.* dream
rêver to dream
révérence *f.* reverence, bow, curtsy
revivre to revive, to come to life again
revoir to see again; **au —** good-bye, till we meet again
revue *f.* review, magazine
Rhin *m.* Rhine
rhum *m.* rum
rhumatisme *m.* rheumatism
rhume *m.* cold; **attraper un —** to catch a cold; **avoir un —** to have a cold
riche rich
rien nothing, not anything; **en —** in any way; **ne . . . rien** not anything, nothing. **Ce n'est — !** You are welcome. Forget it!
rire to laugh; **se — de** to laugh at, to make sport of. **Rira bien qui rira le dernier.** He who laughs last laughs best.
rire *m.* laughter; **— perlé** tinkling *or* musical laughter
risque *m.* risk, peril
rive *f.* shore, bank of a stream
rivière *f.* river (*not flowing into the sea*)
robe *f.* dress
robuste robust, hardy
roi *m.* king
roman *m.* novel
romancier *m.* novelist
rompre to break
rond round
rose *f.* rose
rose *adj.* pink
rosée *f.* dew
roucoulement *m.* cooing
rouge red
rouge-gorge *m.* robin redbreast
rougeur *f.* redness, glow
rougir to blush, to turn red

rouler to roll
route *f.* road, direction; **être en —** to be on the way; **se mettre en —** to set out
rue *f.* street
ruine *f.* ruin, desolation; **tomber en —s** to fall in ruins, to decay, to crumble
rusé sly, resourceful
russe *m.* or *f.* Russian
Russie *f.* Russia

S

sacrifice *m.* sacrifice
sacrifier to sacrifice
sage wise, good, prudent; **un —** a wise man. **Soyez — .** Be good (well-balanced).
sagesse *f.* wisdom
sain sound, wholesome
saisir to seize, to catch
saison *f.* season
salle *f.* room; **— de classe** classroom; **— à manger** dining room
salon *m.* drawing room, reception room
saluer to greet, to bow (*to*)
samedi *m.* Saturday
sang *m.* blood; **se faire du mauvais —** to fret, to worry
sanglant bleeding
sans without; **— que** without
satisfaire (à) to satisfy, to please, to comply (*with*)
satisfait satisfied, pleased
sauce *f.* sauce
saule *m.* willow
sauvage savage, wild
sauver to rescue; **se —** to escape, to run away
savant *m.* scholar, learned person, savant
savoir to know (*when referring to things*), to know how to; to find out, to learn, to discover (*with Perf. and Past Def.*), **Je ne sais que faire.** I don't know what to do. **faire —** to inform; **en — gré à quelqu'un** to be grateful to some one for. **Pas que je sache.** Not that I know of. **un je ne sais quoi** an indescribable something
savoir-faire *m.* tact, ability, skill
savon *m.* soap
scabreux *m.*, **scabreuse** *f.* rough, scabrous, questionable
scélérat *m.* scoundrel
science *f.* knowledge, science
scientifique scientific
seau *m.* bucket
sec *m.*, **sèche** *f.* dry
sèchement dryly, sharply, curtly
second -e second
seconde *f.* second (*time*)
seconder to second, support
secours *m.* aid, relief, succor
secrétaire *m.* secretary
secret *m.* **secrète** *f.* secret
séduire to seduce, to charm, to fascinate
seigneur *m.* lord, nobleman; **le Seigneur** the Lord (God)
seize sixteen
séjour *m.* stay, sojourn
selle *f.* saddle
semaine *f.* week
semblant: faire — de to pretend to
sembler to seem
semestre *m.* semester, half a year
sens *m.* sense, meaning, understanding; **bon —** good sense
sentiment *m.* feeling, emotion
sentir to feel, to smell (*of*); **se —** to feel (well, ill, *etc., i.e.,* something within one's self). **Il se sent bien.** He feels well. **— bon** to smell good
sept seven
septembre September

série *f.* series
sérieux *m.,* **sérieuse** *f.* serious
serpent *m.* snake
serrer to lock, to clasp, to squeeze, to press (together); **— la main** to shake hands
service *m.* service, duty, favor; **à votre —** you are welcome
servir to serve, to aid, to be of use; **se — de** to use, to make use of; **— de** to serve as; **— à** to be used for (to)
seuil *m.* threshold
seul alone, single; **tout —** all alone
seulement only; **non seulement . . . mais encore** not only . . . but also
sexe *m.* sex
si if, whether
si so; yes (*in answer to a question put in the negative*)
siècle *m.* century
sifflet *m.* whistle
signification *f.* meaning
simple simple, plain
sincérité *f.* sincerity
sirène *f.* mermaid, siren
situation *f.* situation, state
six six
sixième sixth
socialiste *m., f. adj.* and *n.* socialist
société *f.* society
sœur *f.* sister
soi *pron.* one's self, self, itself
soi-disant so-called, self-styled
soi-même one's self, itself
soie *f.* silk
soif *f.* thirst; **avoir —** to be thirsty
soigner to take care of
soin *m.* care; **avoir — de** to take care of, to look after
soir *m.* evening; **le (au) —** in the evening; **hier —** last night
Soit! Well and good! Granted! Fine! O.K.!
soit . . . soit whether (either) . . . or; **soit que . . . soit que** *or* **ou que** (*followed by Subj.*) whether . . . or
soixante sixty
soixante-dix seventy
sol *m.* soil
soldat *m.* soldier
soleil *m.* sun. **Il fait du — .** The sun is shining. It is sunny.
solitaire alone
sombre dark, somber
somme *m.* nap; **faire un petit —** to take a little nap
somme *f.* sum, amount; **en —** finally, in short; **— toute** finally, in short
sommeil *m.* sleep; **avoir —** to be sleepy
songer (à) to dream, to think of
sorte *f.* sort, kind; **de la —** in this manner, in that way, so
sortir (de) to go out (*intrans.*), to take out (*trans.*)
sou *m.* sou, cent; **n'avoir pas le —** to be without money, to be broke
soucier: se — (de) to be concerned, to be anxious, to worry about
soucoupe *f.* saucer; **— volante** flying saucer
soudain suddenly
souffrant suffering, ill; **être —** to be ill
souffrir to suffer, to bear, to endure
souhait *m.* wish, desire
souhaiter to wish, to desire, to long for
soulever to raise, to lift up
soulier *m.* shoe

soumettre to submit, to subdue, to subject
soupçonner to suspect
soupe *f.* soup
source *f.* source, spring
sourd deaf; **faire le —** to act (pretend to be) deaf
sourire *m.* smile
sourire to smile
souris *f.* mouse
sous under
soutenir to support, to uphold, to sustain
souvenir: se — (de) to remember, to recall
souvent often
souverain sovereign, supreme
spirituel -lle witty
sport *m.* sport
stupide stupid, dull
stylo *m.* fountain pen
subir to undergo, to put up with, to submit to
subitement suddenly
subsister to subsist
succès *m.* success; **peu de —** lack of success
sucre *m.* sugar
sud *m.* south
sueur *f.* perspiration, sweat
suffire (à, de, pour) to suffice, to be enough (*to, for*). **Cela suffit!** That will do! That's enough!
Suisse *f.* Switzerland
suite *f.* consequence, outcome, sequel; **tout de —** immediately; **de —** in succession
suivant following
suivre to follow; **— un cours** to take a course. **Prière de faire —.** Please forward (*this letter*).
sujet *m.* subject; **au — de** concerning, with regard to; **à mon —** about me
supprimer to suppress
sûr sure, certain
sur on, upon; **sur-le-champ** immediately
sûreté *f.* safety
surprendre to surprise; **— sur le fait** to catch in the act
surtout especially
surveillance *f.* supervision, surveillance
surveiller to supervise, to superintend
survivre to survive
syllabe *f.* syllable
symboliser to symbolize
sympathie *f.* sympathy
sympathique likeable, pleasant, sympathetic

T

tabac *m.* tobacco
table *f.* table
tableau *m.* picture; **— (noir)** blackboard
tablier *m.* apron
tâcher (de) to try, to endeavor
taille *f.* form, stature, build
taire to hush up something; **se —** to keep quiet, to cease speaking, to be quiet *or* to become quiet
talent *m.* talent, faculty, gift
tandis que while, whereas
tant so much, so many; **— bien que mal** rather poorly, somehow; **— mieux** so much the better; **— pis** so much the worse
tante *f.* aunt
tantôt soon, presently. **A — !** Good-by for the present! **tantôt . . . tantôt** sometimes . . . sometimes, now . . . now
taper: *see* **machine**
tapis *m.* carpet, rug
taquiner to tease, to torment

tard late. **Il se fait — .** It is getting late. **plus —** later; **tôt ou —** sooner or later
tarder (à) to delay, to be long (*in*); **— (de)** (*impersonal*) to long for, to be eager to. **Il me tarde de la voir.** I long to see her.
tasse *f.* cup
taxi *m.* taxi
tel such (a); **un — homme** such a man
tempe *f.* temple (A part of the forehead.)
tempérament *m.* temperament, constitution
temps *m.* time, season, weather; **de — à autre** from time to time; **de — en —** from time to time; **en même —** at the same time; **combien de — ?** how long?; **faire un — de chien** to be very bad weather
tenable tenable
tendre *adj.* tender, soft
tendre to stretch out, to hold out
tendrement tenderly
tenir to hold, to keep; **— à** + *Inf.* to be anxious to, to insist on; **— au courant** to keep informed; **s'en — à** to rely on, to stick to; **se —** to stand, to remain
tennis *m.* tennis
tenter to tempt; **— de** to attempt, to try (*to*)
terme *m.* term, limit
terrain *m.* ground, field
terre *f.* earth, land, ground; **par —** on the ground
terreur *f.* terror
terrible terrible, horrible
tête *f.* head
thé *m.* tea
théâtre *m.* theater
thème *m.* theme
thèse *f.* thesis
tiède warm, lukewarm, tepid
Tiens! Is that so! Well! Look here! There!
tiers *m.* third
tigre *m.* tiger
tirer to draw, to pull, to shoot; **se — d'affaire** to get along, to get out of something; **s'en —** to get out of it
tiroir *m.* table drawer
toit *m.* roof
tolérance *f.* tolerance, indulgence
tombeau *m.* tomb
tomber to fall; **— en ruines** to crumble; **— amoureux de** to fall in love with
tondre to shear
tonner to thunder
tordre to twist, to disfigure
tort wrong; **avoir —** to be wrong; **donner — à** to side against
tôt soon, shortly
toucher to touch, to move, to reach, to charm
toujours always, still
tour *f.* tower
tour *m.* tour, trip, trick, turn; **vilain —** mean trick; **faire le — de** to take a stroll through, to go around; **— à —** in turn
tourner to turn
tout (toute, tous, toutes) all, whole, every, quite; **— droit** straight ahead; **— à l'heure** in a little while (*with a verb in the Present or the Fut.*); a little while ago (*with a verb in a past tense*); **tous (les) deux** both; **tous les trois jours** every three days; **— de même** just the same; **— de suite** at once; **— le monde** everybody; **pas du —** not at all; **rien du —** nothing at all; **— à fait** quite,

entirely; — **à coup** suddenly; — **d'un coup** all at once; **à — prix** at any cost. **Voilà — !** That's all!
tout *m.* everything, the whole
tracasser to annoy, to vex, to worry
tracasserie *f.* annoyance, vexation
traduire to translate
trahir to betray
trahison *f.* treachery
train *m.* train, pace; **être en —** to be in good spirits; **être en — de** to be in the act of, on the verge of, busy in
traînant dragging, tiresome
traîner to drag
traiter to treat, to discuss; **— en** to treat as
tramway *m.* streetcar
tranchée *f.* trench
tranquille quiet, calm. **Soyez — !** Don't worry!
transmettre to transmit
travail *m.* work, piece of work, study
travailler to work
travailleur *m.* **-euse** *f.* hard-working
travers: à — through, across; **en —** crosswise; **de —** askew
traverser to cross
treize thirteen
trembler to tremble
trentaine *f.* about thirty, some thirty
trente thirty
très very
trésor *m.* treasure
triompher to triumph
triste sad
tristement sadly
tristesse *f.* sadness, gloom
Troie *f.* Troy
trois three
tromper to deceive; **se —** to be mistaken
trop too much, too many; **être de —** to be one too many, to intrude
trotter to trot
troubler to trouble
trouvaille *f.* something found, discovery
trouver to find; **se —** to find one's self, to be, to happen to be
tuer to kill
tulipe *f.* tulip
type *m.* type, character, fellow; **drôle de —** funny fellow

U

un, une one, a, an; **l'— l'autre** each other; **les —s . . . les autres** some . . . others
uniforme *m.* uniform
univers *m.* universe
université *f.* university
usine *f.* factory
utile useful. **En quoi puis-je vous être — ?** What can I do for you?

V

vacances *f. pl.* vacation, holidays
vache *f.* cow
vain vain; **en —** vainly, in vain
vaisselle *f.* plates and dishes; **(laver) faire la —** to wash the dishes.
valeur *f.* value, worth
valise *f.* valise
valoir to be worth; **— à** to win; **— mieux** to be better; **— la peine** to be worth the trouble; **se —** to be equal, to be as good as
vaniteux *m.* **-euse** *f.* vain
vanter to praise, to vaunt; **se — de** to boast about
vase *m.* vase

vaste vast
veau *m.* calf
venant *m.* comer; **à tout —** to anyone who came along
vendeuse *f.* saleswoman, a store clerk
vendre to sell
vendredi *m.* Friday
venir to come; **— de** + *Inf.* to have just (*cf.* §45); **— à** to happen to, to result in; **en — à** to resort to, to come to the point of
vent *m.* wind. **Il fait du — .** It is windy.
venue *f.* coming, arrival
ver *m.* worm; **— de terre** earthworm
verbe *m.* verb
verger *m.* orchard
véritable true, genuine, real
vérité *f.* truth, veracity
vermisseau *m.* a grub, a small worm
verre *m.* glass; **un petit —** a small glass (of brandy, liqueur)
vers *m.* verse
vers toward
verse *adj.* (*of rain*) in torrents. **Il pleut à — .** It's raining in torrents (cats and dogs).
verser to pour (*out*), to shed, to spill
vert green
vertu *f.* virtue
vêtement *m.* clothing
vêtir to clothe, to dress; (*P.P.*) **vêtu (de)** clothed (*in*)
vêtu (*P.P.* **vêtir**) clothed, dressed; **mal —** improperly dressed, poorly clad.
veuf *m.* widower
veuillez + *Inf.* please. **— vous asseoir!** Please sit down!
veuve *f.* widow
viande *f.* meat
vice *m.* vice, fault
vide empty
vider to empty
vie *f.* life
vieillard *m.* old man
vieillir to grow (to become) old
vieux, vieil *m.* **vieille** *f.* old
vieux *m.* old man, old boy, old fellow, old top
vigoureux *m.*, **vigoureuse** *f.* vigorous
vilain ugly, vile, nasty, mischievous; **— tour** nasty *or* mischievous trick
village *m.* village
ville *f.* town, city; **en —** downtown
vin *m.* wine
vingt twenty
violemment violently
violent violent
violette *f.* violet
vis-à-vis de opposite, facing, face to face with
viser to aim at
visite *f.* visit; **(faire) rendre — à** to call on, to pay a visit to
vite fast, quickly; **— —** very fast
vitesse *f.* speed; **à toute —** at full speed
vitre *f.* window pane, pane of glass
vivre to live; **de quoi —** something (means) to live on. **Vive la République!** Long live the Republic!
vocabulaire *m.* vocabulary
voguer to sail. **Vogue la galère!** Come what may!
voici here is, here are. **Me — !** Here I am! **voici . . . que** for
voilà there is, there are. **Le — !** There he is! **voilà . . . que** for, **— tout!** That's all! **— justement!** That's just it!
voilé veiled, insinuating

voir to see; **faire —** to show
voisin *m.* neighbor
voiture *f.* coach, car, vehicle; **monter en —** to get in (aboard)
voix *f.* voice; **à haute —** aloud; **à — basse** in a whisper, in a low voice; **faire la petite —** to speak humbly, ingratiatingly
vol *m.* theft
voler to steal, to fly
voleur, *m.* thief
volonté *f.* will, intention; **la bonne —** good will
voter to vote
vôtres: être des — to be with you (one of your party)
vouloir to want. **Que voulez-vous?** What do you expect? **— bien** to be willing; **en — à** to have a grudge against. **Veuillez entrer!** Please enter! **Il voudrait vous voir.** He would like to see you. **— dire** to mean
voyage *m.* trip, voyage; **faire un —** to take a trip
voyager to travel
voyageur *m.* traveler
vrai *adj.* true; **à — dire** to tell the truth
vraiment really
vu *prep.* considering
vue *f.* view; **à perte de —** as far as the eye can see

Y, Z

yeux, *m. pl.* eyes; **œil** *sing.*; **faire de grands —** to blink, to look astonished, to stare
zéro *m.* zero, cipher

ENGLISH-FRENCH VOCABULARY

A

a un, une; **two francs a pound** deux francs la livre; **three times a week** trois fois par semaine
able: to be able, can, could pouvoir
aboard à bord
about, de, au sujet de, à, à peu près, environ, vers; **about (it, that, this)** à ce sujet; **about it** en, y
about: to be about s'agir de; **what it was all about** de quoi il s'agissait
above au-dessus de
abroad à l'étranger; **to go —** aller (passer) à l'étranger
absence absence *f.*
absent absent; **— -minded** distrait
accept accepter
accident accident *m.*
accompany accompagner
according to selon, d'après
account (for) rendre compte de; **on — of** à cause de
accustomed: to get — to se faire à
acquainted: to be — with connaître
acquire acquérir
act: in the — of en train de
act agir
address adresse *f.*
address s'adresser à
admire admirer
admit avouer, admettre
advice conseils *m. pl.* avis *m.*
affair affaire *f.*
affirm affirmer
afraid: to be — avoir peur (de); **to be very much — of** avoir grand'peur de
after après
afternoon après-midi *m.* or *f.*
against contre
age âge *m.*
ago il y a (+ *expression of time*); il y a deux mois **two months ago**
agree être d'accord; **to — on** convenir (de)
aim viser
air: in the open — en plein air
air air *m.*
alive vivant
all tout, toute, tous, toutes; **all the more as** d'autant plus que; **not at all** pas du tout
almost presque, manquer de + *Inf.,* faillir + *Inf.*
along: to take along emporter; **to get along (manage)** se tirer d'affaire, s'en tirer; **to get along with** s'entendre avec
already déjà
also aussi
although bien que, quoique
always toujours
a. m. du matin
America l'Amérique *f.*
American américain
amuse amuser, divertir
an un, une
and et
angry fâché; **to get —** se fâcher; **to be —** être en colère
animal animal *m.*

annoy ennuyer
answer répondre (à); **to — for** répondre de
anxious: be — (to) tenir à
any du, de la, de l', des, de; en; **not — more** ne . . . plus; (*in the sense of* **a few)** quelques; (*in the sense of* **just any**) n'importe quel
anybody, anyone quelqu'un, ne . . . personne; (*in the sense of* **no matter who**) n'importe qui
anyhow tout de même, quand même
anyone *cf.* **anybody**
anything quelque chose; **not —** ne . . . rien; **(just) —** (*in the sense of* **no matter what**) n'importe quoi. **He can't do anything about it.** Il n'y peut rien.
anywhere quelque part, ne . . . nulle part; **(just) —** n'importe où
appear paraître, apparaître
appetite appétit *m.*; **to have a good —** manger de bon appétit
applaud applaudir
apple pomme *f.*
apply appliquer
appoint nommer
approach s'approcher de
April avril *m.*
arrival arrivée *f.*
arrive arriver
art art *m.*
article article *m.*
as comme; **as . . . as** aussi . . . que; **as, accordingly as** au fur et à mesure que; **as for** quant à; **as long as** tant que; **as soon as** aussitôt que; **as a Christian** en chrétien. **He died as a Christian.** Il est mort en chrétien.
ashamed: to be — avoir honte (*de*)
aside à part, à l'écart
ask demander; **to — for** demander; **to — a question** poser (faire) une question; **to — someone for something** demander quelque chose à quelqu'un; **to — someone to do something** demander à quelqu'un de faire quelque chose
askew de travers
asleep endormi; **to fall —** s'endormir
assure assurer
astonished étonné
at à, en, dans; **at** (the house, shop, office, *etc.* of) chez; **at my house** chez moi
attack attaque *f.*
attain atteindre, parvenir à
attend assister à
attention attention *f.*; **to pay attention** faire attention
attentively: to listen attentively prêter l'oreille, écouter bien
attitude attitude *f.*
aunt tante *f.*
automobile automobile *f.*
awaken (se) réveiller

B

back: to be back être de retour
bad mauvais
baker boulanger *m.*
bakery boulangerie *f.*
ballerina ballerine *f.*
ballet ballet *m.*
bandit bandit *m.*
banker banquier *m.*
Bastille Bastille *f.*
be être, se trouver;
to be back être de retour;
to be better valoir mieux;
to be far from s'en falloir de beaucoup;

to be a question of (to be about) s'agir de;
to be early être en avance
to be well se porter bien, aller bien
beat battre
beautiful beau, bel, belle
become devenir;
to become (be becoming to) aller à;
to become ill tomber malade.
He became afraid. Il a eu peur. Il eut peur.
bed lit *m.*; **to go to —** se coucher
bedroom chambre *f.*
before *prep.* avant, avant de + *Inf.*; avant que + *Subj.*
before *prep.* devant; (*when speaking of time*) avant
beg prier (de)
begin commencer (à, de), se mettre (à)
behind derrière
believe croire; **to — in** croire à (*with the article*), croire en (*without the article*)
belong appartenir, être à
below au-dessous de
beside à côté de
best *adj.* le meilleur; *adv.* le mieux; **to do my best** faire de mon mieux, faire tout mon possible
bet parier
betray trahir
better *adj.* meilleur; *adv.* mieux; **so much the —** tant mieux; **to be —** valoir mieux
birthday anniversaire *m.*, jour de naissance *m.*
black noir
blackboard tableau (noir) *m.*
blackout obscurcissement *m.*
Blacky Noiraud
blue bleu
blush rougir
boast se vanter de
boat bateau *m.*
bomb bombe *f.*
bonbon bonbon *m.*
book livre *m.*
bore ennuyer
boring ennuyeux
born: to be — naître
borrow emprunter; **to — something from somebody** emprunter quelque chose à quelqu'un
both tous (les) deux; **both . . . and** et . . . et
boy garçon *m.*
break (*to bend, to snap, to disintegrate*) rompre; (*to shatter*) briser; (*to break in two, to render useless*) casser; **to — out** (*fire, laughter, etc.*) éclater; **to — up** rompre
breakfast petit déjeuner *m.*
bring (*carry*) apporter; (*to lead, to conduct*), amener
brother frère *m.* **elder —** frère aîné *m.*
brown brun
brush brosser
bucket seau *m.*
build bâtir; (*in the sense of* **to have built**) faire bâtir
building édifice *m.* bâtiment *m.*
bump into se heurter contre
bus autobus *m.*
busy one's self (with) s'occuper (de)
but mais
butter beurre *m.*
buy acheter
by par, de; **— the way** à propos

C

Caesar César
café café *m.*
cage cage *f.*

cake gâteau *m.*
call appeler; **to — on** rendre visite à, faire visite à
called: be — s'appeler
can pouvoir (*Cf.* **able**)
Canada Canada *m.*
candidate candidat *m.*
cannon canon *m.;* **in cannon range** à portée de canon
capital capitale *f.*
capture prendre, faire prisonnier
car auto *f.*
card carte *f.*
care se soucier (de); **to care for** tenir à
careful: be — to prendre garde à; **be — not to** prendre garde de
carefully soigneusement, avec soin
caress caresse *f.*
cast (a glance) *cf.* glance
cat chat *m.*
catch attraper; **to — a cold** attraper un rhume
cent sou *m.;* **not to have a —** n'avoir pas le sou
century siècle *m.*
certain certain
certainly certainement
chair chaise *f.*
chalk craie *f.*
chase (away) chasser
cheap(ly) (à) bon marché; **cheaper** (à) meilleur marché
checkbook carnet de chèques *m.*
cheese fromage *m.*
cherry cerise *f.*
child enfant *m.* or *f.*
Chinese chinois
choose choisir
Christ Christ; **before —** avant Jésus-Christ, avant J.-C.
Christopher Columbus Christophe Colomb
cigar cigare *m.*
citizen citoyen *m.*
city ville *f.*
class classe *f.*
classroom salle de classe *f.*
clean *adj.* propre
clean nettoyer
climate climat *m.*
close fermer
closely de près; **to look at —** regarder de près
club cercle *m.*
coffee café *m.*
cold froid *m.;* **to be —** (*of weather*) faire froid; **to be —** (*of persons*) avoir froid; **to have** (*catch*) **a —** avoir (attraper) un rhume (être enrhumé)
collar col *m.*
collect recueillir
come venir;
to come down descendre;
to come in entrer (dans);
to come out sortir
complain se plaindre (de)
compromise compromettre
conceive concevoir
concern regarder; **that concerns him** cela le regarde
conduct conduire; **to — one's self as a gentleman** se conduire en homme de bien
conquer conquérir, vaincre
consent consentir (à)
consequently par conséquent
construct construire, faire construire
contain contenir
continue continuer (à, de)
contraband (goods) de la contrebande *f.*
conversation conversation *f.*
convince convaincre
cost coûter; **at any —** à tout prix
country (*political or geographical*) pays *m.*; (*native land*)

patrie *f.*; (*contrasted with city*) campagne *f.*; **in the** — à la campagne
courage courage *m.*
courageous courageux
course cours *m.*; **to take a** — suivre un cours
course: of — bien entendu
cousin cousin(e) *m.*, (*f.*)
cover couvrir
covered: covered with couvert de
cow vache *f.*
criminal criminel *m.*
cross (*to overcome an obstacle*) franchir; traverser
cry pleurer
cry out s'écrier
cup tasse *f.*
cure guérir
curtly sèchement
cut couper

D

dance danser
Danish danois
dare oser
dark obscurité *f.*
darken s'obscurcir
date date *f.*
daughter fille *f.*
day (*unit of time*) jour *m.*; (*unit of accomplishment*) journée *f.*
dead mort
deaf sourd(e)
deceive tromper
decision: to make a — prendre un parti
declare déclarer
defeat vaincre, battre, défaire
defend défendre
deliberately de parti pris
dent: to make a — in ébrécher
describe décrire
destitute dépourvu de
destroy détruire
detest détester
dictator dictateur *m.*
dictionary dictionnaire *m.*
difficult difficile
difficulty difficulté *f.*; **to get out of a** — se tirer d'affaire
dining room salle à manger *f.*
dinner dîner *m.*
dint: by — of à force de
die mourir
direction côté *m.*; **in the — of** du côté de; **from every** — de tous côtés
disappear disparaître
disappointed déçu
disaster désastre *m.*
discourage décourager
discover découvrir, apprendre
disguised déguisé; — **as** déguisé en
dish plat *m.*
dislike: to take a — to prendre en grippe
dismiss renvoyer
display étalage *m.*
displease déplaire (à)
distance: in the — au loin
disturb déranger
do faire;
to do with faire de;
to do without se passer de;
to do good faire du bien (à);
to do one's best faire de son mieux, faire tout son possible
doctor médecin *m.*
document document *m.*
dog chien *m.*
dollar dollar *m.*
door porte *f.*
doubt douter (de)
down: down with à bas;
downstairs en bas;
downtown en ville;
to get down descendre
dozen douzaine *f.*

draw dessiner
drawing room salon *m.*
dress robe *f.*
dress habiller; **to — one's self** s'habiller
drink boire; (*when speaking of prepared beverages*) prendre
drive conduire
drug store pharmacie *f.*
dryly sèchement
dumb, sot, stupide
during pendant
duty devoir *m.*

E

each *adj.* chaque; **each** *pron.* chacun(e); **each other** *pron.* se; l'un l'autre
early de bonne heure; (*ahead of time*) en avance
earn gagner
earth terre *f.*
easily facilement
easy facile
eat manger
economize économiser, faire des économies
edge bord *m.*
effort effort *m.*
egg œuf *m.*
eight huit
eighty quatre-vingts
either ou; **either . . . or** soit . . . soit, ou . . . ou; **not either . . . or** ne . . . ni . . . ni; (*after a negative*) non plus
elect élire
elephant éléphant *m.*
else: or — ou bien; **something —** autre chose
end: at the — of au bout de
endeavor chercher à, essayer de
enemy ennemi *m.*
England Angleterre *f.*
enjoy trouver bon, jouir (de)
enough assez; **to be —** suffire; **to have — of** en avoir assez
enter entrer (*before a noun* — dans)
entire tout(e); entier(-ère); **the — house** toute la maison
envelope enveloppe *f.*
erase effacer
escape s'évader (de), s'échapper (de); **to have a narrow —** l'échapper belle
eternal éternel
even même; **— if** même si; quand (même) + *Cond.* (*Cf.* §100.)
evening soir *m.*; **in the —** le (au) soir
ever jamais
every tous les, toutes les; **— citizen** tous les citoyens; **— house** toutes les maisons
everybody tout le monde
everything tout
exactly exactement; au juste
examination examen *m.*
examine interroger
example exemple *m.*
excellent excellent
exercise exercice *m.*
exhausted: to be — n'en pouvoir plus
expect s'attendre à. **What do you — ?** Que voulez-vous? **I do not know what to expect.** Je ne sais pas à quoi m'en tenir.
expensive cher, chère
explain expliquer
extinguish éteindre
extremely extrêmement
eye œil *m., pl.* yeux

F

face figure *f.*
fact: the — is . . . c'est que . . .
fail manquer à + *noun,* — de + *Inf.*

faint s'évanouir
fall (*capture*) prise *f.*; **Fall of the Bastille** Prise de la Bastille; (*season*) automne *m.*
fall tomber; **to — in love** tomber amoureux (de), s'énamourer (de); **to — asleep** s'endormir; **to — ill** tomber malade
famous célèbre
far from il s'en faut de beaucoup que, loin de
fashionably à la mode
fast vite
fat, gras, grasse
fat: to grow — engraisser
father père *m.*
father-in-law beau-père *m.*
fault défault *m.*; faute *f.*
fear craindre, avoir peur (de); **for — of** de peur de; **for — that** de peur que
feeble faible
feed nourrir, donner à manger
feel sentir; **to — like** avoir envie (de)
few peu de; **a —** quelques; *pron.* quelques-uns(-unes)
field champ *m.*
fifteen quinze
fifth cinquième; **three fifths** les trois cinquièmes
fight se battre; lutter; combattre
finally enfin; finir par + *Inf.*
find trouver; **to — out** apprendre; (*in past tenses other than the Imperf.*) savoir
fine beau, bel, belle, beaux, belles
fine! à la bonne heure!
finger doigt *m.*
finish finir
fire feu *m.*; incendie *m.*
first *adj.* premier (-ère); *adv.* d'abord
fish poisson *m.*
fishing pole canne à pêche *f.*
five cinq
flask gourde *f.*
flatter flatter
floor plancher *m.* **to take the —** prendre la parole
florist fleuriste *m.* or *f.*
flower fleur *f.*
fly mouche *f.*
flying saucer soucoupe volante *f.*
follow suivre; **it —s that . . .** il s'ensuit que . . .
fond: to be — of aimer beaucoup
for *prep.* pour; *conj.* car; (*during*) pendant, depuis, par, à; **for (during) some minutes** pendant quelques minutes. **I have been here for ten minutes.** Je suis ici depuis dix minutes.
Ford Ford *f.* (*automobile*)
forehead front *m.*
foreign étranger -ère; **— language** langue étrangère
foreman chef d'équipe *m.*
foresee prévoir
forget oublier (de)
former *adj.* ancien; *demons. pron.* celui-là, *etc.*
formerly autrefois
fortune fortune *f.*
fortunately heureusement
forward: Please forward (*this letter*). Prière de faire suivre.
franc franc *m.*
France France *f.*
Francis François
French français(e)
Frenchman Français *m.*
fresh frais, fraîche
friend ami(e) *m.*, (*f.*)
frighten faire peur à
from (*origin*) de; (*out of*) dans; (*off of*) sur; **from . . . on** à partir de, dès
front: in front of devant
fruit fruit *m.*

fun: to make fun of se moquer de
fundamentally au fond
furnish fournir
furniture meubles *m. pl.*
furthermore en outre, de plus
future avenir *m.*; **in the —** à l'avenir

G

garage garage *m.*
garden jardin *m.*
gather cueillir
Gaul Gaule *f.*
general général *m.*; **in —** en général
genius génie *m.*
gentle doux, douce
gentleman monsieur *m.*
German allemand
get obtenir, procurer;
  to get accustomed se faire à;
  to get along (manage) s'en tirer;
  to get along with s'entendre avec;
  to get angry se fâcher;
  to get down descendre;
  to get fat, old, etc. *cf.* **grow**
  to get married se marier (avec);
  to get out sortir;
  to get out of it, s'en tirer;
  to get through with en finir avec;
  to get up se lever;
  to get well guérir;
  to get: to go and get aller chercher
girl jeune fille *f.*
give donner; **— back** rendre
glad content
glance coup d'œil *m.;* **to —** jeter un coup d'œil (sur, à)
glory gloire *f.*
glove gant *m.*
go aller;
  to go away s'en aller, partir;
  to go to bed se coucher;
  to go back to bed se recoucher;
  to go (and) get aller chercher;
  to go in entrer (dans);
  to go back into rentrer;
  to go on (occur) se passer
  to go out sortir;
  to go upstairs monter (en haut);
  to go with aller avec, accompagner
goat chèvre *f.*, bouc *m.*
God Dieu *m.*
golf golf *m.*
good bon(-ne)
good: to do — faire du bien
government gouvernement *m.*
grade note *f.*
gradually: gradually as à mesure que, au fur et à mesure que
grain grain *m.*
grammar grammaire *f.*
grandfather grand-père *m.*
granted! soit!
grasp étreindre
grateful: to be — to (*someone for something*) savoir gré à (quelqu'un de quelque chose); être reconnaissant
grave grave
gray gris
great deal of beaucoup de
greet saluer
groan geindre
grocer épicier m.
grocery épicerie *f.*
grouchy de mauvaise humeur; maussade
grow pousser; (*of children*) grandir;
  to grow fat engraisser;
  to grow old vieillir
  to grow thin maigrir;
  to grow younger rajeunir.

grudge: to have a — against en vouloir à
guess deviner

H

habit habitude *f.*, coutume *f.*
haircut: to get a — se faire couper les cheveux
half moitié *f.*; *adj.* demi(e); **a half hour** une demi-heure; **an hour and a half** une heure et demie; **half pound** demi-livre *f.*
hand main *f.*; **on the one —** d'un côté; **on the other —** de l'autre côté, d'autre part; **helping —** coup de main *m.*
hand (to *or* in) remettre
happen arriver, se passer; **to happen** (*by chance*) venir à + *Inf.*; **to happen to be** se trouver
happy heureux
hard dur -e; difficile
hardly ne . . . guère, à peine
haste: in great — en grande hâte, à toute vitesse
hasten se hâter (de), s'empresser (de), se dépêcher (de)
hat chapeau *m.*
have avoir; **to — to** (*necessity*) il faut que; **to — a good time** s'amuser; **to — someone do something** faire + *Inf.*; **to — nothing to do with** (*not to be involved in*) n'y être pour rien
head tête *f.*
hear entendre, écouter; **to — of** entendre parler de
height hauteur *f.*
hello bonjour
help assistance *f.*, aide *m.*
helping hand coup de main *m.*
henceforth désormais
Henry Henri
her *adj.* son, sa, ses; *pron.* la; **to —** lui
here ici; **— is, are** voici; **— he is** le voici
hero le héros *m.*
hers *poss. pron.* le sien, la sienne, *etc.* **This pen is hers.** Cette plume est à elle.
high haut
his *adj.* son, sa, ses; *pron.* le sien, la sienne, *etc.* **This book is his.** Ce livre est à lui.
hold tenir
hold out tendre
home: at — chez moi, *etc.*; à la maison
hope espérer
hopeless sans espoir, désespéré
horse cheval *m.*
hot: It is — . Il fait chaud. **He is — .** Il a chaud.
hotel hôtel *m.*
hour heure *f.*
house maison *f.*
how comment; **— long?** depuis quand? **— much, many?** combien (de)? **— tall you are!** Comme (que) vous êtes grand!
however cependant; *cf.* §110(3) for use with *Subj.*
hundred cent
hungry: to be — avoir faim
hurry se dépêcher
hurt faire mal à; **to — one's self** se faire mal (à)
husband mari *m.*
hussar houssard *m.*

I

I je, j', moi
icebox réfrigérateur *m.*
idea idée *f.*
idiom idiotisme *m.*
ill malade
illness maladie *f.*
imitation imitation *f.*, **imitation jewelry** parure fausse

immediately tout de suite, sur-le-champ, immédiatement
important important
improve faire des progrès, améliorer
in dans, à, en; (*after a superlative*) de; **in it, in there** y; **in which** où; **in the evening** le soir; **in spring** au printemps; **in 1940** en 1940
in order to pour; afin de
in spite of malgré
inform informer, renseigner, mettre au courant, faire savoir; **to be informed** être au courant; **to keep informed** tenir au courant
insect insecte *m.*
inside dedans, là-dedans
insincerity peu de sincérité *m.*; mauvaise foi *f.*
insist on tenir à
instead of au lieu de
intend avoir l'intention de; compter; penser
interest intérêt *m.*
interest intéresser; **to be interested in** s'intéresser à
interesting intéressant
interminably à n'en plus finir
interpreter interprète *m.*
introduce présenter
invitation invitation *f.*
invite inviter (à); **to get one's self invited** se faire inviter
it il, elle, ce; le, la; cela. **It is he.** C'est lui. **to it, in it** y; **of it, from it, about it** en; **to think of it** y penser
Italian italien (-ne)
Italy Italie *f.*

J

Japan Japon *m.*
Japanese japonais
jewel bijou *m.*
job metier *m.*
John Jean
join joindre; (*reunite those separated*) rejoindre
judge: to be a good — of se connaître à *or* en
jump sauter
June juin *m.*
just: — now tout à l'heure; **— the same** tout de même; **to have —** venir de (*Pres. Ind.*) + *Inf.*; **had —** venir de (*Imp. Ind.*) + *Inf.*

K

keep garder, tenir; **— quiet** se taire; **to —** (*something*) **quiet** taire; **to — informed** tenir au courant (de)
kill tuer
kitchen cuisine *f.*
knife couteau *m.*
know (*facts*) savoir; (*persons or objects in the sense of* **to be acquainted with)** connaître; **to know about** savoir de
knowledge: without my — à mon insu

L

lack manquer de (*Cf.* Idioms, page 161.); **for — of** faute de
lady dame *f.*
lake lac *m.*
lamb agneau *m.*
landmark borne *f.*
language langue *f.*
last dernier (-ère), passé; **— night** hier soir; **— summer** l'été dernier (passé)
late tard; **to be —** (*behind schedule*) être en retard
later plus tard
latter: the — celui-ci, *etc.*
laugh rire; **to — at** (se) rire de
learn apprendre (à)

least *adj.* moindre; *adv.* moins; **at —** (*quantity*) au moins; **at —** (*concession*) du moins
leave (*of an object*) laisser; (*persons or places*) quitter; (*to depart, to go away*) partir, s'en aller;
to leave alone laisser tranquille;
to leave for partir pour;
to leave up to s'en rapporter à;
we still have . . . left il nous reste toujours . . .
lecture conférence *f.*
left gauche *f.*; **to the —** à gauche; **we have one —** il nous en reste un
leisure loisir *m.*
lemonade citronnade *f.*
lend prêter
lesson leçon *f.*
let laisser; permettre (à quelqu'un de faire quelque chose)
letter lettre *f.*
library bibliotheque *f.*
lie mensonge *m.*
lie mentir
life vie *f.*
lift lever
light lumière *f.*
like aimer; **I should —** je voudrais
liking: to my — à mon gré
limit: to the — à outrance
listen écouter; **to — attentively** prêter l'oreille, écouter bien
literature littérature *f.*
little petit; **— by —** peu à peu; **a —** un peu (de)
live (*to be alive, to exist*) vivre; (*to live in a street, district, etc.*) demeurer à; (*to reside*) habiter + *dir. obj.*
living vivant; **to be still —** être toujours vivant
loafer badaud *m.*, fainéant *m.*
lock fermer à clef (*or* clé)
long long, longue; **a long time** longtemps; **as — as** aussi longtemps que; **in the — run** à la longue
longer plus longtemps; **no —** ne . . . plus
look regarder;
to look after s'occuper de, soigner;
to look at regarder, avoir l'air;
to look at closely regarder de près;
to look for chercher;
to look out regarder par, (*meaning to be careful*) prendre garde
to look well avoir bonne mine
lose perdre; **to — sight of** perdre de vue
lot: a — (of) beaucoup (de)
loud haut
love amour *m.*; **to fall in —** tomber amoureux, s'énamourer (de)
love aimer; **in making her — him** à se faire aimer d'elle
lower baisser
luck chance *f.*, veine *f.*

M

magazine *i.e.*, **a periodical** revue *f.*
magnificent magnifique
make faire;
to make fun of se moquer de;
to make happy rendre heureux;
to make progress faire des progrès;
to make up one's mind prendre son parti
to make a decision prendre un parti;
to make a speech prononcer (faire) un discours

mama maman *f.*
man homme *m.*
manner façon *f.*, manière *f.*, sorte *f.*; **in that manner** de cette facon; — **of living** façon de vivre
marble (*for playing games*) bille *f.*
March mars *m.*
mark marque *f.*
marmalade marmelade *f.*, confiture *f.*
marriage mariage *m.*
marry épouser, se marier avec; **to — off** marier
Marseilles Marseille
Mary Marie
matter importer. **What's the — ?** Qu'est-ce qu'il y a? **no — how (much) I try . . .** j'ai beau essayer . . .
me me, moi
meadow pré *m.*, prairie *f.*
meal repas *m.*; **evening** — repas du soir *m.*
mean *adj.* méchant
mean vouloir dire
meanwhile en attendant
meat viande *f.*
meet (*by accident*) rencontrer; (*by agreement*) rejoindre, retrouver; (*meaning to become acquainted with* [*anyone*]) faire la connaissance de; **to go to —** aller à la rencontre de; **to come to meet** venir à la rencontre de
Mexico Mexique *m.*
midnight minuit *m.*
milk lait *m.*
mind: to make up one's — prendre un (son) parti
minded: absent-minded distrait
mirror miroir *m.*
miserable misérable
miss manquer (*Cf.* Idiomatic Expressions, page 161.)
mistaken: to be — se tromper
modern moderne
modest modeste
moment moment *m.*
Monday lundi
money argent *m.*
month mois *m.*
more plus; — **and** — de plus en plus; **all the — as, because** d'autant plus que
moreover en outre, de plus, d'ailleurs
morning matin *m.*; **in the —** le (au) matin; **yesterday —** hier matin; **at five in the —** à cinq heures du matin
most le plus; — **men** la plupart des hommes
mother mère *f.*
mother-in-law belle-mere *f.*
mountain montagne *f.*; **mountain water** l'eau de montagne
mountaineer montagnard(e) *m.*, (*f.*)
mouth bouche *f.*
move (*to change residence*) déménager; (*to stir*) remuer; (*emotionally*) émouvoir
moved ému
movie film *m.*, cinéma *m.*
much beaucoup (de); **so —** tant (de)
must devoir (*cf.* §*138*); falloir (*cf.* §*141*)
my mon, ma, mes
mysterious mystérieux

N

name nom *m.* **What is your — ?** Comment vous appelez-vous?
narrow étroit; **to have a — escape** l'échapper belle
near près de, auprès de

necessary nécessaire; **to be —** falloir (*Cf.* §*141*)
necklace collier *m.*, parure *f.*
necktie cravate *f.*
need avoir besoin (de); falloir + *noun* (*Cf.* §*141*)
neighbor voisin(e) *m.*, (*f.*)
neither . . . nor ne . . . ni . . . ni
neither one ni l'un ni l'autre
never ne . . . jamais
nevertheless néanmoins, quand même
New Orleans La Nouvelle-Orléans
New York New York *m.*
newspaper journal *m.*
next prochain(e); **— week** la semaine prochaine; **the — lesson** la prochaine leçon; **the — day** le lendemain
nice gentil(le). **It is — weather.** Il fait beau.
night nuit *f.*; **last —** la nuit dernière, hier soir, cette nuit
no non; (*in the sense of* **not one**) ne . . . aucun; **no longer** ne . . . plus; **no one** ne . . . personne; **no more** ne . . . plus
nobody ne . . . personne; (*subject*) personne . . . ne
none ne . . . aucun, ne . . . nul
nonsense! allons donc!
noon midi *m.; at* **— sharp** à midi précis
nor ni; **— I either** ni moi non plus
North America Amérique du Nord *f.*
northwind bise *f.*
nose nez *m.*
not ne (n') . . . pas (point), non, pas; **— at all** pas du tout; **— yet** pas encore. **Why — ?** Pourquoi pas? **— only** non seulement. **Is it — (so)? Is he — ? Will he — ?** *etc.*, N'est-ce pas?
nothing ne . . . rien; **to have — to do with** n'y être pour rien; **— but . . .** ne (rien) . . . que
notice s'apercevoir de, remarquer
novel (*a book*) roman *m.*
now maintenant, à présent; **now . . . now** tantôt . . . tantôt; **just now** tout à l'heure; **right now!** plus vite que ça!
nowhere nulle part
nurse infirmière *f.*

O

obey obéir (à)
occasion: on several —s à plusieurs reprises
o'clock heure(s) *f.*; **at eight o'clock A. M.** à huit heures du matin
offer offrir
officer officier *m.*
often souvent
old vieux, vieil, vieille; **to be five years old** avoir cinq ans; **to get** *or* **grow old** (*older*) vieillir
older plus âgé, plus vieux; **—** (*brother*) aîné
on sur, à, de, en; **— that day** ce jour-là; **from that day —** à partir de ce jour; **— it** là-dessus; **— the other side** de l'autre côté; **— Monday** le lundi; **— what day?** Quel jour?; **— July 14th** le quatorze juillet
once une fois; **at —** a l'instant, tout de suite
one un(e); *indef. pron.* on
only ne . . . que, seulement; **not only . . . but also** non seulement . . . mais encore
open ouvrir; **in the — air** en plein air; **— on** donner sur

opinion avis *m.*; opinion *f.*
opportunity occasion *f.*, opportunité *f.*
opposite en face de, vis-à-vis (de)
or ou; **either . . . or** ou . . . ou; **or else** ou bien
order ordre *m.*; **in — to** pour; **in — to (so that)** pour que
other autre
ought devoir (*Cf.* §138.)
our notre, nos
ours le nôtre, la nôtre, les nôtres; à nous
out dehors;
to look out regarder par; (*meaning* **be careful**) prendre garde;
to get out sortir;
to go out sortir;
to set out se mettre en route, partir pour;
to wear out user.
overcast: to become — s'obscurcir
over there là-bas
owe devoir (*Cf.* §*138.*)
own *adj.* propre (*preceding a noun*); **his own father** son propre père

P

paint peindre
palace palais *m.*
papa papa *m.*
paper papier *m.*; **newspaper** journal *m.*
parent parent *m.*
Paris Paris *m.*
park parc *m.*
park (*vb.*) stationner
passenger voyageur *m.*
pay payer; **to — attention** faire attention
peace paix *f.*
pear poire *f.*
pen plume *f.*, **fountain pen** stylo *m.*
people gens *m.* or *f.*; on; personnes *f. pl.*
perfectly à merveille, parfaitement
perhaps peut-être
permit permettre (à quelqu'un de faire quelque chose)
personally personnellement
piano piano *m.*
picnic pique-nique *m.*; **to go on a —** faire un pique-nique
picture tableau *m.*
piece morceau *m.*
pilot pilote *m.*
pistol pistolet *m.*
pity dommage *m.*; **it is a —** c'est dommage
pity plaindre
place endroit *m.*, lieu *m.*; **to take —** avoir lieu
plan penser, compter, projeter
plane avion *m.*
play (*games*) jouer à; (*musical instruments*) jouer de; **to — dumb, dead** faire le sot, le mort
please plaire, faire plaisir à; **— do it** Veuillez le faire. **If you —**. S'il vous plaît.
pleasure plaisir *m.*; **to take — in** se plaire à; **to give —** faire plaisir à
pocket poche *f.*
pocketbook porte-monnaie *m.*, portefeuille *m.*; bourse *f.*
poem poème *m.*
poison poison *m.*
poker poker *m.*
police police *f.*
policeman agent (de police) *m.*
polite poli
political politique
poplar peuplier *m.*
poor pauvre

poorly mal; **rather —** tant bien que mal, assez mal
Portuguese portugais
possession: to take — of s'emparer de; **to regain — of** rentrer en possession de
possible possible
possibility possibilité *f.*
posted: to be well — être au courant (de); **to keep —** tenir au courant (de)
pound livre *f.*
pour verser; **to — down rain** pleuvoir à verse
prefer aimer mieux, préférer
preference préférence *f.*
premier premier ministre *m.*
prepare préparer
presence présence *f.*
present actuel
presently tout à l'heure
president président *m.*
prestige prestige *m.*
pretend faire semblant (de), prétendre; **to — to be dead** faire le mort
price prix *m.*
primitive primitif; **in a — state** dans l'état de nature
prize prix *m.*
problem problème *m.*
produce produire
professor professeur *m.*
progress progrès *m.*; **to make —** faire des progrès
promise promesse *f.*
promise promettre
pronounce prononcer
pronunciation prononciation *f.*
properly comme il faut
propose proposer
prosecute poursuivre
protestation protestation *f.*
pull tirer
purse bourse *f.*, sac à main *m.*
pursue poursuivre
put mettre; **to — on** mettre; **to — to sleep** endormir

Q

quarter quart *m.*; **a — past noon** midi et quart
quality qualité *f.*
question question *f.*; **it is a — of** il s'agit de
quiet: to keep — se taire
quite tout à fait, assez, tout

R

rain pleuvoir
raincoat imperméable *m.*
raise augmentation *f.*
raise lever, élever
range: in — à portée (de)
rarely rarement
raspberry framboise *f.*
rather assez; **— poorly** tant bien que mal, assez mal
read lire
realize se rendre compte de
rear élever
receive recevoir
recognize reconnaître
recover se remettre (de)
red rouge
reduce réduire
refresh rafraîchir. **This drink is wonderfully refreshing.** Cette boisson rafraîchit à merveille.
refreshing rafraîchissant
refuse refuser (de). (Also *cf.* vouloir.)
reign régner, dominer
remain rester
remember se souvenir de, se rappeler
Renaissance Renaissance *f.*
rent louer
repeat répéter
reread relire
rescue sauver

resemble ressembler à
resort (to) en venir à
respect: in this — à cet égard
responsible responsable
restaurant restaurant *m.*
retake reprendre
return revenir, rentrer, retourner, rendre
revolution revolution *f.*
rewrite récrire
rich riche
right droite *f.*; **to be —** avoir raison; **to the —** à droite. **— now!** Plus vite que ça!
ring bague *f.*; **wedding —** alliance *f.*
river (*flowing into a sea or an ocean*) fleuve *m.*; (*flowing into a* fleuve) rivière *f.*
road chemin *m.* route *f.*
roll petit pain *m.*
roof toit *m.*
room (*general*) pièce *f.*; (*private*) chambre *f.*; (*public*) salle; **dining —** salle à manger *f.*; **bath —** salle de bain *f.*; **bed- —** chambre *f.*
rose rose f.
rule régner
rum rhum *m.*
run courir;
in the long — à la longue;
to run away se sauver;
to run over (*to crush*) écraser;
to run through *or* **over** parcourir;
to run up accourir
Russian russe

S

saleswoman vendeuse *f.*
same (*preceding the noun*) même; **the — day** le même jour; **just the —** tout de même, quand même
sandwich sandwich *m.*
say dire; **that is to —** c'est-à-dire
scarcely ne . . . guère, à peine
school école *f.*; **at —** à l'école
science science *f.*
scold gronder
scratch gratter
sea mer *f.*
search: in — of à la recherche de; **in — of her (him, it)** à sa recherche
seated assis
second (*of only two*) second; (*of more than two*) deuxième
secret secret *m.*
secretary secrétaire *m.* or *f.*
see voir; **to — again** revoir; **— here!** Voyons! **— you soon** à bientôt
seek chercher à
seem sembler, paraître, avoir l'air (de). Il a l'air bien portant. **He seems well.**
seize saisir, s'emparer de
sell vendre
send envoyer; **to — away** renvoyer; **— for (to get)** envoyer chercher
sentence phrase *f.*
serious sérieux *m.*, sérieuse *f.*
serve servir; **to — as** servir de
service service *m.*
set out partir (pour), se mettre en route
seven sept
several plusieurs; **on — occasions** à plusieurs reprises
sharp précis; **at eight —** à huit heures précises
shave se raser
she elle
shear tondre
sheep mouton *m.*
sheltered à l'abri (de)
shirt chemise *f.*

shoot fusiller
shore rive *f.*; rivage *m.*
short court; **in —** bref, somme toute
shot coup *m.* (de fusil, de pistolet)
show spectacle *m.*; (*movie*) cinéma *m.*
show montrer
sick malade
side côté *m.*; **on this — of** de ce côté de; **on the other — of** de l'autre côté de; **to — with** donner raison à
sight vue *f.*; **to lose — of** perdre de vue
since depuis; **— when (how long)** depuis quand
sing chanter
single seul
sir monsieur
sister sœur *f.*
sit down s'asseoir; **to — — again** se rasseoir
sitting: to be — être assis
situation situation *f.*
sky ciel *m.*
sleep dormir; **to go to —** s'endormir; **to put to —** endormir
sleepy: to be — avoir sommeil
slowly lentement
sly: on the — à la dérobée
smell sentir
snow neige *f.*
snow (*vb.*) neiger
so si, aussi, tellement; **— much, — many** tant; **— to speak** pour ainsi dire
soldier soldat *m.*
solitude isolement *m.*, solitude *f.*
solve résoudre
some du, de la, de l', des; (*before an adjective and the object of a negative verb*) de, d'; (*pron. when no noun follows*) en; (*meaning* **a few**) quelques
someone quelqu'un(e); personne *f.*
something quelque chose; **— else** autre chose *f.*
sometimes quelquefois
somewhere quelque part
son fils *m.*
soon bientôt; **see you —** à bientôt
sooner plus tôt
sorry: to be — regretter, être fâché
soul âme *f.*
sound bruit *m.*
South America Amérique du Sud *f.*
Spaniard Espagnol *m.*
speak parler; **so to —** pour ainsi dire
speech discours *m.*; **to make a —** prononcer (faire) un discours
speed vitesse *f.*, **at full —** à toute vitesse
spend (*money*) dépenser; (*time*) passer
spite: in — of malgré, en dépit de
spring (*water*) source *f.*; (*season*) printemps *m.*; **in the —** au printemps
spy espion *m.*
stable (*for cows*) étable *f.*; (*for horses*) écurie *f.*
stake: to be at — y aller de. **My life is at —.** Il y va de ma vie.
star étoile *f.*
state état *m.*; **in a primitive —** dans l'état de nature
station gare *f.*
stay rester
step pas *m.*; **in —** au pas
still *adv.* toujours, encore
stop arrêter, s'arrêter, cesser (de); **to — at a hotel** descendre à un hôtel

store magasin *m.*
story histoire *f.*; (*tale*) conte *m.*; (*short story*) nouvelle *f.*
stranger inconnu *m.*
strawberries fraises *f. pl.*
stroll se promener; **to take a —** faire une promenade
strong fort
struggle lutter, s'exercer
student étudiant(e) *m.*, (*f.*)
study étude *f.*
study étudier
stupidity stupidité *f.*, bêtise *f.*
style mode *f.*; **in —** à la mode, bien mise
submarine sous-marin *m.*
succeed réussir (à), pouvoir (*cf.* §*137*, Idioms). **Will he succeed in making her love him?** Réussira-t-il à se faire aimer d'elle?
success succès *m.*
succession: in rapid — coup sur coup
such tel, telle; **— a book** un tel livre
suddenly subitement
suffer souffrir
suffice suffire
sufficient: to be — suffire
sugar sucre *m.*
summer été *m.*; **in the —** en été; **next —** l'été prochain
Sunday dimanche *m.*
sure sûr
surprise surprendre
surprised surpris(e)
surrender se rendre
survive survivre (à)
suspect se douter de
sweep balayer
sweet doux
swim nager
Switzerland Suisse *f.*

T

table table *f.*
tail queue *f.*
take prendre
to take along emporter;
to take a course suivre un cours;
to take a dislike to prendre en grippe;
to take the floor prendre la parole;
to take from prendre dans, sur;
to take place avoir lieu;
to take pleasure in se plaire à.
It would take you two days to go there. Il vous faudrait deux jours pour y aller.
talk parler
teacher professeur *m.*; maître *m.*
tear larme *f.*
telegram dépêche *f.*, télégramme *m.*
tell (*to say*) dire; (*to tell a story*) raconter; **to — the truth** à vrai dire
ten dix
tenant locataire *m.*
tender tendre
terrain terrain *m.*
than que; (*before numerals*) de; **more —** plus que, plus de
thanks (to) grâce (à)
the le, la, l', les
their *poss. adj.* leur, leurs
theirs *poss. pron.* le leur, la leur, les leurs; à eux, à elles
them les; **to —** leur; **of —** en; **in —** y
then (*at that time*) alors; (*afterwards, denoting a succession of incidents*) puis; (*next*) ensuite; *conj.* (*therefore, so*) donc
there là, y; **— is, are** (*pointing*) voilà; **— is, are** (*referring to something*) il y a; **over —** là-bas

therefore par conséquent
thereupon là-dessus
these *dem. adj.* ces, ces . . . (-ci) *dem. pron.* ceux (-ci), celles (-ci)
thesis thèse *f.*
they ils, elles; (*impersonal*) on
thief voleur *m.*
thin maigre; **to grow —** maigrir
thing chose *f.*
think penser; **to — about** (*turn one's thought toward*) penser à; **to — of** (*have an opinion of*) penser de
third tiers *m.*
thirsty: to be — avoir soif
thirty trente
this *dem. adj.* ce, cet, cette
this *dem. pron.* ce, c', ceci; **— one** celui(-ci), celle(-ci); **— is** voici, c'est
those *dem. adj.* ces, ces . . . (-là); *dem. pron.* ceux(-là), celles (-là)
thousand mille; (*with dates*) mil
three trois
threshold seuil *m.*
through par, à travers; **to get (be) — with** en finir avec
throw jeter; **to — away** jeter; **to — out of the door** jeter à la porte
Thursday jeudi *m.*
time (*duration in general*) temps *m.*; (*occasion*) fois *f.*; (*specific time*) heure *f.*;
at the same time à la fois, en même temps;
at the time of lors de;
at what time? à quelle heure?
from time to time de temps en temps, de temps à autre;
to have a good time s'amuser;
in our time de nos jours;
it is time to il est temps de;
on time à l'heure, à temps;
What time is it? Quelle heure est-il?
tired fatigué
tobacco tabac *m.*
today aujourd'hui; **a week from —** d'aujourd'hui en huit
tomb tombeau *m.*
tomorrow demain; **day after —** après demain; **— morning** demain matin
tonight ce soir
too aussi; **— much** trop (de)
tool outil *m.*
tooth dent *f.*
towards vers, du côté de
town ville *f.*; **in (down) —** en ville
train train *m.*
translate traduire
travel voyager
treasure trésor *m.*
tree arbre *m.*
trip voyage *m.*
trouble chagrin *m.*; peine *f.*; **to be worth the —** valoir la peine; **the — is . . .** il y a que . . . **What is the — ?** Qu'y a-t-il?
trout truite *f.*
true vrai
trunk malle *f.*; **to pack one's —** faire sa malle
trust se fier à
truth vérité *f.*
try essayer (de), tâcher (de), vouloir (*Cf.* §*137*, Idioms); **Try as she may . . .** Elle aura beau essayer . . .
twenty vingt
twenty-first vingt et unième
twice deux fois; **— a day** deux fois par jour
two deux
type (*write*) taper à la machine
tyranny tyrannie *f.*

U

umbrella parapluie *m.*
unable: **to be —** ne pas pouvoir
uncle oncle *m.*
under au-dessous de; **— it** là-dessous
understand comprendre
undertake entreprendre
unfortunately malheureusement
United States Etats-Unis *m. pl.*
unless à moins que + *Subj.*; à moins de + *Inf.*
until (*with noun*) jusqu'à; (*with clause*) jusqu'à ce que; (*with* attendre + *Subj.*) que *E.g.*, J'attends qu'ils le fassent
unwell: **to be —** être souffrant, aller mal, se porter mal
upstairs en haut
use: **what's the — ?** A quoi bon (+ *Inf.*)?
use se servir de, employer
used: **to get — to** se faire à; **to be — for** servir à. *Expressed by Imperf. Ind., cf.* §*2*, §*13*, §*22*, §*42*, §*43*.
useful utile
useless: avoir beau (*Cf.* Idioms, page 43.)
usually d'ordinaire, d'habitude, généralement

V

vacations vacances *f. pl.*
valise valise *f.*
very très, bien, fort; **— much** beaucoup; **the — place** la place même
vest gilet *m.*
vex ennuyer
vice vice *m.*
village village *m.*
visit (*in the sense of* **inspect**) visiter; (*persons*) faire (rendre) visite à

W

wait attendre; **to — for** attendre; **to — until** attendre que + *Subj.*
walk marcher, aller à pied
want vouloir
war guerre *f.*
warm chaud; **to be —** (*said of persons*) avoir chaud; **to be —** (*said of the weather*) faire chaud
warn avertir
wash (se) laver
water eau *f.*
way chemin *m.*; manière *f.*; **by the —** à propos; **on the —** chemin faisant; **in this —** de cette façon, de la sorte
we nous; **— French** nous autres Français
weakness faiblesse *f.*; côté faible *m.*
wear porter; **to — out** user
weather temps *m.*; **the — is nice (bad, *etc.*)** il fait beau (mauvais, *etc.*)
week semaine *f.*; **a — from today** d'aujourd'hui en huit
welcome accueillir, souhaiter la bienvenue
well bien, eh bien, tiens! **to be —** aller bien, se porter bien
what *rel. pron.* ce qui, ce que, quoi; *interrog. pron.* que, qu'est-ce que, qu'est-ce qui, quoi; *interrog. adj.* quel, quelle, quels, quelles; *interrog. adv.* comment? **What is his name?** Comment s'appelle-t-il?
when quand, lorsque; (*in a question*) quand?
where où; **from —** d'où
whether si; **whether . . . or** soit . . . soit; soit que . . . soit que

(*Subj.*). soit que . . . ou que (*Subj.*)

which *rel. pron.* qui, que; **of which** dont (duquel, de laquelle, *etc.*); **in which** où, dans lequel; **(that) which** ce qui, ce que; *interrog. pron.* **which (one, ones)** lequel, laquelle, *etc.*; *interrog. adj.* quel, quelle, *etc.*

while pendant que; (with *Pres. Part.*) en; **in a little —** tout à l'heure

whisper: in a — à voix basse

white blanc, blanche

who *interrog. pron.* qui? qui est-ce qui?; *rel. pron.* qui

whole tout, toute; **the — factory** toute l'usine

whom *interrog. pron.* qui? qui est-ce que? *rel. pron.* que

whose *rel. pron.* dont, de qui, duquel; *interrog. pron.* à qui? de qui?

why pourquoi

wife femme *f.*

willing: to be — vouloir bien

win gagner; l'emporter; **to — three times out of four** gagner trois fois sur quatre. **He will try to win her love.** Il essayera de (mériter, gagner son amour) se faire aimer d'elle.

window fenêtre *f.*

windy: It is — . Il fait du vent.

winter hiver *m.;* **in —** en hiver

with avec, auprès de; **— its finger in its mouth** le doigt à la bouche

without sans; *with Subj.* sans que; **to do —** se passer de

woman femme *f.*

wonder se demander

wonderfully à merveille

word mot *m.*; parole *f.* **He gives us his word.** Il nous donne sa parole.

work (*the action of working*) travail *m.*; (*single work completed*) ouvrage *m.*; (*work of artistic merit*) œuvre *f.*

work travailler

worn out usé(e)

worth: to be — valoir

wound (*physically*) blesser; (*in the sense of* **offend**) offenser

write écrire

writer écrivain *m.*

wrong: to be — avoir tort

Y

yard cour *f.*

year (*unit of time*) an *m.*; (*duration of time*) année *f.*

yes oui; **why —** mais oui; (*in contradiction*) si, mais si

yesterday hier; **day before —** avant hier

yet encore; **not —** pas encore

young jeune

your votre, vos; ton, ta, tes

yours le vôtre, la vôtre, les vôtres; à vous

INDEX

(References are to articles unless otherwise stated)

Oct. 5 - review -er verbs; Exercises Chapt. I
vocabulary notebook

Oct. 12 - 2nd lesson - review for 2 hrs. lesson I
Oct. 19 - 2nd lesson - know verbs; exercises
study reflexive

Oct. 26 - 3rd lesson - reflexive + verbs
a, b, c, d, e

Nov. 2 - Test on 3 chapters - verbs
irregular verbs

Nov. 9 - Chapter 4
Nov. 16 - write F - quiz

Book report - Tues. 24th 3:00 p.m.

Nov. 23 - Lesson 5, pg 54, ABDE + G
Dec. 7 - Lesson 6, pg. 69 ABCD, 70 Ea.
Verb devoir

Dec. 14 - Translation H

Jan. 4 A, B, C, D, pg. 84

G

Jan. 11 - chapter 8
pg. 87 (study thoroughly)
pg. 91 - article 68
pg. 96 - A, B, C, D, E